Pivoting Your Instruct

This practical guide for college and university instructors explains how to design and prepare your courses to be adaptable for a full range of learning environments— whether that's online, hybrid, or face-to-face traditional campus teaching.

Author Bruce M. Mackh unpacks a comprehensive instructional design approach to curriculum and instruction that is suitable for all modalities and allows you to pivot quickly, regardless of how the course will be delivered. Chapters provide quick takeaways and cover challenges and opportunities, adapting high-impact practices across instructional models and fostering a culture of care. The book also encourages faculty members to adopt a student-centered mindset as they employ the principles of Design Thinking, User Experience Design, Instructional Design, and Learning Experience Design to create a high-quality course.

The strategies at the heart of this book will help both new and experienced faculty save time, ensure instructional continuity during transitions, and achieve excellence in teaching.

Bruce M. Mackh is the Department Head of Art and Design and Associate Professor at Valdosta State University, USA. He is the author of *Higher Education by Design: Best Practices for Curricular Planning and Instruction* (Routledge, 2018).

Pivoting Your Instruction

A Guide to Comprehensive Instructional Design for Faculty

Bruce M. Mackh

Routledge
Taylor & Francis Group

NEW YORK AND LONDON

First published 2022
by Routledge
605 Third Avenue, New York, NY 10158

and by Routledge
2 Park Square, Milton Park, Abingdon, Oxon, OX14 4RN

Routledge is an imprint of the Taylor & Francis Group, an informa business

© 2022 Taylor & Francis

Library of Congress Cataloging-in-Publication Data
Names: Mackh, Bruce M. author.
Title: Pivoting your instruction : a guide to comprehensive instructional
    design for faculty / Bruce M. Mackh.
Description: New York, N.Y. : Routledge, 2021. | Includes bibliographical
    references.
Identifiers: LCCN 2021007570 (print) | LCCN 2021007571 (ebook) |
    ISBN 9781032015927 (hardback) | ISBN 9781032017099 (paperback) |
    ISBN 9781003179726 (ebook)
Subjects: LCSH: Education, Higher—Curricula. | Education,
    Higher—Computer-assisted instruction. | Instructional systems—Design. |
    College teaching. | Student-centered learning.
Classification: LCC LB2361 .M34 2021 (print) | LCC LB2361 (ebook) |
    DDC 378.1/99—dc23
LC record available at https://lccn.loc.gov/2021007570
LC ebook record available at https://lccn.loc.gov/2021007571

ISBN: 978-1-032-01592-7 (hbk)
ISBN: 978-1-032-01709-9 (pbk)
ISBN: 978-1-003-17972-6 (ebk)

Typeset in Perpetua
by Apex CoVantage, LLC

Access the Support Material: www.routledge.com/9781032017099

Contents

Preface

John Adams famously said, "Every problem is an opportunity in disguise." I'm fairly certain that everyone in higher education would agree that the COVID-19 pandemic has caused significant problems in our colleges and universities. Nevertheless, the opportunity waiting in disguise is what we learned from this extraordinary experience. In *Pivoting Your Instruction*, I walk with faculty on a journey to mobilize their hard-won skills and knowledge by employing the principles of design to create effective student-centered courses that can easily pivot from one instructional model to another.

When I wrote *Higher Education by Design: Best Practices for Curricular Planning and Instruction* (Routledge, 2018), my goal was to support faculty in applying design thinking to the task of planning and teaching a course. Since then, my experiences as an administrator charged with the task of leading faculty, staff, and students through what may be the most widespread crisis higher education has encountered prompted me to take my original premise a step further. Well-designed courses housed entirely in the institution's learning management system (LMS) allow us to shift easily between instructional models to maintain educational continuity despite whatever may befall us. Even better, this approach increases students' access to education, fosters students' academic achievement, contributes to continuous curricular improvement, and facilitates program review and assessment, all of which should be among every educator's goals.

The book leads faculty through a process of identifying and examining our underlying beliefs about teaching and attitudes toward our students. We'll consider the principles of design and what it means to adopt a design-thinking approach to building a course, and then examine the characteristics of a high-quality course built in the LMS. We'll also look at seven instructional models and think about how we can build High-Impact Practices into the courses we're designing. Finally, we'll return to the idea of empathy, the first step of design thinking, reflecting on how a student-centered perspective allows us to be genuine change agents in our students' lives and within our institutions. The following short chapter summaries provide a bit more explanation of the journey we'll undertake.

INTRODUCTION

The pandemic of 2020 left an indelible mark on higher education. Even though we may wish we could return to normal, our reality no longer matches our treasured dreams and memories. Now our challenge is to recognize how we might use what we've learned from this crisis to grow and change, moving beyond the histories and traditions that formerly limited us.

CHAPTER 1: THE INTERSECTION OF IDENTITY AND PHILOSOPHY

Self-knowledge helps us recognize our motivations and modify our behavior when we see that our past actions have not yielded the results we wanted to achieve. Our first task is a thoughtful examination of whether we hold a faculty-centered or student-centered philosophy of education. We also need to recognize the hidden bias of college readiness before we can become student-ready educators. Our students are far more diverse than ever before, and a student-ready, student-centered mindset allows us to meet students' need for an education that empowers them to reach for their goals and dreams. The better we understand ourselves and our students, the more we increase our ability to see beyond deeply ingrained aspects of faculty culture and move toward practices that support students' success.

CHAPTER 2: STUDENT CENTERED BY DESIGN

The tools of design help us re-envision our work from a student-centered perspective. They provide a framework in which we can engage in pedagogical and curricular innovation that establishes empathy for our students as the central tenet of our work as educators. Ideation and innovation in curricular and pedagogical design require fresh approaches to our work in creating courses that improve upon the instructional norms of the past. When we implement UX design, instructional design, learning experience design, design thinking, and backward course design, we enact a continuous, productive, and beneficial cycle of empathize-define-ideate-prototype-test each time we teach. This knowledge is fundamental to developing flexible courses that deliver effective learning experiences.

CHAPTER 3: BUILDING A COURSE ONLINE

Without a doubt, building a new course online or adapting a previous course for online delivery involves a substantial investment of time and creative energy, using strategies for empathy and ideation to create content that delivers the requisite instruction while also exhibiting best practices in pedagogical and curricular design. The LMS is a powerful tool that expands our instructional options and allows us to prioritize our students' success regardless of how the course is delivered. Quality Matters and OSCQR define standards for reviewing the quality of online courses. The Quality Recommendations in Chapter 3 synthesize these ideas and reorder them into a checklist that all instructors can use to plan and evaluate their online courses' design.

CHAPTER 4: PIVOTING BETWEEN MODELS OF INSTRUCTIONAL DELIVERY

Students rightfully expect that the institution and its instructors will uphold their responsibilities within higher education's social contract. Providing continuity by being prepared to pivot helps ensure we have the capacity to fulfill our end of the bargain. Chapter 4 offers a shared understanding of terms relating to seven instructional models spanning a continuum from fully online to fully face to face, providing a definition, strengths and weaknesses, and strategies for implementing each one. Building the course into the LMS before the first day of class using Comprehensive Instructional Design goes a long way toward ensuring quality and continuity, no matter which model or models we use.

CHAPTER 5: ADAPTING HIGH-IMPACT PRACTICES ACROSS INSTRUCTIONAL MODALITIES

High-Impact Practices are proven to support students' success, reflecting the student-centered philosophy of teaching at the heart of user experience design and design thinking. We don't employ high-impact practices because they make our job as educators easier—we build them into our courses and programs because we care about delivering the best educational experience within our power. Each instructor can use the strategies and suggestions in this chapter to define how they can include High-Impact Practices in their courses.

CHAPTER 6: A CULTURE OF CARE

Empathy is central to design thinking, but it is also the heart of teaching. Higher education is a fundamentally human enterprise built on the relationships between faculty, students, staff, administrators, and the community. Prioritizing these relationships by caring for ourselves, our students, our colleagues, and our institutions aligns our priorities and places our focus where it belongs—on providing our students with the best educational experience it is within our power to deliver. The idea of the "trim tab"—a small part of a ship's rudder that helps guide even an enormous ocean liner—tells us that each of us can make a significant difference in the lives of others. Every person, no matter what our circumstances, can change the world for the better. Small actions by instructors can significantly impact students' experience in our classrooms, especially when these are motivated by care.

EPILOGUE PART 1: A LETTER TO ADMINISTRATORS AND ACADEMIC LEADERS

Our institutions were already in need of innovation and transformation before COVID-19 because they have not kept pace with the world outside our doors. Administrators should be prepared to lead our institutions to pivot between operational models just as faculty can move fluidly between instructional models. We are called to redefine our institutions even as society redefines what it means to be an educated person, leading with vision, passion, courage, and empathy as we help our colleges and universities transform from what they've always been to what they must become.

EPILOGUE PART 2: A LETTER TO FACULTY

The world does not stand still. Sometimes all we can do is choose how we will respond to the forces surrounding us, thinking deeply about how our actions as educators intersect with the world outside our doors. Our beloved histories and traditions may no longer be the best way to help our institutions achieve the primary mission of making the world a better place through the advancement of knowledge. Adopting Comprehensive Instructional Design will help us through whatever we face, allowing us to provide continuous, high-quality instruction, whether we teach online, on campus, or a blend of both. We all have the power to be change makers, one step at a time.

As you read this book, I hope you'll see that *Pivoting Your Instruction* isn't only about course design. Its central message is that we should learn from our valued histories and traditions but not allow ourselves to be constrained by them. I believe it's time to open our minds to innovation in higher education, approaching our work as educators with grit and a growth mindset shaped by the principles and practices of design and fueled by a student-centered student-ready perspective and culture of care. The longer you've been working in higher education, the more challenging this may be, yet I can wholeheartedly assure you that the rewards are well worth the effort it requires.

Tables and Figures

TABLES

FIGURES

BOXES

Introduction

Challenges and Opportunities

Higher education's difficult forced transformation that began in the spring of 2020 upended our tradition-bound methods of teaching and learning. Our institutions' long-term sustainability depends on developing our capacity for adaptability and agility, preparing us to navigate an uncertain future.

****

DREAMS AND REALITY

The picture is so clear in our minds: graceful campus landscapes filled with stately brick buildings flanked by tree-lined walkways. Inside, students listen attentively to their professors' lectures, study in quiet libraries, work in state-of-the-art laboratories and studios, and relax in comfortable dormitories. Faculty steadily pursue eminence through their high-profile research or creative practice, serve on meaningful committees, and teach in classrooms full of admiring students. The predictable excitement of annual events like Freshman Move-in Day, Homecoming, and Commencement punctuate the unchanging rhythm of campus life. It's a beautiful dream permanently etched in our memories, shaping our ideal of what college should be.

Outside our ivy-covered walls, emerging technologies, evolving cultural norms, and shifting demographic patterns have dramatically changed our lives. Consider a few facts from 2005:[1]

- George W. Bush began his second term as president.
- Hurricane Katrina struck the Gulf Coast of the United States.
- YouTube was founded.
- There were still no "smartphones"—people used separate devices for phone calls, music players, and cameras. In 2005, Samsung was the first

company to offer a two-megapixel camera integrated into a cell phone. The iPhone would not be available for another two years, and the iPad would not exist for another five.

■ Blockbuster and other video rental services were the primary way people watched movies at home.

Since 2005, we've undergone major socio-cultural shifts as well: the Marriage Equality Act, states' legalization of marijuana, the "Me Too" era, mass shootings, ongoing conflict in the Middle East and Afghanistan—all these and more have had a decided impact on our way of life. Furthermore, changing demographics are poised to affect higher education in the coming decade.

■ Population growth has slowed overall, with the South and West far out-pacing the Northeast and Midwest.[2]

■ The percentage of US residents age 65 and older is the fastest-growing segment of the population.[3]

■ Only half the population under age 18 are non-Hispanic white, compared to 76% of those ages 65 and older.[4]

Higher education tends to respond slowly to changes occurring outside our walls. Demographic shifts will have a decided impact on us in the near future as the population of available students shrinks, especially in certain regions. Longstanding presumptions about who our students are and what we can expect of them must change as well. Many institutions have not yet begun to feel these demographic fluctuations, but most have faced significant problems due to dramatic decreases in state funding and their commensurate impact on tuition, which have raised serious questions about the cost of a degree versus its benefits.

■ State funding for two-year and four-year colleges fell by nearly $10 billion between 2008 and 2016. States averaged a reduction of 18%, with nine states decreasing by 30% or more.[5]

■ The average cost of tuition at a public in-state college or university in 2005 was $4,633. In the fall of 2019, it was $11,260[6]—nearly triple the cost in only 15 years.

Lynn Pasquerella, president of the Association of American Colleges and Universities and former president of Mount Holyoke College, addressed this problem during an interview in May of 2020.

We have for a hundred years relied on the same model of higher education, and in the past few decades have implemented what is an unsustainable financial model, where we continue to raise tuition and have burgeoning loan burdens, which result in growing economic and therefore racial segregation in higher education. So I think this crisis will force us to look at new ways to deliver a curriculum at a time when we're recognizing an education will be more important than ever.[7]

COVID-19 thrust institutions of higher learning into a situation they could not ignore. They suddenly had little choice but to navigate the unfamiliar waters of online instructional delivery. Students clamored for tuition refunds, saying they had signed up for an on-campus experience, not online learning. Enrollment plummeted, with students choosing to wait to resume their studies until the campuses reopened sometime in the future. Many institutions scrambled to deal with these financial woes by cutting positions, furloughing faculty and staff, and slashing budgets—upheavals that revealed the tenuous state of their finances. Uncertainty and anxiety became our constant companions.

Nevertheless, this unprecedented experience is not without concurrent opportunity, giving us a chance to upgrade our approaches to instructional delivery and critically examine the organizational and philosophical structures that have shaped higher education for generations.

THE BENEFITS OF CRISIS

Growth and entropy are natural processes, but genuine metamorphosis seldom occurs without a catalyst. People tend to stay in the same workplace, live in the same house, and go about their lives until something happens to push them in a different direction. Sometimes a catalyst is positive: a promotion at work could lead to a higher income, allowing the purchase of a larger, better home. Sometimes a catalyst comes in the form of a crisis: job loss, serious illness, injury, or natural disaster can leave us no choice in the matter—change must occur whether we welcome it or not. In a TED talk titled "The Upside of Crisis" (2014), leadership coach Joseph Logan stated,

Winston Churchill said we should never let a good crisis go to waste. There's an opportunity in chaos that isn't there in stable times. We don't get to choose the crisis, but we do get to choose what happens next. Those choices resonate throughout our lives.[8]

For the sake of illustration, let's first consider an example outside academia. My friend Jo[9] worked at the same job for 30 years, experiencing growth in her career, rising into increasingly responsible professional roles, and serving as a peer leader. Although Jo had known a few workplace hardships over the years, she fully expected to finish her career where it began. Cue the catalyst: a management change rendered her position intolerable. Worse, losing her job would decimate her expected retirement income. Although it was an emotionally wrenching decision made with great reluctance, Jo transferred to a different unit within the organization. She would never have sought this change and grieved that it had become necessary. However, she proved to be surprisingly resilient and adaptable, expanding her professional skill set and making new friends. Best of all, her new supervisor valued her as a human being. In hindsight, Jo realized that the upside of her professional crisis outweighed the trauma it initially brought into her life.

Fink, Beak, and Taddeo (1971) set the standard for understanding how both individuals and organizations respond to times of crisis, a four-stage process beginning with an initial period of shock followed by defensive retreat, acknowledgment, and finally adaptation and change.[10] We can see this play out in Jo's story. She was certainly shocked to learn that her new manager was actively working toward removing her from the organization. She retreated, searching for ways she could defend herself from the manager's unfounded criticism. Nevertheless, Jo eventually acknowledged that she would have to leave the workplace where she'd spent three decades, despite how painful this would be, because choosing to stay posed too great a risk to her financial future. Adapting to the changes of beginning anew in a different location was not easy for her, but it eventually brought about a better outcome than Jo would have experienced if she'd stayed.

Higher education is even more opposed to change than my friend Jo. We cling tenaciously to our valued histories and traditions. They are part of our collective and professional identities. They shape our departmental cultures and distinguish our institution from its peers. That's all well and good . . . until something catastrophic happens. When we cannot loosen our grip on the past, we bog down in the stage of "defensive retreat," placing ourselves in jeopardy. For instance, arts and humanities programs have been under fire for the past decade or more, with political leaders questioning their validity compared to STEM disciplines, pointing to their low enrollment and poor alumni outcomes.[11] Increasing financial pressure prompts universities to seek opportunities to cut costs, often targeting underperforming, under-enrolled programs. In the spring of 2018, the University of Wisconsin at Stevens Point announced a plan to close its programs in American studies, art, French, geography, geoscience, German, music literature, philosophy, political science, sociology, and Spanish, leaving only portions of history, English, and social sciences as required for teacher certification.[12]

Similarly, Emory University closed its Division of Educational Studies, the Department of Physical Education, the Department of Visual Arts, and the Program in Journalism in 2012.[13] The same story has played out elsewhere. Faculty and administrators of threatened programs tend to respond with defensive retreat, attempting to marshal convincing evidence in support of their disciplines' intrinsic value to the university in hopes it will avert the crisis so they can continue with business as usual. Indeed, the College Art Association offers similar advice to programs facing potential closure in its standards and guidelines.

> Using [your] depth of knowledge in the field, craft a statement specifically tailored to the individual institution, setting forth a well-reasoned rationale as to why visual arts, art history and related programs are important to the institution, the region, state, nation, and is of particular importance to developing an informed global perspective. The statement should articulate why a population educated in humanities is advantageous to our culture and the development of a skilled workforce.[14]

The CAA's guidelines also direct faculty and staff to understand factors that led to the proposed change and explore and suggest alternatives or solutions to program closure. Nevertheless, focusing energy on persuading upper administrators not to close a program is a preservationist stance that fails to acknowledge the program's role in precipitating the problem or suggest what the program could do to solve the problem from within. Academic units that maintain sufficient enrollment to sustain their operations and produce graduates who find gainful employment in their major fields seldom encounter an existential crisis when funding cuts must occur. Conversely, those that depend on the university's largesse for their continued existence cannot trust that their inherent value to culture or society will be sufficient to merit their survival. When the crisis descends, faculty and administrators of these units often demonstrate fierce determination to keep things the way they've always been rather than taking steps to address challenges. They resist suggestions to alter their longstanding habits and practices and meet proposed innovations with disdain or even outrage. To say the least, defensive retreat is unproductive and potentially self-destructive when we refuse to accept the situation and move forward.

Before entering higher education, I worked in the insurance industry, where I witnessed the full crisis-to-recovery process play out time and again. Property owners who had experienced a devastating loss were usually still in shock when I first spoke with them. They would look around at their damaged belongings in bewilderment, trying to find something they could salvage. Only after they had accepted the reality of the loss were we able to discuss what they must do to move forward. Letting go is hard. No one wants to see their belongings pitched into a dumpster or watch as their home is gutted, but once the restoration was complete, many of these property owners were better off than before the damage occurred. A home with a deteriorating roof damaged by hail now sported a brand-new roof. New paint and flooring upgraded the appearance of a dingy office space ravaged by fire and smoke. A fresh start doesn't erase a loss we've suffered, but it helps us move on to something better.

Perhaps the best example of managing a crisis comes from Tulane University's response to Hurricane Katrina in 2005 when virtually the entire city of New Orleans was submerged beneath floodwaters. Tulane had to turn away its 12,000 students, and its leadership team operated out of a hotel suite 300 miles away. Tulane's president emeritus, Scott Cowen, spoke to Philip Rogers of the American Council on Education's "Engage" about his experiences with Katrina (March 27, 2020),[15] just as US campuses had sent their students home and were moving into Emergency Remote Teaching. Cowen explained,

> The most important thing we were thinking about at the time was the safety and welfare of all of our students, faculty and staff and their families. That was first and foremost in everything we did because we were deeply concerned about them.

He outlined the three steps Tulane took to manage the crisis.

- [We continued] to pay all faculty and staff for as long as we could, even though we were not going to be open, that turned out to be important because we knew that they were going through their own personal crisis, and they were anxious because they had lost their homes. We didn't want them to think they were going to lose their job or their salary. Making that investment, which costs us about $40 million a month for about five months, was very significant.
- We decided that we would just declare that we would re-open in January 2006, even though we had no idea that we would be able to re-open [because] we wanted to give a sense of hope . . . [something] everybody could think about, and could look forward to in the midst of all this tragedy.
- [Third], I reached out to all the higher education associations in America and asked them to [let] our students come for this fall semester of 2005 but don't let them transfer at all because if they transfer, they would never come back. And, if possible to let them come for free.

Amazingly, many colleges and universities responded to Cowen's plea for help, allowing Tulane's students to attend classes at no charge in the fall 2005 semester. Cowen's actions to take care of Tulane's people, instill hope, and recruit help all served Tulane well. Decisions made during the crisis were unprecedented, but they allowed Tulane to reopen in January 2006 despite the work ahead, beginning a process of rebuilding and recovery that was not completed for almost a decade. Cowen and his leadership team approached the seemingly insurmountable problem one step at a time, breaking it down into the smallest parts they could. Each day, they reviewed what they had accomplished the day before and made a new plan for what they would accomplish that day, focusing on action steps that were under their control rather than those that were beyond their reach.

TECHNOLOGY, OPINION, AND EXPERIENCE

Crisis sometimes forces us beyond our perceived limits. At more than one of the institutions at which I've served, certain faculty adamantly insisted they could not possibly teach their discipline online without sacrificing quality. Twice, at two different universities, the topic came up in a department meeting, ending with a colleague storming out of the conference room, distraught at the mere suggestion of offering a variation of their courses online—utterly convinced that doing so would "erode the discipline forever." COVID-19 had no respect for such sentiments—programs across the country went online without regard for faculty preferences or beliefs. Lo and behold, nearly all of us found we were able to complete our teaching for the semester fully online. The pandemic led us to discover resources within ourselves that we would not otherwise have known we possessed.

In 2005 or even 2010, the feats we accomplished in 2020 would have been impossible. All we could have done was go home and wait until it was safe to return to campus because the requisite technologies simply didn't exist at that time, were far too costly, or weren't widely available for immediate implementation back then. Even as remarkable as our present technologies have been and what we've been able to achieve, when the crisis hit, the majority of faculty and students were notably inexperienced in the use of their campus learning management system (LMS), video conferencing such as Zoom or Microsoft Teams, and other of the tools that facilitated our instructional transformation. Consider the following:[16]

- More than 19 million students were enrolled in US higher education at the start of the 2019–2020 academic year.
- Of those, between 12 and 13 million were taking courses only on campus.
- Another 3.5 to 4 million were taking both online and on-campus courses.
- Finally, 3.2 to 2.5 million were taking all their courses online.

Faculty numbers show slightly more disparity: of the 1.5 million faculty members teaching in higher education, 1 million had never taught online before the spring of 2020.

Considering that approximately two-thirds of students and faculty had little to no prior experience with teaching and learning online, the fact that institutions were able to respond so quickly to the abrupt closure of their campuses is nothing short of extraordinary.

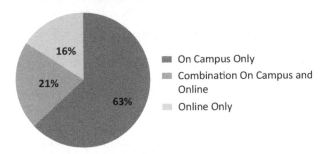

Student Enrollment

- On Campus Only
- Combination On Campus and Online
- Online Only

FIGURE 0.1 Student Enrollment Type

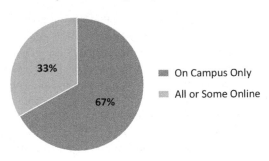

Faculty Teaching Experience

- On Campus Only
- All or Some Online

FIGURE 0.2 Faculty Teaching Experience

Statistics about prior online experience came as somewhat of a surprise to me. I've taught online for many years and designed courses that could be offered online, on-campus, and as a blend of the two. Furthermore, it's no secret that online education has been growing for the past two decades, but perhaps it didn't seem personally relevant to those accustomed to teaching and learning exclusively on campus. Implementation of online instructional delivery was imperfect at most institutions, particularly concerning students' access to necessary technologies and faculty inexperience in the use of the institution's LMS. Fortunately, the pace of development in educational technology has not slowed. Between my writing of this sentence and your reading of this book, more innovations will have occurred. I sincerely hope we will have solved the problems of ensuring that every student has sufficiently fast Wi-Fi connections at home and up-to-date computers with built-in cameras and microphones, facilitating synchronous online meetings and remote learning.

THE HUMAN ELEMENT

COVID-19 may have been the first pandemic to force us to close the campus and work from home, but it is unlikely to be the last time we face disruption. Our ability to cope with the next crisis doesn't rest in new and better technologies, although these will assuredly come our way. Rather, our task is to reskill and upskill the people who work with them. Even the best tools are useless if we're unable or unwilling to use them, so training in the "hard skills" required for technological competence is important. Nevertheless, this is just part of the answer since the rapid pace of technological innovation will require frequent skills updates for all users. We also need to focus our energies on developing essential "soft skills"—increasing our aptitude for adaptability and developing the capacity to learn new skills with ease. More importantly, we need to maintain a positive attitude toward educational innovation and fortify our professional curiosity. Intrinsic motivation to remain at the forefront of our professions, never ceasing in our pursuit of excellence, is among the qualifications essential for any educator in this rapidly changing world. Many of us don't want to hear this. We'd like to think we can turn our backs on the painful experiences we've had and settle back into our comfortable routines as though nothing ever happened. Of course, that's an option, but it's probably not the best choice we could make. Instead, we can grow stronger, more resilient, more open, and more willing to capitalize on the benefits of the crisis we experienced.

Management experts Becky Frankiewicz and Tomas Chamorrow-Premuzic echo these thoughts in an article for the *Harvard Business Review*.[17]

> Human beings are the common denominator to the concept of future-proofing, whether it's as a complement to the technology being unleashed for remote working, or whether it's because we possess the soft skills and leadership needed to navigate a historic crisis, or because we have the insights needed to drive slow success or fast failure for a cure. It all starts with each and every one of us, and those we are responsible for developing. The key is to nurture curiosity, so we have options, even outside of a crisis.

WHAT'S NEXT?

This book is not about the pandemic. Rather, its purpose is to leverage the lessons we can learn from that shared experience and address areas where we can strengthen our skills as educators so that we are prepared to meet whatever challenges come our way while continuing to provide an optimal learning experience to our students.

In the chapters that follow, we'll examine topics including:

- Developing a student-centered mindset through User Experience Design, Instructional Design, Learning Experience Design, and Design Thinking.
- Creating courses designed for flexibility using Quality Matters, TILT (Transparency in Teaching and Learning), and "backward" design.
- Teaching from a student-centered mindset, incorporating High-Impact Practices, guided learning, and a culture of care.
- Moving easily between online, hybrid, and on-campus formats, fueled by a growth mindset and grit.

I wrote this book because I firmly believe that *every* faculty member can make a difference to the students we teach and to our colleagues as we embrace the challenges and opportunities that lie before us. We can lead by example, sow seeds of inspiration, and be a force for good in our programs, departments, colleges, schools, and universities.

Without a doubt, our institutions can and should take steps to become more resilient, agile, and future proof. Visionary leadership, investment in high-quality faculty development, improved LMS and communication technologies, and ensuring adequate access for *every* learner will be crucial in this regard. However, few of these considerations fall under the control of individual faculty members.

I believe the future of higher education belongs to people just like us—caring educators who can honor the histories and legacies of the past without being bound by them. We can move forward with confidence in our skills and abilities as knowledgeable disciplinary experts and empathetic instructors, driven by curiosity and the desire to change the world one student at a time.

Notes

[1] Beres, D. (2017, December 6). What your favorite tech gadgets looked like 10 years ago. *HuffPost*. Retrieved from www.huffpost.com/entry/2005-tech-gadgets_n_7215718; The People History. (2005). Retrieved from www.thepeoplehistory.com/2005.html

[2] Pollard, K., Jacobsen, L., & Mather, M. (2020, February 18). The US population is growing at the slowest rate since the 1930s. *Population Research Board*. Retrieved from www.prb.org/the-u-s-population-is-growing-at-the-slowest-rate-since-the-1930s/

[3] Mather, M., Jacobsen, L., Jaroz, B., et al. (2019, June 12). What the 2020 census will tell us about a changing America. *Population Research Board*. Retrieved from www.prb.org/what-the-2020-u-s-census-will-tell-us-about-a-changing-america/

[4] Mather, M., Jacobsen, L., Jaroz, B., et al. (2019, June 12). What the 2020 census will tell us about a changing America. *Population Research Board*. Retrieved from www.prb.org/what-the-2020-u-s-census-will-tell-us-about-a-changing-america/

[5] Mitchell, M., Leachman, M., & Masterson, K. (2016, August 15). Funding down, tuition up: State cuts to higher education threaten quality and affordability at public colleges. *Center on Budget and Policy Priorities*. Retrieved from www.cbpp.org/research/state-budget-and-tax/funding down tuition up

[6] Boyington, B., & Kerr, E. (2019, September 19). 20 years of tuition growth at national universities. *U.S. News & World Report*. Retrieved from www.usnews.com/education/best-colleges/paying-for-college/articles/2017-09-20/see-20-years-of-tuition-growth-at-national-universities

[7] Schermele, Z. (2020, May 21). Higher education will be transformed by the coronavirus pandemic. Politics. *Teen Vogue*. Retrieved from www.teenvogue.com/story/higher-education-coronavirus

[8] Logan, J. *The upside of crisis*. TEDxBoulder. Retrieved from www.youtube.com/watch?v=rVtMYpOSNmA&feature=youtu.be

[9] Name has been changed.

[10] Fink, S. L., Beak, J., & Taddeo, K. (1971). Organizational crisis and change. *The Journal of Applied Behavioral Science*, 7(1), 15–37. https://doi.org/10.1177/002188637100700103

[11] For more information, see Mackh, B. (2016). *Connecting the dots*. Presented at the Conference on the Liberal Arts, Jackson State University, Mississippi, October 2016. Available on Academia.edu https://independent.academia.edu/BruceMackhPhD

[12] Flaherty, C. (2018, March 6). U Wisconsin-Stevens Point to eliminate 13 majors. *Inside Higher Ed*. Retrieved from www.insidehighered.com/quicktakes/2018/03/06/u-wisconsin-stevens-point-eliminate-13-majors

[13] Seiderman, N. (2012, September 14). Emory college announces new directions. *Emory News Center*. Retrieved from https://news.emory.edu/stories/2012/09/EmoryCollege-Plan/campus.html

[14] Guidelines for Addressing Proposed Substantive Changes to an Art, Art History or Design Unit or Program at Colleges or Universities. (2018, October 28). *Standards & guidelines*. Retrieved from www.collegeart.org/standards-and-guidelines/guidelines/changes

[15] Rogers, P. (2020, March 27). *Interview with Scott Cowen. American Council on Education,* "engage." Retrieved January 2, 2021, from www.facebook.com/page/1734477186870105/search/?q=scott%20cowen

[16] Statistics from the National Center for Education Statistics "Fast Facts: Distance Learning." https://nces.ed.gov/fastfacts/display.asp?id=80. Cited by Jeff Seaman, director of Bay View Analytics in the webcast "The Great (Forced) Shift to Remote Learning: A Survey of Instructors and Campus Leaders," hosted by Inside Higher Ed. (4/24/2020).

[17] Frankiewicz, B., & Chamorro-Premuzic, T. (2020, May 6). Digital transformation is about talent, not technology. Developing employees. *Harvard Business Review*. Retrieved from https://hbr.org/amp/2020/05/digital-transformation-is-about-talent-not-technology

The Intersection of Identity and Philosophy

CHAPTER 1 SUMMARY

- Faculty Identities
- Philosophies of Teaching
- Student Identities
- From College Ready to Student Ready
- Student-Centered Institutions
- Student-Centered Educators
- Reflection and Review
- Grit and Growth Mindset

Let's embark upon a journey together. I imagine you chose this book because you're a faculty member who cares about your students and wants to improve your practice as an educator. (If that's not true, then this book probably isn't for you. I'll understand if you choose to stop reading now, although I hope you'll continue.)

The first stage of our journey will begin before we take a single step. This chapter will help us find our bearings—to locate the little dot on the map labeled "You Are Here" so we can plot a course that will take us to our destination. Therefore, we'll start by developing an understanding of the identities, values, and beliefs that guide our work as educators. We'll also examine who our students are and how their identities have changed. The knowledge we'll gain prepares us for the work in which we'll engage throughout our journey, leading toward our development of student-centered and student-ready philosophies of teaching and a more accurate understanding of our students.

FACULTY IDENTITIES

Imagine you're at a social gathering. You strike up a conversation with a new acquaintance who asks, "So, what do you do?" How would you respond?

Many faculty might say, "I teach ____ [name of subject] at ____ [name of institution]," or "I'm a professor of ____ [name of subject] at ____ [name of institution]."

Connections between work and identity are particularly strong for professionals: when we're asked how we see ourselves, we commonly respond with statements about our jobs, as in the previous examples.[1] Clearly, the act of teaching takes priority in these statements, but the phrasing is somewhat curious. To say, for example, "I teach molecular biology" usually means "I teach students the theories and practices of molecular biology," but we seldom phrase it this way. The same is true of saying, "I am a professor of music." To profess is to boldly state a claim, which implies the existence of an audience. To whom are you professing your knowledge? The habit of omitting students from our statements of identity may be nothing more than a verbal mannerism or figure of speech, but it's also indicative of our perceptions and attitudes toward our work. After all, teaching is not an activity conducted in isolation, nor does the subject we teach have anything to learn from us. Although we may not be aware of it, leaving students out of our statements of professional identity reveals that, at least for many faculty, our focus remains firmly on our discipline.

We include the name of the place we teach when someone asks, "So, what do you do?" because the institution plays a significant role in our professional identities. Its reputation, status, history, and brand shape how others perceive us and how we perceive ourselves. Likewise, our role within the institution affects those perceptions, including the degrees or titles we hold, our academic rank, tenure status, and affiliations with groups within the institution. It's all part of our professional identity, defining who we are and how others think of us.

Most faculty develop a professional identity in graduate school, where we absorb the values, attitudes, and disciplinary norms of the faculty under whom we study. Terminal degree programs place a primary emphasis on research or creative practice. Graduate students may work as teaching assistants or graduate instructors, but a demonstration of competence in teaching is seldom required for graduation. Instead, our studies lead to qualification as disciplinary experts. Then, equipped with this new status, we obtain work as educators—a job for which we've had little to no prior training.[2]

Our experience as graduate students transmits implicit expectations about how teaching works. Most of the faculty from whom graduate students learn tend to rely on lectures or direct instruction as their primary teaching method. As a result, their students emulate this technique once they become faculty members themselves. Graduate students and new faculty members also internalize faculty

2

cultures that value and reward engagement in research or creative activity over the pursuit of excellence in teaching, mirrored in the systems by which faculty achieve professional distinction through peer-reviewed publication, exhibition, or performance. Furthermore, institutional systems for retention, promotion, and tenure often include a peer-review component whereby faculty evaluate one another, usually emphasizing disciplinary achievement over excellence in teaching.[3] It should come as no surprise, then, that many (if not most) faculty hold their research or creative practice in higher esteem than their work as educators.

PHILOSOPHIES OF TEACHING

Institutions of higher learning frequently include the term "student centered" in their mission and vision statements, strategic plans, and promotional materials. Do our institutions' public claims of being student centered align with our own attitudes toward teaching? The answer lies in our professional identities and philosophies of education, both of which exist within the highly institutionalized environment of higher education.

First, a common understanding of the meaning of the term "student centered" might be helpful. The Glossary of Educational Reform defines "student-centered learning" as "a wide variety of educational programs, learning experiences, instructional approaches, and academic support strategies that are intended to address the distinct learning needs, interests, aspirations, or cultural backgrounds of individual students and groups of students."[4]

It's one thing for an institution to declare that it's student centered, but this philosophy is nothing more than an attractive slogan until faculty come to see themselves as both disciplinary practitioners *and* educators, understanding that one identity need not displace the other. Institutions can facilitate this change by providing professional development, time to create and revise curriculum and pedagogies as an established and protected staple of a faculty member's load, and incentives that persuade faculty to take action to become better educators. However, developing a student-centered philosophy of education primarily depends on changing our minds about what we do as educators, influenced by the extent to which we retain a traditionally faculty-centered perspective.

Faculty-Centered vs Student-Centered Models of Education

What springs to mind when you picture teaching and learning in higher education? Many of us immediately envision a middle-aged white man standing at the front of a lecture hall. There's a projected presentation on a large screen behind him, and he's facing a sizeable group of students seated in theatre-style rows, all taking notes. It's a cliché, I know, but how many times a day does this scene play

3

out on nearly every campus? Most of us sat in these lecture halls when we were in college, and many of us still teach in them today.

Since time immemorial, higher education has focused both literally and figuratively on the instructor, whose status as a disciplinary expert imparts a high degree of prestige as well as autonomy over the pedagogies and curricula they choose to employ. We're quite comfortable with the instructor as the center of attention. Given the path that most of us took to the professorate, it's no surprise that we would presume this is simply how education has always been and will always be.

Faculty-Centered Teaching

Faculty seldom spend much time contemplating their philosophy of teaching unless we're asked for a written statement to accompany a job application, nor is this a requirement of most graduate programs outside the field of education. Nevertheless, our explicit and implicit teaching philosophies drive our approaches to the pedagogies and curricula we choose to use in our classrooms, labs, and studios. In Chapter 2 of *Higher Education by Design*, I presented a brief overview of educational philosophy, including the following (emphasis added):

> Traditional approaches to education might be termed **"instructivism,"** rooted in John Locke's Essay Concerning Human Understanding (1689), in which Locke proposes that the human mind is a blank slate at birth, filled by accumulated experience. Education has, therefore, historically been predicated on the belief that students' minds are empty until filled by the instructor, who carefully plans and organizes a program of study on behalf of the learner. Learners must first become literate and gain a measure of self-discipline in order to pay attention to the information presented by the instructor and to remember concepts they do not understand, including rote memorization of information.[5] Clearly, this is an **instructor-centered**[6] model of learning, with the student remaining a passive recipient of transmitted knowledge.

Similarly, the Glossary of Educational Reform defines this as "teacher-centered learning."

> Teacher-centered typically refers to learning situations in which the teacher asserts control over the material that students study and the ways in which they study it—i.e., when, where, how, and at what pace they learn it. In classes that would be considered teacher-centered, the teacher tends to be the most active person in the room and do most of the talking (e.g., by lecturing, demonstrating concepts, reading aloud, or issuing instructions),

while students spend most of their time sitting in desks, listening, taking notes, giving brief answers to questions that the teacher asks, or completing assignments and tests. In addition, in teacher-centered classrooms, teachers may also decide to teach students in ways that are easy, comfortable, or personally preferred, but that might not work well for some students or use instructional techniques shown to be most effective for improving learning. These descriptions probably sound very familiar. They reflect the way most of us were taught when we were students, and for many of us, they define our preferred pedagogical approaches.

Student-Centered Learning

At the opposite end of the spectrum, "student-centered learning" shifts a classroom's focus away from faculty expertise in a given discipline. Student-centered learning relies on constructivist theory as proposed by Jerome Bruner (1960),[7] who identified learning as an active process through which students build new knowledge upon prior learning. Constructivism is consistent with discoveries in cognitive neuroscience, explaining how the human brain learns.[8] We cannot retain new content unless we have an existing schema, or mental model, upon which to build.

Instead of the passivity that characterizes students' presence in a faculty-centered learning environment, student-centered pedagogies employ active participation in the learning process. Students might design their own projects, explore topics of interest, and work collaboratively with one another. The classroom environment itself looks different, too. Chairs in a room used for lectures generally face the front of the room so that students can keep their eyes on the instructor. On the other hand, student-centered classrooms might feature furniture arranged to accommodate group discussions and collaborative projects. Indeed, learning activities might not occur in a classroom at all: students might participate in self-guided learning experiences or activities such as internships, apprenticeships, independent research, study abroad, service learning, community engagement, and more.[9]

Although student-centered learning can encompass a broad array of approaches and strategies, a few common characteristics usually exist:

1. Instruction in a given content area or discipline accommodates learners' goals, needs, interests, aspirations, and cultural backgrounds.
2. Assessments measure students' acquisition of the knowledge, skills, and competencies specified in the course objectives and outcomes.
3. Learning activities reflect student voice and choice: students determine how, what, where, and when they will learn, subject to parameters determined by the instructor and the institution.

5

Faculty-centered philosophies might lead some readers to be suspicious of student-centered approaches to teaching and learning. However, before you jump to the conclusion that student-centered learning is a slippery slope descending into educational anarchy, it's important to clarify a few points. Being student centered does not imply that students should control every aspect of the learning environment. The instructor remains a subject-area expert, establishes expectations for learning within the classroom, and evaluates students' work, as is the case in nearly every classroom, lab, or studio. However, student-centered learning seldom casts students as mere recipients of transmitted knowledge. Rather, the instructor sets the purpose for learning and provides background information sufficient to empower students on their journey of discovery. Students engage in tasks designed by the instructor but driven by student interest, active learning, and the construction of knowledge and skill within a discipline. We will look at specific teaching strategies later on. For now, the point is to understand the philosophical differences between maintaining a focus on the instructor and focusing on students' learning.

Synthesis and Comparison

Table 1.1 compares faculty-centered and student-centered models of education.[10]

TABLE 1.1 Comparison of Faculty-Centered and Student-Centered Models of Education

	Faculty-Centered	Student-Centered
What is the priority?	What's best for faculty.	What's best for student learning.
How are decisions made?	By faculty.	Students choose from among available options determined by faculty or the institution.
What is the primary role of faculty?	To design and teach curricula, which remains under the faculty member's control.	To guide and facilitate student learning.
What shapes instruction?	Individual faculty preferences.	Students' interests and goals.
How are students taught?	Primary reliance on lecture; faculty teach as they were taught; same instructional approach employed for all students.	Engaged learning, cooperative problem solving; students pursue their own interests within a framework created by the instructor.

	Faculty-Centered	Student-Centered
How is curriculum selected and presented?	Faculty select curricular materials; presentation generally covers a large quantity of material and emphasizes memorization of facts and information.	The instructor provides a framework of foundational knowledge to facilitate students' independent learning. Students discover knowledge through interest-based inquiry.
What is the role of the student?	To passively receive information transmitted by faculty.	To actively engage in the learning process.
What is the role of the instructor?	To plan instruction, create instructional materials, deliver instruction, and assess students' mastery of course content.	To facilitate student learning through a combination of methods and approaches designed to promote students' discovery of knowledge and its application to settings outside the learning environment.
How is learning assessed?	Formal exams, usually multiple-choice, measure students' acquisition of knowledge presented during lectures and in required readings.	Student self-assessment; peer assessment/critique; instructor analysis of student learning through observation, critique/ evaluation. Assessment measures student achievement of stated objectives and outcomes.
What is the philosophy regarding student success?	Faculty present material that students must learn; it is up to students to learn it or not. Individual students' success is not a priority.	Faculty demonstrate concern for the well-being and success of all students; instructional materials are adapted to meet individual students' needs.
What types of learning are assessed?	Memorized facts; reflection of the instructor's attitudes and beliefs as communicated through lectures.	Fundamental knowledge, critical thinking, collaboration, communication, creativity, skills and competencies, ability to apply knowledge to practical situations or settings.
What characterizes graduates?	They have completed their studies and have been exposed to a body of knowledge within a discipline.	They understand what they have learned and can apply it to solve problems, communicate in real-world settings, and maintain the ability to be self-motivated, lifelong learners.

In the grand scheme of higher education, the student-centered philosophy is a relative newcomer, whereas faculty-centered philosophies have existed quite literally for millennia. Nevertheless, the same is true of motorized transportation when compared to centuries of travel by horse-drawn conveyances. Continued adherence to anachronistic practices exists, of course. The Amish still travel by horse and buggy and have compelling religious reasons for doing so. Likewise, some faculty retain their longstanding belief that their presence at the center of attention in the classroom is not just a tradition but an imperative, believing it's their job to fill students' heads with the disciplinary expertise they possess.

Defining our professional identities and understanding how they affect our teaching philosophy can help us become better educators, but this is only half the task before us. Our next step is to understand our students' identities better since they are the direct recipients of our actions.

STUDENT IDENTITIES

Who are our students? Under a faculty-centered model of education, this question might be seen as irrelevant because the faculty-centered model operates on two core presumptions. First, the instructor's job is to teach their subject. Second, students ought to be ready for college and, therefore, able to meet the instructor's expectations. Under a faculty-centered model, then, it doesn't really matter who our students are. They come to us ready to learn, and we teach them what we know.

For generations, admissions practices led faculty to presume that their students had proven themselves worthy by earning excellent grade point averages in high school, achieving stellar scores on standardized testing, and demonstrating they are "well rounded" through their exemplary participation in extracurricular activities, volunteering or community service, and other measures of individual achievement. The more selective the institution, the more outstanding its applicants must prove themselves to be. Faculty could trust their students' capacity to be independent learners who didn't require additional assistance from their instructors.

Expectations that students must demonstrate a certain level of merit before earning admission to a college or university grew from the fact that higher education was formerly a privilege available only to those whose families were sufficiently affluent to pay for college out of pocket. The GI Bill of 1944 and the establishment of the National Defense Student Loan (now the Perkins Loan) in 1958 broadened access to higher education,[11] but elitist attitudes remain. For example, in *Assault on American Excellence* (2019), former dean of the Yale Law School Anthony Kronman upholds the aristocratic ideal of higher education above considerations of equity or equality, justifying his stance by saying, "an aristocratic education promotes the independent-mindeness that is needed to combat the tyranny of majority opinion."[12] At first glance, this might ring true: many of

8

us who work in academia believe that one of the purposes of higher education is to produce well-informed citizens who can think critically—the "indepen-dent-mindedness" that Kronman suggests. However, we also believe this ought to be a benefit for *everyone* who receives a liberal arts education. Kronman's use of the word "aristocratic" that, he acknowledges, implies some people "are more fully developed as human beings—more fully human, one might say,"[13] than oth-ers conveys an attitude that I find inexcusable. Higher education has many bene-fits, but I truly believe that even a completely uneducated person is just as fully human as a person with several advanced degrees.

Similarly elitist attitudes have been part of US higher education since its founding. The nine original colonial colleges were established by religious groups to train young men for the ministry, based on the widespread belief that an edu-cated and well-informed clergy was crucial to society, producing many of the political, social, and religious leaders of the time.[14] All these institutions are still in operation today.

Harvard University (1636)—Puritan
College of William and Mary (1693)—Anglican (Church of England)
Yale University (1701)—Congregationalist
College of New Jersey (now Princeton University) (1746)—Presbyterian
King's College (now Columbia University) (1754)—Anglican (Church of England)
College of Philadelphia (now the University of Pennsylvania) (1755)—nondenominational
College of Rhode Island (now Brown University) (1764)—Baptist
Queen's College (now Rutgers University) (1766)—Dutch Reformed Church
Dartmouth College (1769)—Congregationalist

In time, the colonial colleges expanded to include instruction in law and medi-cine, but the course of study continued to mirror the classical European model. All students were white, male, and Christian, and most were from relatively privileged families. Graduates were few: scholars estimate that no more than one in one thousand colonists attended college, with perhaps only 3,000 living grad-uates in a population of about 2.5 million in 1775.[15]

As the nation grew over the next century, more colleges opened their doors, given a boost in 1862 with the passage of the Morrill Act, which prompted the creation of land-grant colleges and universities in every state. These shared "the primary goal of educating the common rural American"[16] and fostered scientific research into agriculture and the mechanical arts (engineering) "in order to pro-mote the liberal and practical education of the industrial classes in several pur-suits and professions in life"[17]—a far cry from the elitism of the colonial colleges.

The Industrial Age rapidly spawned new technologies, leading to increasing specialization in the sciences and demanding a better-educated workforce. Just as the colonial colleges served a dual purpose in providing a broad classical education coupled with preparation for careers in ministry, medicine, and law, the land-grant colleges served the same function across a wider variety of fields, professionalizing agriculture and engineering while continuing to uphold the value of instruction in the liberal arts.

The impulse to broaden access to higher education in the mid-1800s, "to build up a people's institution, a great free University, eventually open and accessible to the poorest [person] in the land, who may come and receive an education practical and suitable for any business or profession in life" (Kentucky University, 1866), echoes today's conversations. A century and a half later, we're still debating issues of the intrinsic and instrumental value of a college education, but we might see the impulse toward open access and inclusiveness, affordability, and practical preparation for careers as a return to our roots rather than a betrayal of traditional values. Both purposes remain essential, and we should recognize that both have been present in higher education since the beginning.

Questions of access, exclusivity, expense, and purpose continue to shape higher education, resulting in gaps between institutions that are both wide and deep. Seven of the nine colonial colleges now comprise the Ivy League (excluding the College of William and Mary and including Cornell University, founded in 1865), remaining prohibitively exclusive and extraordinarily expensive. For instance, Harvard admits around 5% of applicants, and its total cost of attendance for one year is $67,580.[18] In contrast, Bridgewater State, a regional comprehensive public university located just 43 miles from Harvard, admits 81% of applicants, and a year of tuition is slightly more than $10,000.[19] Room and board can at least double the cost of attendance, so students increasingly choose to live at home and commute to class. For example, less than 25% of students live in campus housing at Valdosta State University in Georgia,[20] whereas 97% of Harvard students choose to live on campus for all four years.[21]

Discrepancies such as these characterize the diverse selection of colleges and universities available to prospective students. Public versus private, nonprofit versus for profit, faith based versus secular, small liberal arts colleges versus enormous Research-1 universities, historic bricks-and-mortar campuses versus solely online programs, highly selective admissions versus open enrollment, and unlimited points along these parallel spectrums present a dizzying array of options for potential students.

Selectivity

Elite colleges and universities remain powerfully influential, conferring considerable prestige upon their faculties and alumni. Daniel Markovits, a professor of law at Yale, offers a contradictory viewpoint to Kronman. In his book *The Meritocracy Trap* (2015), Markovits points to the establishment of a meritocracy via the self-perpetuating cycle of wealth and access to elite education, noting inequities that result: "In recent years, the 'Ivy Plus'[22] colleges have enrolled more students in the top 1 percent of income distribution than from the entire bottom half."[23] Graduates of elite institutions dominate prestigious, high-paying career fields. The more affluent a family is, the more resources they can devote to providing their children with an outstanding education from preschool onward. They pay for sports, art lessons, and music lessons. They live in wealthy neighborhoods where school districts spend as much as $30,000 per pupil per year, versus the median public school expenditure of $15,000,[24] and ranging to just under $7,000 in the poorest school districts.[25]

Markovits cites sobering statistics from the College Board (2016) linking parental finances to educational outcomes.[26]

- Students whose parents earned over $200,000 were 35 times more likely to score above 750 on the SAT's critical reading test than students whose parents earned less than $20,000.
- Students with a parent who held a graduate degree were 140 times more likely to score over 750 than students whose parents did not complete high school.
- Twelfth-graders whose parents have college degrees spend 25% more days volunteering than those whose parents have a high school education or less.
- High–socioeconomic status twelfth-graders are twice as likely as low-status twelfth-graders to participate in and captain interscholastic sports teams.

Perceptions (and misperceptions) about elite universities shape our unconscious ideals about what college ought to be like. Nevertheless, these institutions are the exception, not the rule. Less than 1% of all undergraduates are enrolled at a highly selective institution (those accepting less than 10% of applicants), and just 3% attend selective institutions (accepting less than 25% of applicants).[27] Statistics from the Pew Research Center (2019) paint a similar picture.[28] A small minority of institutions are prohibitively selective, while the majority admit two-thirds or more of students who apply.

Figure 1.1 demonstrates that just 3% of all institutions admit less than 20% of applicants; another 17% admit between 20% and 50% of applicants, and 70% admit 50% of applicants or more. Less selectivity means these institutions enroll greater numbers of students who don't match the profile of a traditional "college-ready" student that the selective institutions rely upon—students who demonstrate merit through their high standardized test scores and grade-point average, completion of college-preparatory or honors classes, and extracurricular participation in high school.

Percent of Institutions / Acceptance Rates

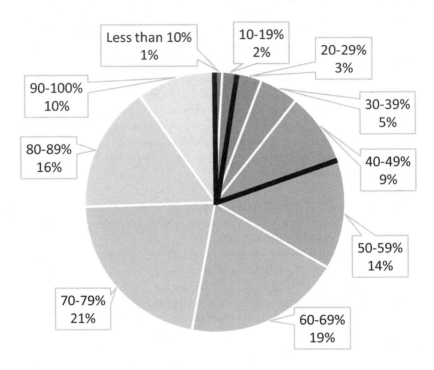

FIGURE 1.1 Student Acceptance Rates

College Readiness

Public education in K–12 remains under pressure to produce high school gradu-ates who are college ready, but correlations between school systems' geographic, demographic, and socioeconomic characteristics lead to the general observation that students who demonstrate the highest degree of so-called college-readiness share a set of similar characteristics linked to wealth and race.

- Graduates of high schools located in relatively affluent neighborhoods
- Financially secure
- At least one parent graduated from college
- More likely to be white

Conversely, graduates of comparatively weaker school systems also tend to come from lower-income households. Their parents are less likely to have graduated from college. They are more likely to be among racial or ethnic minorities, and they are statistically less likely to exhibit the qualities associated with being college ready.

The roots of these inequalities run deep into the founding of our nation. In 1813, Thomas Jefferson wrote to John Adams, suggesting the cultivation of a "natural aristocracy" built on an educational system that would identify individuals with inborn talents and intelligence, sorting "the best and brightest toward their proper station in society" (Carnavale, Schmidt, and Strohl, 2020). Adams disagreed, saying. "Artificial aristocracy, and monarchy, and civil, military, political, and hierarchical despotism, have all grown out of the natural aristocracy of 'virtues and talents' " such as Jefferson proposed. Adams warned that implementing Jefferson's proposal would result in "the very sort of system we had chosen to reject in rebelling against monarchy," but he tempered this alarming prediction by adding, "We, to be sure, are far remote from this. Many hundred years must roll away before we shall be corrupted." Nevertheless, Adams acknowledged the danger of a meritocracy: "Mankind has not yet discovered any remedy against irresistible corruption in elections to offices of great power and profit."[29]

More than 200 years later, Jefferson's dream and Adams's fears both seem to have been realized. Our higher education system is stratified into a small "upper track that is dominated by the wealthy and white, and a lower track that disproportionately serves those students who are members of racial and ethnic minority groups or from families of modest means"(p. 22),[30] the vast majority of whom face a high likelihood of not graduating at all. The elitist, college-ready mindset shrugs this off, saying in effect, "Well, those students just weren't college material."

Although many faculty would prefer to believe that our students pursue a college degree simply because of its intrinsic value, most students choose to go to college because they believe earning a degree is a pathway leading to a well-paying career and all that comes with it. According to a 2018 Strada-Gallup poll:

Fully 72% of those with postgraduate educational experiences say getting a good job is their top motivation, as do 60% of those on a technical or vocational educational pathway. Four-year degree holders (55%), two-year degree holders (53%), and non-completing students (50%) are also most likely to identify work and career motivations.[31]

Carnavale et al. caution that this aspiration is valid, but its attainment is far from a given.

By going to college, a person can change his or her lot in life, but only if the system is based on opportunity, fairness, and merit. Instead of realizing that ideal, we as a country have built a system that is committed to

sustaining a class- and race-based aristocracy through intense and unbal-
anced competition.

(p. 20)

Higher education straddles the two conflicting principles of merit and opportunity. How can we resolve the idea that college should be reserved for those who
possess certain levels of talent and intelligence (ostensibly, as defined by grade-
point average, the quality of one's high school, standardized test scores, and so
on) or that it should be accessible to everyone, period? It's as though our system
exists along a geological fault line, with two tectonic plates grating against one
another. As a result, we see vast disparities in the quality of education students
receive, graduation rates, and career outcomes.

For decades, we in higher education have accepted these realities without question, often disguised as college readiness. Byron White, the Vice President of University Engagement and Chief Diversity Officer at Cleveland State University, addressed
"The Myth of the College-Ready Student" (*Inside Higher Ed*, March 21, 2016).

[Students are] either college-ready or [they're] not, we reasoned. And if
you're not, don't blame us. The fact that those who did not make it were
disproportionately less economically privileged and more likely to be a racial or ethnic minority was simply the way it was.

Colleges and universities, for the most part, have been equipped to serve
one fairly narrow population of students, which institutions have conve-
niently defined as college-ready. Meanwhile, for decades, higher education
has passively accepted the conventional wisdom that minority, low-income,
and first-generation students disproportionately underperform other students because they are the unfortunate casualties of inadequate systems—
low-achieving public school systems, poor neighborhoods, unsophisticated
households—that leave them woefully unprepared for college success.[32]

Many educators hold a set of expectations about what it means for their students
to be college ready without understanding its roots in the aristocratic, elitist her-
itage of higher education. We also assume our students are 18 to 22 years old, single, childless, dependent on their parents for financial support, and (most likely)
white. These expectations were valid until the second half of the 20th century. But
is this who our students are today?

Enrollment Trends

Patterns of educational enrollment have changed dramatically in the past century
or so. Very few Americans even graduated from high school, let alone earned a
college degree, until well into the 20th century. In 1900, only about half of

5-to-19-year-olds were enrolled in school at all, and just 2% of 18-to-22-year-olds were in college. By the 1950s, about 50% of students completed high school, and about 24% enrolled in college.[33] The upward trend continued in 1980, with a 72% high school completion rate and 49% college enrollment. As of 2018, 88% of students completed high school, and recent high school graduates' college enrollment had risen to 70%.[34] In other words, about three-fourths of all high school graduates did *not* go to college in 1950, whereas today, nearly three-fourths *do* go to college.

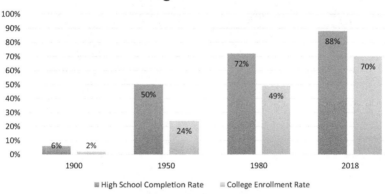

FIGURE 1.2 High School Completion and College Enrollment Trends

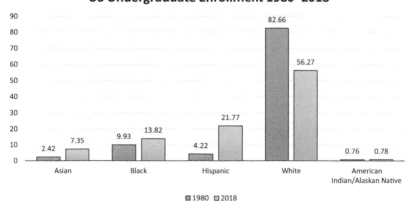

FIGURE 1.3 US Undergraduate Enrollment 1980–2018

Black students were vastly underrepresented in higher education for most of the 20th century. For instance, the Air Force Academy graduated three black students in 1963, and the same year, Tulane University in New Orleans admitted its first black student.[35] By 1980, however, undergraduate students' demographic profile had become more diverse, and by 2018, trends toward greater diversity were becoming increasingly evident.[36]

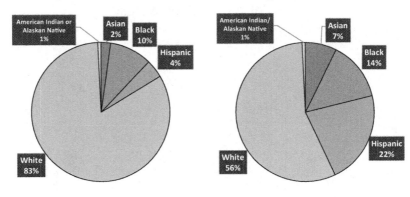

FIGURE 1.4 Comparative US Undergraduate Enrollment 1980 and 2018

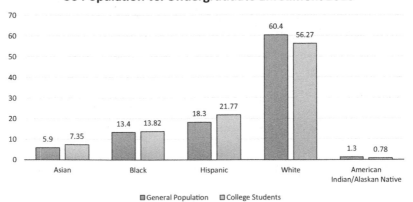

FIGURE 1.5 US Population vs. Undergraduate Enrollment 2018

Today's enrollment figures more accurately reflect the racial composition of the US. Except among American Indian or Alaskan Native students, each category shows slightly higher levels of diversity than among the general population.[37]

However, we should not presume these levels of diversity are the norm across all colleges and universities. Individual institutions exhibit widely different demographics. The Universities of Wisconsin at Stout, River Falls, and Eau Claire, for example, remain approximately 88% white. Howard University in Washington, DC, is 94% black.[38] These figures alone don't point to systemic attempts at segregation, though. The three Wisconsin universities mainly serve the region where they are located, which happens to be much less diverse than some other areas of the nation. Howard University is an HBCU (Historically Black College or University), founded specifically to educate black students. Even though discrimination based on race has been illegal since the landmark *Brown v. Board of Education* case of 1954,[39] looking beneath admissions criteria such as test scores reveals disproportionate associations with race and income.

Dependent and Independent Students

Just as overall racial demographics have come to reflect the US population more closely, student enrollment also reflects increased egalitarianism. FAFSA (the Free Application for Federal Student Aid) classifies students as either dependent or independent when calculating their financial aid eligibility. Dependent status means that the student relies on financial support from their parents. Dependent students are also high school graduates under 24 years of age who are unmarried and childless. This description also matches our perceptions of "traditional" college students.

Formerly, we referred to all other students as "non-traditional," but the FAFSA category of "independent" is a more accurate descriptor because, at 51% of all undergraduates, this group is now the majority. Qualification for independent status means the student demonstrates one or more of the following characteristics.[40]

- Age 24 or older
- Married
- Veteran or active-duty member of the armed forces
- Ward of the court or state, orphan, or in foster care since age 13
- Has legal dependents other than a spouse
- Emancipated minor
- Homeless or at risk of being homeless

Looking more closely at statistics about independent students reveals information that should be of great concern to us as educators.

17

- The median age is 29 years old.
- Independent students have lower levels of income:
  - 42% live at or below the federal poverty line.
  - 63% of single mothers who are in college live in poverty.
  - 88% of single parents have incomes at or below 200% of the poverty line.[41]
- 57% work at least 20 hours per week while in school.
- 25% work full time while attending school full time.
- Independent students are 70% less likely to graduate within six years.
- 51% of independent students are parents.
  - 71% of students with dependent children are women.
  - Ethnicities of women in college who are parents:
    - 47% of Black women.
    - 41% of American Indian/Native Alaska women.
    - 39% of Native Hawaiian/Pacific Islander women.
    - 32% of Hispanic women.
    - 29% of White women.
    - 18% of Asian women.
- 60% of single parents in college are raising their children without the support of a partner, spouse, or other family member.
- 72% of student parents have unmet financial needs even after financial aid, grants, and family contributions.
- The student loan debt a single mother owes is at least $5,000 greater than male graduates with no children.

Taking all this data into account, Table 1.2 presents a profile of what we know about our students.[42]

TABLE 1.2 Student Identity Profile

Descriptor	Dependent	Independent	Mean
Median age	20 yrs.	29 yrs.	24.5 years
Have dependent children	0%	50%	25%
Are single parents	0%	26.5%	13%
Live at or below the poverty line	17%	42%	39%
Live at or below 200% of poverty line	36%	66%	51%
Work 20+ hours/week	39%	57%	48%
Attend only part time	19%	44%	31.5%
Complete a 4-yr. degree within 6 yrs.	56%	33%	44.5%

Does this information fit our concept of a traditional/dependent student? No. Does it align with elitist notions that only individuals from certain social classes (a pejorative belief disguised as college readiness) "belong" in college? No.

Instead, if we were to take this information and attempt to calculate a mean upon which to build a portrait of an average student, it would be someone who is well into adulthood, has dependent children, is financially insecure, and works part time. These are the very students who have the most to gain by earning an education, yet they face a considerable risk of not graduating within six years.

Non-traditional, independent students will play an increasingly prominent role in the near future. Enrollment data and national demographic trends as described by Nathan Grawe in *Demographics and the Demand for Higher Education* (2018)[43] point to a significant decline in the numbers of traditional students available to enroll in our institutions, particularly in the North and East regions in the US (interestingly, where most of the "Ivy Plus" institutions are located). Meanwhile, numbers of non-traditional, minority, low-income, and first-generation students are expected to rise, especially in the South and West. We cannot forget about our traditional/dependent students, but we ought to expand our concept of who our students are to recognize that more than half of them won't align with our assumptions.

FROM COLLEGE READY TO STUDENT READY

The belief that our students will (or should) meet our expectations for college readiness doesn't just mask implicit bias—it is an unattainable fantasy for faculty at all but the small percentage of very selective institutions. Most faculty cannot presume their students developed the skills associated with college readiness while in high school nor that they have retained those skills by the time they enroll in college later in life. Neither can we presume our students had opportunities for meaningful participation in extracurricular activities like sports, clubs, religious or community organizations, or volunteer work that helped them develop the core competencies we used to take for granted like collaboration, communication, or creativity. Our students are seldom among the privileged elite, and most of them graduated below the top percentiles of their high school class. Only a comparative few possess the athletic, artistic, or academic prowess to qualify for a merit scholarship. Instead, the faces that greet us in our classrooms, labs, and studios belong to typical, everyday people. Each one has a special blend of strengths and weaknesses, talents and deficits.

It is high time to shed our belief in college readiness. Regardless of whether we think our students ought to be ready for college, we must recognize they're already in college, necessarily having met existing admissions criteria before registering for our courses. Despite our legitimate and understandable frustrations

19

when students fail to meet our expectations, it's time to stop asking, "Why aren't my students ready for college?"

Faculty-centered models of education cannot produce a satisfactory response. For decades, we've reasoned that if students were ready for college, they would achieve passing grades in our courses and make it through to graduation by themselves. We've believed that students could take full responsibility for their learning, leaving us free to focus on presenting the disciplinary information we want our students to absorb.

It's impossible to ignore the reality that these attitudes do not support student success. True, at elite institutions accepting less than 25% of applicants, the six-year graduation rate for first-time, full-time undergraduates is 87%, but this is a far cry from the dismal reality that only 31% of first-time, full-time undergraduates graduate within six years from institutions with open admissions policies.[44] Most of our institutions proclaim their support for access, diversity, equity, and inclusion, yet what does it tell us about our traditional models of education when the very institutions that provide the greatest access to higher education for all learners fail to fulfill their promise to more than two-thirds of their students?

Ultimately, your views about student success come down to your philosophy of education. If you espouse a merit-based, faculty-centered point of view, you're likely to believe that only students deemed worthy of a college education by virtue of their superior intellect, talent, or ability belong in college. You see yourself primarily as a disciplinary expert while sharing your knowledge with students is a lesser part of your job. You believe learning is the student's responsibility, and students should internalize your teaching simply for its own sake.

Conversely, if you hold an opportunity-based, student-centered point of view, you're likely to believe that everyone deserves an education. You know that students have different strengths and weaknesses, and you consider those differences when planning how and what you will teach. You see yourself primarily as an educator who helps students learn about the discipline in which you achieved expertise. You believe that your course content has intrinsic value, but you also recognize that it serves an instrumental purpose in preparing students for productive careers after graduation.

Before you read another word, stop and ask yourself: *which of these philosophies most closely describes my views?* Perhaps neither accurately reflects how you feel, or maybe your views are a mixture of both. Whatever the answer, the point is to begin thinking about these issues and recognize how your implicit beliefs create a lens through which you see your students.

STUDENT-CENTERED INSTITUTIONS

Our institutions' public statements and our private beliefs influence our choices and actions. Colleges and universities have begun to recognize that traditional approaches to higher education don't consistently yield positive outcomes for the majority of their students, undertaking systemic changes to improve service to incoming students at all levels of ability through new requirements for credit hour loads or creating credit-bearing courses that provide built-in support for struggling students. For instance, some institutions discovered that requiring students to complete non-credit remedial courses far too frequently caused students to discontinue their studies altogether, so they restructured their remedial courses to focus on student success. Institutions have also begun to re-examine general education requirements, instructional delivery systems, and more.

We might identify a set of common characteristics among student-centered institutions.[45]

- They express a sincere belief in all students' ability to learn. This conviction characterizes the entire institution, shaping its values, ethos, and identity—upholding a foundational belief in all students' capability for academic and professional success.
- They embrace a culture of full inclusion and share an appreciation for all stakeholders' diverse perspectives, whether faculty, staff, or students.
- They prioritize excellence across teaching, learning, student development, institutional functions, and engagement with local and global communities.
- All these efforts involve the entire campus community in ongoing conversations about how best to support students' success.

Nevertheless, even the most visionary and progressive institutions cannot establish a student-centered model without their faculty's support. Educators accustomed to having a great deal of autonomy within their departments and classrooms may balk at the notion that they should no longer operate from a position of "what's best for us" but "what's best for our students," since this contradicts the longstanding faculty-centric norms and practices that shaped their departmental cultures.

To be willing to make a fundamental change, we should remember that understanding is the key to motivation—when we know *why* we should do something, it prompts us to take action. So why should we choose to adopt a student-centered mindset?

First, a student-centered approach benefits the entire institution for which we work. Every college or university is tuition dependent, no matter how large its endowment or how much funding it attracts through research and development. As mentioned previously, the supply of future students will diminish over the coming decades,[46] and prospective students have many options when choosing where they will study. Given these realities, it's clearly in our institutions' best interest to establish an attractive internal culture that garners positive student

21

reviews, achieves favorable retention and graduation statistics, and produces robust alumni outcome data flowing from a focus on student success. Furthermore, graduates who are satisfied with the educational experience they received develop positive associations with their alma mater, especially when they achieve a measure of career success. These graduates form strong alumni networks and increase the institution's base of prospective donors. In short, their success fuels our capacity to continue our work. Adopting a student-centered mindset isn't only good for our students—it's good for everyone in the institution, both now and into the future.

STUDENT-CENTERED EDUCATORS

Next, why should faculty choose to alter their preferred teaching practices and adopt a student-centered instructional model? To answer this question, we might begin by taking a step back to consider the big picture of what it means to be an educator. Teaching is a service-oriented profession, comparable to fields such as medicine and law. We serve our students by providing them with an education. We serve the institution by meeting our contractual obligations for service, such as participation on committees. We also serve our professional field by training the next generation of scholars and through the disciplinary contributions of our research or creative practice.

The relationship between the provider and the recipient of the provider's services—be it patient, client, or student—is crucial to service-oriented professions. When we're injured or unhealthy, we don't just want to see doctors who are medical experts—we also want our doctors to treat us with respect and care about us as people. If we need a legal service such as drawing up a will, we want a lawyer who's skillful in writing legal documents, considers our needs as individual human beings, and keeps our best interests in mind throughout the transaction. We hope that our doctors care whether we live or die. We hope that our lawyers care that the legal services they perform are effective. Just so, it's reasonable to hope that faculty members care whether or not their students learn their course content and can apply what they've learned in the real world.

A mindset of professional service doesn't mean catering to the every whim of those we serve. Instead, this should be a relationship of mutual respect. A medical doctor has a reasonable expectation that the patient will respect their expertise and authority, but the doctor should reciprocate by treating the patient with dignity and respect, no matter what combination of ethnicity, income, social status, or other identity factors make the patient who they are. The same is true of lawyers and clients or faculty and students.

Becoming a student-centered educator means growing beyond the natural human tendency to serve our own interests. Caring about our students and their learning requires us to shift our focus from the faculty-centered norm of "What's best for me?" to the student-centered thought of "What's best for my students?" We do *not* have to say yes to every student request, nor does caring about students imply diluting academic rigor. Nevertheless, becoming student centered leads us to prioritize students' well-being over personal convenience or forgo strict enforcement of our classroom policies. It means setting aside our implicit expectations of where we think students *should* be and meeting them where they *are*.

All this leads us to the central questions we'll revisit in the next chapters: what will it take for you to become a student-centered, student-ready educator? How can we design our curricula to reflect this mindset? And how can we adapt our instruction to meet our students' needs while also preparing to cope with sudden changes to our instructional delivery systems?

REFLECTION AND REVIEW

Part of my job as an academic administrator involves advising faculty about their job performance. One member of a department I formerly led, whom I'll call Joseph, regularly received poor student evaluations and demonstrated significantly higher withdrawal and failure rates in his classes than other department members. The more I worked with Joseph, the more I realized that his core philosophy of education prevented him from being the instructor his students needed. This institution required instructors to submit academic alerts when students failed to turn in their work or acquired a certain number of absences, but Joseph often neglected to do this or waited until the last week of the term when it was too late to intervene. On more than one occasion, I respectfully suggested that Joseph should be more proactive and should try to meet his students where they are. He did not understand. "Of course I'm meeting them where they are. I'm here. They're here. We interact in the classroom. It's where we are." He resisted my suggestion to reach out to students who had late or missing work beyond occasionally sending one email reminder and nothing more, and he angrily objected to making accommodations for struggling students. Furthermore, the institution's generous enrollment policies meant that many of our students demonstrated gaps in the basic knowledge and skills necessary for college-level work, but Joseph was uninterested in helping them meet his courses' requirements, saying, "That's their job, not mine."

Now that you've read this chapter, I hope you can see where Joseph was: firmly entrenched in a faculty-centered, college-ready mindset that made no allowances for the difficulties his students might have been experiencing. We can also see where the students were: in need of much more help than he was willing to give. One such student (whom I'll call Ahmad) had failed Joseph's required course three times and was enrolled for a fourth. This was supposed to be Ahmad's last semester, but he couldn't graduate unless he earned a passing grade. With the provost's permission, I intervened in the situation, transferring Ahmad into a "rescue

23

section" of the course, which I then taught myself. Ahmad and I met in person and online. I called and emailed him several times a week to make sure he was staying on track. I quickly discovered that the cause of his previous three failures had been the course's required research paper, which he found so daunting he just gave up. Having diagnosed the problem, I broke the paper down into smaller parts and helped him complete it one step at a time. I also connected him to the campus writing center for additional tutoring. In the end, Ahmad completed the research paper, passed the course, and received clearance to graduate. When he introduced me to his family at commencement, his mother thanked me and cried. (I even misted up a bit, myself.) I realize this story might sound a little hokey, but every word is true. The joy I felt at seeing Ahmad graduate and the happiness it brought to his family are honestly among the highlights of my career.

I've attended or worked at institutions of higher learning across the spectrum: a two-year community college, two four-year private colleges, a regional comprehensive university, a Research-2 university, and two public Research-1 universities. Some of those institutions were on the more exclusive end of the spectrum, and others had more open admissions policies. At every one of these institutions, I encountered students who both confirmed and confounded faculty expectations, just as I met faculty, staff, and administrators who were inflexibly faculty centered and others who placed the highest priority on their students' success. If my experiences may serve as an example, our teaching philosophies are not so much a reflection of the institutions with which we're affiliated as alumni or employees. Rather, they result from how we've internalized our experiences in higher education and integrated them with our professional identities. Student-centered educators can work for the most elite institutions, just as faculty-centered educators work at institutions that openly espouse a student-centered model.

I'd like to emphasize that I intend no disrespect to the Ivy League, Ivy Plus, or other highly selective institutions, nor to their faculty or students. I know good people who work at these institutions and genuinely care about their students. Likewise, even the wealthiest, best-prepared students can experience heartbreak, failure, or complications that imperil their studies. Nevertheless, we must also recognize the role these institutions have played in the stratification of higher education and, by extension, our entire society. Of course, not all the rich and powerful people in the US attended an Ivy League institution, but before the election of Joe Biden, we had to look back to Ronald Reagan 40 years ago to find a US president who wasn't an Ivy League grad.[47]

Given the length of many faculty members' careers, it's unsurprising that antiquated belief systems such as college readiness continue to be passed down. Think of it this way: if you're a 40-year-old faculty member, you might have attended graduate school about 15 years ago. The professors under whom you studied likely earned their graduate degrees up to 30 years earlier, and the same is true of the faculty members under whom your professors would have studied. In just three faculty generations, then, we're back to the norms and expectations of the 1950s, when student identities were far different than they are today. We unconsciously transmit our philosophies from one generation to the next without pausing to recognize these beliefs or question whether they are beneficial, relevant, or accurate.

This chapter's goal was to present a countervailing point of view: to uncover the faculty-centric philosophy that has dominated higher education since its founding and hold it up to the implicit bias and discrimination that lurk within the standards of college readiness that our colleagues and institutions have long upheld.

Before we move on, I'd like to suggest a different approach that I first proposed in *Higher Education by Design*.

Student learning occurs at the intersection of three factors shown in Figure 1.6: the instructor, the course content, and the student, all of which exist within the larger context of an academic discipline, which itself is an important part of the university. Each of these five components exerts an influence over the

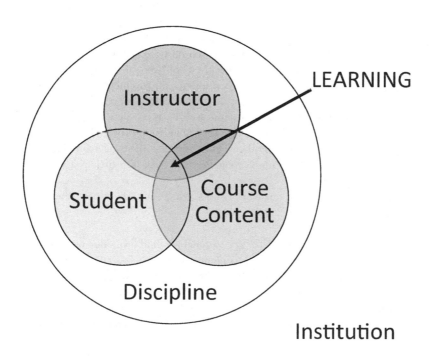

FIGURE 1.6 The Learning-Centered Model of Instruction

25

teaching and learning that occurs, but the most important contact point is at the center, as the student and instructor engage with the course content. We'll revisit this graph when we talk about teaching in a subsequent chapter because specific pedagogical strategies can be found in the areas where the circles overlap.

Meanwhile, I hope you've been able to locate yourself along the continuum of faculty-centered to student-centered and college-ready to student-ready belief systems. I also hope you now have a better understanding of who your students are and why they might not meet the expectations you've held.

For the rest of this book, I'll presume that you, like me, embrace a student-centered and student-ready philosophy of teaching and are ready and willing to do what it takes to meet your students' needs as you provide the best educational experience it is within your power to deliver.

GRIT AND GROWTH MINDSET

Two additional concepts can help us make this leap—first, the character trait of grit, as explained by Angela Duckworth.[48] In a nutshell, grit is the ability to achieve one's goals through persistent effort. As a society, we revere individuals who seem to have been born with extraordinary gifts intellectually, athletically, or artistically. However, talent is only half the story, according to Duckworth. One can possess talent and still not achieve much. High achievers may or may not be naturally talented, but virtually all demonstrate grit. Grit consists of four traits. First, people with grit love what they do. Next, they engage in deliberate practice and pursue a process of continuous improvement. They also have a purpose above and beyond self-interest: their work is personally fulfilling and contributes to others' well-being in some way. Last, people with grit are driven by hope. They keep practicing because they hope to improve. They keep working because they hope to help others. Hope sustains them through failures and setbacks. It gets them back up on their feet and back into their practice, again and again.

How does grit relate to our work as educators? Let's take a look, one component at a time.

> **Interest and Passion**: As faculty, we ought to find joy in our work as educators. Our interactions with students should be a source of delight, not an onerous chore. If you can't say, "I really love teaching," then the work ahead is going to be that much more difficult for you.
>
> **Deliberate Practice**: Teaching is inherently iterative, but it doesn't need to be repetitive. Yes, we teach the same course over and over again, sometimes for many years. Developing a mindset of continuous improvement—engaging in the "deliberate practice" that's part of grit—allows us to make the course better every time we teach it.

Purpose: Holding a student-centered mindset gives us our purpose. We teach because we're helping our students achieve our courses' objectives and outcomes, which we believe will help them have a better life.

Hope: We keep going year after year because we never lose hope that our work is valuable and meaningful. We never stop working to become better educators, and we never lose our passion for our work. Everyone has days when they're tired. Everyone goes through times when we feel like we've lost our spark. Grit is what gets us back into the classroom the next day, helping us push through the hard times until we regain our passion and sense of purpose.

Grit is closely related to having a growth mindset, a concept developed by Carol Dweck.[49] Each of us has an internal monologue—a small voice in our heads that reacts to what we experience and affects the way we perceive and interpret what happens to us. In people with a fixed mindset, that little voice passes judgment on us. It condemns us when we make a mistake. On the other hand, people with a growth mindset look for what they can learn after a mistake so that they don't repeat it. A fixed mindset insists that people possess a given set of skills and competencies that do not change. "No, I can't do the statistical analysis on this project—I'm bad at math," or "Just give me a summary of this policy—I don't have time to read." Someone with a growth mindset is aware of their shortcomings but is willing to work to overcome them. "I don't have much experience with statistical analysis, but I'm willing to try," or "Sure, I'll read this policy document, but I'd like to ask you a few questions about it afterward, if I may."

A fixed mindset keeps us trapped in our routine. It won't loosen its grip on our habits because the thing it loves best is "the way it's always been." A growth mindset is willing to consider the possibility of change. It can look at the prospect of trying something new without becoming angry or immediately rejecting it out of hand. As we embark upon our journey in this book, we'll need the tools of grit and a growth mindset, just like someone running a marathon needs a good pair of running shoes and socks that won't chafe. Together, they will help us reach our destination successfully!

The job of a faculty member is far from easy even under normal circumstances. We're pulled in at least three directions between our teaching, our service to the institution, and the pursuit of our research or creative practice. I'm glad you've chosen to take this journey, because it speaks to your willingness to push beyond your limits despite the demands on your time, reaching out with grit and a growth mindset to become a better educator.

Our next chapter introduces the concept of design, as found in User Experience Design, Instructional Design, Learning Experience Design, and Design Thinking, which will support our course development efforts and inform our work as educators.

27

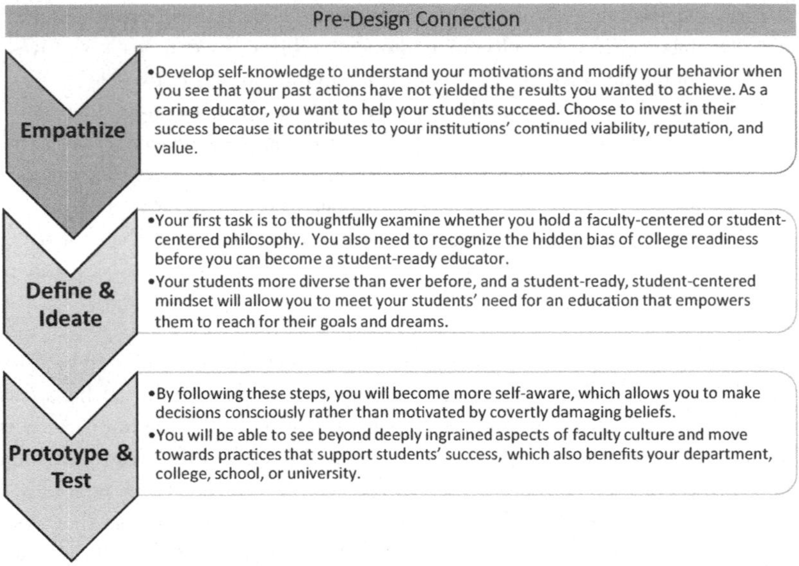

FIGURE 1.7 Chapter 1 Pre-Design Connection

Each chapter in this book concludes with a "Design Connection." However, as we haven't yet delved into theories of design, we'll call this one a "Pre-Design Connection."

Notes

[1] Reay, T., Goodrick, E., Waldorff, S., & Casebeer, A. (2017). Getting leopards to change their spots: Co-creating a new professional role identity. *Academy of Management Journal, 60*(3), 1043–1070. doi:10.5465/amj.2014.0802; Pratt, M., Rockmann, K., & Kaufmann, J. (2006). Constructing professional identity: The role of work and identity learning cycles in the customization of identity among medical residents. *Academy of Management Journal, 49,* 235–262.

[2] Brownell, S. E., & Tanner, K. D. (2012). Barriers to faculty pedagogical change: Lack of training, time, incentives, and . . . tensions with professional identity? *CBE Life Sciences Education, 11*(4), 339–346. https://doi.org/10.1187/cbe.12-09-0163

[3] Brownell, S. E., & Tanner, K. D. (2012). Barriers to faculty pedagogical change: Lack of training, time, incentives, and . . . tensions with professional identity? *CBE Life Sciences Education, 11*(4), 339–346. https://doi.org/10.1187/cbe.12-09-0163

[4] Glossary of Educational Reform. (2014). *Student-centered learning.* Retrieved from www.edglossary.org/student-centered-learning/

[5] Hase, S., & Kenyon, C. (2001). *From andragogy to heutagogy*. Retrieved from www.psy.gla.ac.uk/~steve/pr/Heutagogy.html

[6] The terms *faculty*, *instructor*, *educator*, and *teacher* should be considered synonymous in this book, indicating any person employed to teach students, without regard for that person's rank, contractual status, tenure, or the level of students taught.

[7] Bruner, J. (1966). *Toward a theory of instruction*. Cambridge, MA: Harvard University Press.

[8] Jang, C. S., Lim, D. H., Yoo, J., & Yim, J.-H. (2019). *An analysis of research trends in brain-based learning in adult education and HRD fields: The content analysis and network text analysis*. Adult Education Research Conference. Retrieved from https://newprairiepress.org/aerc/2019/papers/33

[9] Glossary of Educational Reform.

[10] Information is drawn from Blumberg, P. (2004). Beginning journey toward a culture of learning-centered teaching. *The Journal of Student Centered Learning*, *2*(1), 69–80; Mackh, B. (2018). *Higher education by design: Best practices for curricular planning and instruction*. Abingdon: Routledge, and from personal experience.

[11] Lumina Foundation. (n.d.). *History of federal student aid, Chapter 1*. Retrieved from www.luminafoundation.org/history-of-federal-student-aid/chapter-one/

[12] Kronman, A. (2019). *The assault on American excellence* (p. 10). New York: Simon & Schuster. See also:

  a. Roth, M. (2019, August 23). A yale professor frets about a waning aristocracy. Outlook: Review. *The Washington Post*. Retrieved from www.washingtonpost.com/outlook/a-yale-professor-frets-about-a-waning-aristocracy/2019/08/23/99b70bd8-acb5-11e9-bc5c-e73b603e7f38 story.html

  b. Lemann, N. (2019, August 20). Two views of the tumult on American campuses. Books: Nonfiction. *The New York Times*. Retrieved from www.nytimes.com/2019/08/20/books/review/assault-on-american-excellence-anthony-kronman.html

[13] Kronman, A. (2019). *The assault on American excellence* (p. 7). New York: Simon & Schuster.

[14] Shriver, P. (1972). *The colonial colleges*. Address to the 77th Winter Court of The Society of Colonial Wars in the State of Ohio. Retrieved from www.colonialwarsoh.org/files/forms/Trilogy/Colonial_Trilogy_1/2._The_Colonial_Colleges.pdf

[15] Shriver, P. (1972). *The colonial colleges*. Address to the 77th Winter Court of The Society of Colonial Wars in the State of Ohio. Retrieved from www.colonialwarsoh.org/files/forms/Trilogy/Colonial_Trilogy_1/2._The_Colonial_Colleges.pdf

[16] Sternberg, R. (Ed.). (2014). *The modern land grant university*. West Lafayette, IN: Purdue University Press.

[17] Sternberg, R. (Ed.). (2014). *The modern land grant university*. West Lafayette, IN: Purdue University Press.

[18] Harvard University. (2020). *Harvard at a glance*. Retrieved from www.harvard.edu/about-harvard/harvard-glance

[19] Bridgeview State University. (2020). *Admissions: Cost of attendance*. Retrieved from www.bridgew.edu/admissions-aid/cost-attending

29

[20] Valdosta State University. (2020). *Housing and international students*. Retrieved from www.valdosta.edu/academics/international-programs/student-information/housing.php

[21] Harvard University. (2020). *Harvard at a glance—student life*. Retrieved from www.harvard.edu/about-harvard/harvard-glance/student-life

[22] The Ivy League plus Stanford, Duke, the University of Chicago, and the Massachusetts Institute of Technology (MIT).

[23] Markovits, D. (2019, September 12). American universities must choose: Do they want to be equal or elite? *Time*. Retrieved from https://time.com/5676174/universities-equality-eliteness/

[24] Markovits, D. (2019, September 12). American universities must choose: Do they want to be equal or elite? *Time*. Retrieved from https://time.com/5676174/universities-equality-eliteness/

[25] Lin, G. (2019, March 7). States that spend the most and least on education. *Yahoo Finance*. Retrieved from https://finance.yahoo.com/news/states-spend-most-least-education-090000945.html

[26] Lin, G. (2019, March 7). States that spend the most and least on education. *Yahoo Finance*. Retrieved from https://finance.yahoo.com/news/states-spend-most-least-education-090000945.html

[27] Wong, A. (2019, April 10). College-admissions hysteria is not the norm. *The Atlantic*. Retrieved from www.theatlantic.com/education/archive/2019/04/harvard-uchicago-elite-colleges-are-anomaly/586627/

[28] DeSilver, D. (2019, April 9). A majority of US colleges admit most students who apply. Fact tank: News in the numbers. *Pew Research Center*. Retrieved from www.pewresearch.org/fact-tank/2019/04/09/a-majority-of-u-s-colleges-admit-most-students-who-apply/

[29] Carnavale, A., Schmidt, P., & Strohl, J. (2020). *The Merit Myth: How our colleges favor the rich and divide America*. New York: The New Press.

[30] Carnavale, A., Schmidt, P., & Strohl, J. (2020). *The Merit Myth: How our colleges favor the rich and divide America*. New York: The New Press.

[31] Strada-Gallup. (2018, January). Why higher ed? Top reasons U.S. Consumers choose their educational pathways. *The Atlantic*.

[32] White, B. (2016, March 21). The myth of the college-ready student. *InsideHigherEd.com*. Retrieved from www.insidehighered.com/views/2016/03/21/instead-focusing-college-ready-students-institutions-should-become-more-student

[33] Snyder, T. (1993, January). *120 years of American education: A statistical portrait*. US Department of Education, Center for Education Statistics. https://nces.ed.gov/pubs93/93442.pdf

[34] Chart data aggregated from Snyder, T. (1993, January). *120 Years of American education: A statistical portrait*. US Department of Education, Center for Education Statistics. Retrieved from https://nces.ed.gov/pubs93/93442.pdf; NCES Table 187—College Enrollment rates of high school graduates. Retrieved from https://nces.ed.gov/programs/digest/d99/tables/PDF/Table187.pdf; NCES Digest of Education Statistics Table 100, 2007 Table and Figures. Retrieved from https://nces.ed.gov/programs/digest/d07/

tables/dt07_100.asp; Simon, K., & Grant, V. (1965). *Digest of educational statistics*. Office of Education, Bulletin 1965 No. 4. US Department of Health, Education, and Welfare, Washington, DC.

[35] Titcomb, C. (2020). Key events in black higher education: JBHE chronology of major landmarks in the progress of African Americans in higher education. *The Journal of Blacks in Higher Education*. Retrieved from www.jbhe.com/chronology/

[36] Education Data.Org. (2018). *College enrollment & student demographic statistics*. Retrieved from https://educationdata.org/college-enrollment-statistics/

[37] United States Census Bureau. (2018). *Quick facts. Race and Hispanic origin*. Retrieved from www.census.gov/quickfacts/fact/table/US/IPE120218

[38] Data from 24/7 Wall Street, a USA TODAY content partner. Retrieved from www.usatoday.com/story/money/2020/02/13/these-colleges-have-the-least-diverse-student-bodies/41152235/

[39] Franklin, V. (2005). Introduction: Brown v. Board of education: Fifty years of educational change in the United States. *The Journal of African American History*, 90(1/2), 1–8. Retrieved June 7, 2020, from www.jstor.org/stable/20063972

[40] Being a graduate or professional student of any age or actual dependency level also qualifies a student for independent status for the purpose of financial aid. However, our discussion here focuses on undergraduate students.

[41] As of January 2020, 200% of the poverty line is an annual income of $25,520 for a one-person household, or $52,400 for a family of four. (US Health and Human Services Federal Poverty Guidelines. https://aspe.hhs.gov/poverty-guidelines).

[42] Institute for Women's Policy Research. (2018, February). *Understanding the new college majority* (IWPR #C462). Retrieved from https://iwpr.org/wp-content/uploads/2018/02/C462_Understanding-the-New-College-Majority-BP_2.8.18-clean.pdf

[43] Grawe, N. (2018). *Demographics and the demand for higher education*. Baltimore, MD: Johns Hopkins University Press.

[44] U.S. Department of Education, National Center for Education Statistics. (2019). The Condition of Education 2019. (NCES 2019–144), Undergraduate Retention and Graduation Rates.

[45] McNair, A., Cooper, M., & Major, N. (2016). *Becoming a student-ready college: A new culture of leadership for student success*. San Francisco, CA. Jossey-Bass and Association of American Colleges and Universities.

[46] Grawe, N. (2018). *Demographics and the demand for higher education*. Baltimore, MD: Johns Hopkins University Press.

[47] Reagan, R. (1980)–Eureka College; Bush, G. H. W. (1988)–Yale; Clinton, W. (1992)–Yale; Bush, G. W (2000)–Yale and Harvard; Obama, B. (2008)–Columbia and Harvard; Trump, D. (2016)–University of Pennsylvania; Biden, J. (2020)–University of Delaware and Syracuse University. Statistics from Presidents of the United States: Education Level. Retrieved from www.potus.com/presidential-facts/education-level/

[48] Duckworth, A. (2016). *Grit: The power of passion and perseverance*. New York: Scribner.

[49] Dweck, C. (2016). *Mindset: The new psychology of success*. New York: Random House.

Chapter 2

Student-Centered by Design

CHAPTER 2 SUMMARY

- Student-Centered Curricula and Pedagogies
- Characteristics of Student-Centered Teaching and Learning
- By Design: User Experience Design, Instructional Design, Learning Experience Design, and Design Thinking
- Course Design Fundamentals: Backward Design
- Reflection and Review

****

Now that we've begun to develop a student-centered teaching philosophy, we'll learn how to use the tools for design to build a student-centered course. First, let's consider what we mean when we apply the descriptor "student-centered" to the teaching and learning that occurs in our classrooms.

STUDENT-CENTERED CURRICULA AND PEDAGOGIES

McNair, Albertine, Cooper, McDonald, and Major (*Becoming a Student-Ready College*, 2016, p. 89)[1] suggest that a student-centered institution should "prepare students for the kinds of challenges they will confront in work, in life, and as citizens, both US and global, and to help them integrate and apply their knowledge and skills to complex and unscripted problems." I'll call this Priority One. We can measure students' academic achievement by assessing learning outcomes that reflect this central purpose. However, neither the institution nor its students will be successful if Priority One is nothing but attractive verbiage in a mission statement—it has to become the lived reality of every member of the institution, beginning with faculty.

Indeed, it's impossible to underestimate the importance of faculty in students' learning experience. Let's consider this comparison. The only thing that connects a vehicle to the road is a small area of each tire called the "contact patch." A parked car has a contact patch that's roughly a six-inch by six-inch square.[2] However, when the vehicle is in motion, multiple forces act on the tire that cause the contact patch to become even smaller. The car's performance depends on the contact patch, which is affected by the amount of force the vehicle's engine generates, the resiliency of the material the tire is made of, the tire's inflation, tread depth, the weight of the vehicle, the weather and road conditions, the driver's handling of the vehicle, and more. When we step into a vehicle weighing between 3,000 and 5,000 pounds and propel it down the highway at speeds of 55 to 75 miles per hour, we're trusting our very lives to that tiny contact patch where the tires meet the pavement.

Just so, faculty are the "contact patch" between students and their educational experience. The most renowned university probably won't keep its reputation long if its faculty are not comparably excellent. A beautiful campus and championship athletics program may increase the institution's public recognition, but its true worth depends far more on the tone and quality of daily interactions occurring between faculty and students.

The Big Six

The importance of faculty is borne out by the 2014 Gallup-Purdue Index,[3] which concluded that *where* a student goes to college is far less important than *how* they go to college. This survey of more than 30,000 graduates measured workplace engagement, elements of well-being (purpose, financial, social, community, and physical), and alumni attachment to alma mater. Researchers identified six factors that are "so strongly related to graduates' lives and careers [it] is almost hard to fathom . . . yet few college graduates achieve the winning combination."[4] Only 3% of all those surveyed reported having all six of these key experiences, but even those who had just three or more experienced higher degrees of well-being and career engagement. Gallup-Purdue dubbed these factors the "Big Six."

- Professors who made students feel excited about learning
- Professors who cared about students as people
- A mentor who encouraged students to pursue their goals and dreams
- The opportunity to work on a long-term project
- Taking part in an internship or job where students could apply what they were learning in the classroom
- Being extremely active in extracurricular activities and organizations during college

33

Each of these factors is well within faculty members' capacity to provide. Furthermore, all are aspects of a student-centered approach to higher education. The first three speak to students' relationships with faculty, and the last three reflect their participation in educational opportunities faculty can facilitate or encourage. Let's look at each of these more closely.

First, we should never underestimate the impact that **instructors' attitudes and demeanors** have on their students' experience.[5] Our passion for our discipline is contagious—the more excited we are about what we teach, the greater the positive effect on our students. Sharing our ongoing research or creative practice; bringing interesting examples to class that we've gleaned in our professional development activities, such as an article from a new professional journal that we can't wait to share with students; or demonstrating enthusiasm for our course content can dramatically affect students' perceptions of the instructor and the course.

Next, no matter how upbeat or enthusiastic we might be with the whole group, our **connections with individual students** can make or break their learning experience.[6] Students need to know that we care about them individually.[7] Every interaction, no matter how insignificant it might be to us as instructors, can have a marked impact on students. For example, when a student emails the instructor about a late assignment, we face a choice of whether we will remain firm on our stated policies or respond with empathy and kindness. We might be within our rights to insist that a penalty will apply, but compassion has a much more positive effect on the student and their subsequent views of their experience in our classrooms.

Mentoring relationships often develop formally or informally between faculty and students, especially those who major in our department. Students should feel that someone on the faculty understands their hopes and dreams and is willing to help achieve them. Mentorship goes well beyond standard duties for student advising, where we meet with students only to help them select the courses they'll need to take in the next semester or when the student is in danger of failing. Mentors, in contrast, take a personal interest in the student. They ask what the student plans to do after graduation. They work with the student to explore graduate programs, complete grant applications, or write their resumes. They write letters of recommendation, celebrate their students' successes, and help them through their disappointments. They express belief in their students' potential to succeed. The more skillful we are in building appropriate mentoring relationships with our students, the better the chance that students will view their educational experience positively. Mentoring need not involve a formal commitment, however. Even casual, non-classroom interactions between students and faculty produce a markedly positive effect on students' motivation and academic achievement, promoting cognitive gains, raising students' academic self-concept, and increasing their engagement.[8]

Long-term projects (those lasting for a semester or more) allow students to engage deeply with a topic of investigation.[9] Projects are even more impactful when they can mobilize the "Four Cs":

- Collaboration and the ability to work well with others
- Communication across contexts and audiences
- Critical thinking and the ability to solve complex problems
- Creativity and innovation

We might also expand this list to include additional "Cs" characteristic of well-educated students who are prepared for success in their lives and careers.

- Content-area knowledge
- Confidence
- Curiosity
- Citizenship
- Character
- Competency
- Compassion
- Courage
- Commitment
- Coping with complexity and ambiguity
- Cross-cultural understanding

These skills and characteristics aren't limited to long-term projects. We can embed them across the curriculum and in every academic discipline, but it doesn't happen by chance—it requires a deliberate effort to do so. We should not underestimate the importance of these so-called "soft" skills, either. Google conducted a study titled Project Aristotle that examined their most innovative and productive teams. Google's A-teams were comprised of top scientists, most of whom were graduates of elite universities with highly specialized technical knowledge and proven abilities to engage in cutting-edge innovation. Contrary to the company's expectations, the study revealed that the A-teams underperformed compared to its B-teams, whose members exhibited skills such as equality, generosity, curiosity about teammates' ideas, empathy, emotional intelligence, and most importantly, psychological and emotional safety. They felt empowered to speak freely, knew their ideas would be heard, and felt safe taking risks and making mistakes. As a result, Google changed its hiring practices, seeking employees with backgrounds in humanities, arts, and business as well as STEM—a notable departure from their previous approach to staffing. Reporting on this study for the *Washington Post*, author Valerie Strauss concluded,

> Broad learning skills are the key to long-term, satisfying, productive careers. What helps you thrive in a changing world isn't rocket science. It may just well be social science, and, yes, even the humanities and the arts that contribute to making [students] not just workforce ready but world-ready.[10]

35

Providing students with practical experience through **internships**, externships, co-op, and practicum requirements allows them to apply prior learning to settings they're likely to encounter in the workplace after graduation. Furthermore, such opportunities help build the student's professional network, broaden their understanding of career options, and introduce them to workplace norms, all of which are essential to professional success.[11]

Co-curricular engagement might seem like an unnecessary distraction, taking time away from study. However, research by scholars such as Astin (1993), Cress, Astin, Zimmerman-Oster, and Burkhardt (2001), Kuh (2008), Wolf-Wendel, Ward, and Kinzie (2009) demonstrates that students who participate in purposeful co-curricular activities experience positive effects on their academic success, retention, and persistence. George Kuh (1995 and 2011) also reported positive outcomes such as an enhanced sense of belonging, capacity for humanitarianism, and growth in student's interpersonal and intrapersonal competence.[12,13]

We tend to measure an institution's success by its alumni outcomes: their employment statistics, their graduate school placement rates, or their annual salaries. These might be useful metrics, but do they reflect the missions of our institutions? Do they tell us about our graduates' quality of life? Narrowing our considerations to employment and salary leads to the results we expect to see: graduates of highly selective institutions tend to fare better than others. The Gallup-Purdue Index's more holistic measurements revealed a counterintuitive truth: "where graduates went to college—public or private, small or large, very selective or not selective—hardly matters at all to their current well-being and their work lives in comparison to their experiences in college."[14] What matters is whether they received the experiences of the Big Six, which correlate with a student-centered perspective. Faculty have the greatest potential to enact these student-centered strategies. We care about our students, make them feel excited about learning, and serve as formal or informal mentors. We build long-term projects and experiential learning into our courses. We encourage students to deepen their educational experience through participation in internships and extracurricular and co-curricular activities. If we had to distill the Big Six into a single statement, it would be this: no single factor is more important to students' futures than working with student-centered faculty who provide these core experiences.

Characteristics of Student-Centered Teaching and Learning

Author Sabine Holden, in *Student-Centered Learning Environments in Higher Education Classrooms* (2017), explains that student-centered learning depends on a constructivist philosophy of education that facilitates knowledge building and construction of meaning, demonstrated by five key characteristics.

1. The instructor communicates subject-area knowledge through learning activities that foster higher-order thinking rather than rote memorization.
2. Learning activities accommodate students' differences as learners, allowing for student choice, which increases motivation, engagement, and participation in the learning process.
3. The instructor establishes the classroom environment as a community of learners that supports all members and fosters collaboration, respect for others' perspectives, exploration, and reflection.
4. The instructor provides ongoing formative assessment and constructive feedback on students' work. Criteria for assessments are clear and align with the course's objectives and outcomes.
5. The instructor adapts instruction to meet students' needs, both for the whole group and for individual students. Instructors remain flexible in their approaches to instruction and engage in continuous reflection and improvement of their curricula and pedagogies.

A student-ready educator or institution is prepared to meet all students' needs, not just the ones who fit our implicit assumptions or expectations. Maintaining a student-centered perspective goes hand-in-hand with this goal. McNair, Albertine, Cooper, McDonald, and Major (*Becoming a Student-Ready College: A New Culture of Leadership for Student Success*, 2016) rightly state that "without clearly defined action steps, becoming a student-ready college will quickly become one of the many catchphrases in higher education that everyone agrees with but no one really understands."[15] These action steps include:

1. **Making excellence inclusive** by delivering courses designed to accommodate learners' differences. Access to higher education is no less than a social justice issue. It is incumbent upon all educators to take this matter seriously and to address systemic inequities by making their classrooms a welcoming and supportive environment in which all students can learn.
2. **Remaining deeply committed to learning about our students as individuals** and supporting their success through whatever means are within our reach. The impact of a caring adult on students' learning is well-documented, not only by Gallup-Purdue but in the work of Harvey, 2007; Kramer and Gardner, 2007; Lerner and Brand, 2006; and McClure, Yonezawa, and Jones, 2010.[16] Not every instructor can be a mentor or counselor for every student. Rather, we have a choice in every interaction to be kind, empathetic, and supportive toward our students. What if we stopped to consider that our students' problems might not arise from deficits in the students themselves, but from problems in our institution, our society, or perhaps even in ourselves. Becoming a student-centered,

37

student-ready educator means that each of us makes a personal decision to take responsibility and ownership for student success—the polar opposite of longstanding faculty-centered attitudes that take responsibility only for "setting the table," leaving students to succeed or fail by themselves.

3. **Engaging in continuous reflection** about our instruction's efficacy, particularly about meeting the needs of our most diverse students or those with the greatest levels of need. We reject deficit-minded perspectives that see problems as residing in the student, recognizing them, instead, as an outgrowth of implicit biases such as believing that certain groups of students lack the intellectual capacity for advanced study or that people who live in poverty have little to no income because they are lazy or financially illiterate. "Deficit-minded thinking involves blaming the students for being underprepared, rather than blaming the social systems that perpetuate inequities in education."[17]

4. **Measuring students' success** by assessing the level to which they meet course objectives and outcomes. These should align with the institution's mission, which itself reflects Priority One. Even if only the instructor upholds Priority One, we can still make a positive difference to our students' academic achievement and career success by aligning instruction with objectives and outcomes supporting this key goal. Faculty and students should understand that success is not defined as earning a passing grade for the course but *learning* what the course was designed to teach. Assessment criteria should explain how students could demonstrate their achievement of the course objectives and outcomes. A student-centered instructor provides a rationale for those objectives and outcomes and makes explicit connections to students' lives outside the classroom, resulting in a transparent and clearly defined assessment process.

5. **Incorporating High-Impact Practices** (HIPs) into their instruction, including first-year experiences, common intellectual experiences, learning communities, writing-intensive courses, collaborative assignments and projects, undergraduate research, diversity/global learning, service-learning, community-based learning, internships, capstone courses, and projects, all of which can increase students' persistence and raise grade-point averages.[18] Although some HIPs appear to be institution-level strategies, we can scale them to our individual classrooms. We'll explore HIPs in greater depth later on in this book.

The Gallup-Purdue study, Holden's recommendations for creating student-centered learning environments, and the characteristics of being student ready noted by McNair et al. share many commonalities. All emphasize the importance of caring faculty who are committed to their students' success. They also promote teaching approaches that prioritize students' learning through transparency in assessment and strategies including internships, long-term projects, and other practices known to support students' success.

The next question, then, is: how do we create courses that enact a student-centered, student-ready mindset? The answer: by learning how to implement strategies for design.

BY DESIGN

As a noun, *design* simply refers to a plan; as a verb, it means planning something with a purpose in mind. Therefore, to design is to plan purposefully as opposed to allowing things to occur organically. Although design is an academic and professional field encompassing art, engineering, architecture, fashion, advertising, and the development of new products, services, technologies, and much more, it's also something most of us do in our daily lives. If you've ever decided how you'll rearrange the furniture in your living room or sketched the layout for a new garden, you've designed something. As educators, we engage in curricular and pedagogical design when we deliberately build instruction around students' learning of course objectives and outcomes. We'll focus on specific approaches to design—User Experience Design, Design Thinking, and Learning Experience Design—to learn how they can help us create student-centered courses.

User Experience Design

User Experience Design (UX) normally focuses on the relationship between a technological product and the person who uses it, seeking to create "digital experiences that not only empower but delight users."[19] Nevertheless, the creators of anything from a toothbrush to a commercial aircraft pay attention to each facet of the user experience. Apple might serve as the penultimate example of UX design—their products are elegant in their simplicity, intuitive to use, and intended to elicit an emotional response. Many of us have owned an Apple product, whether an iPhone, iPad, iPod, or Macintosh computer, and can recall the surprise, joy, and delight of discovering what these devices could do. Apple builds the user's experience first, then designs around that intention.[20]

The field of design has come a long way, accelerated by the exponential growth of technology. In decades past, the user wasn't given much consideration. When Henry Ford built the Model T automobile, he quipped to the design team, "The customer can have a car painted any color that he wants so long as it is black."[21] Today, consumers demand a much higher degree of customization and amenities in the products or services they purchase. The 2019 Subaru Ascent, for example, had 19 cup holders, reflecting changing lifestyles in which people increasingly use their vehicles as living space.[22]

Today's consumers are also more selective, partly due to the ease with which we can access product information. Not so long ago, shoppers made a concerted effort to research a product before purchasing it, often consulting product reviews by such venerable publications as *Consumer Reports* magazine or looking for the "Good Housekeeping Seal of Approval." E-commerce has seen a proliferation of users' product reviews, which have become staples of retailers' websites. I imagine many of us have received an email invitation to review a product we purchased online. Positive and negative reviews can sway potential customers' decisions, so companies have a strong interest in increasing the number of positive reviews by listening to their customers and designing products that will not only sell but will be well received.

Higher education is subject to comparisons and reviews as well. Annual rankings in publications such as *U.S. News and World Report*, *Forbes*, and the *Wall Street Journal / Times Higher Education* or on websites like *Niche* fuel competition between colleges and universities. It's a simple matter to find websites that propose to help prospective students and their families decide which college or university might be the best fit, comparing two or more institutions based on multiple factors such as the cost of tuition, alumni outcome data, diversity scores, available scholarships, student success rates, and more. These sites may also include present and former students' comments about the institutions.

None of this information is meant to suggest that higher education should be treated as a commodity or a commercial transaction like purchasing a new car, nor that we should think of our students as customers or bow to their whims as consumers. A certain amount of comparison shopping occurs when students are looking for a college, but it's logical when contemplating a decision with an attached price tag that might be larger than the market value of the family's home. Perhaps we should frame the transactional aspect of higher education by comparing it to purchasing a gym membership. The user signs a contract and pays a fee to become a gym member, much as a student enrolls in the institution and pays tuition. The gym provides the facility, equipment, and instruction that its members might require. It might even offer amenities like a juice bar, sauna, hot tub, and so on. However, the purchaser of the membership must put in the work if they want to see results. They have to use the equipment, attend Zumba or spin classes, consult with a personal trainer, and apply significant perseverance and effort. If not, they will fail to achieve their fitness goals. In higher education, we have an implicit social contract with our students. They enroll and pay tuition and fees. In return, institutions provide instruction and the buildings, equipment, and amenities that facilitate students' education. Nevertheless, students must also uphold their end of the bargain by attending class, doing their assignments, studying for tests, and participating in campus activities. Higher education is very much a two-way street.

40

A student-centered viewpoint asks us to consider higher education through a new set of lenses, in marked contrast to previous generations of faculty-centered practices where students barely registered on their instructors' radar. UX can be quite helpful in this regard because it prioritizes the user's experience.

UX design outside higher education, particularly in a business context, answers seven questions about the relationship between prospective customers, called "users," and a product or service.[23] When we apply these questions to higher education, we'll modify the "user" to students and the "product" to the education we provide. *Allow me to emphasize: education is emphatically not a product*, but we can find useful models outside higher education that can be adapted to our purpose as educators.

1. Useful: does the product serve a purpose?
2. Usable: can users effectively and efficiently use the product for themselves?
3. Findable: can the user find the product to purchase it?
4. Credible: does the user believe that the product will do what it's advertised to do?
5. Desirable: does the product inspire the user to want to purchase it?
6. Accessible: can persons with disabilities use the product?
7. Valuable: does the product deliver value to the person who purchases it and the company that produces it?

Few institutions of higher learning focus on creating a user experience for students. Their systems and procedures grew and evolved rather than being consciously designed to work well together, let alone operating from the standpoint of serving students' needs. By applying UX design, we can do better. Let's recast those seven questions to reflect a student-centered model of higher education.

1. **Useful: how will this _____ (course, assignment, experience) be personally useful to the student?**
   Everything students encounter in higher education has a purpose, but we're not always diligent about articulating this to our students. We generally assume that students automatically understand why we're asking them to do something, or we expect them to discover the purpose for themselves. However, when we take the time to articulate *why* we're asking students to do something, they're better able to learn from that experience. This process takes about two minutes, but it's a powerful tool for enhancing students' learning. "Today, we're going to learn about _____ because it's the key to understanding _____." Or "This lesson will help you develop your skills in _____, which are essential to success in the workplace after you graduate." Perhaps you'd want to add a bit more

41

explanation, but even short statements such as these go a long way to prime students' minds for the instruction that's about to occur.

2. **Usable: how can the student use the available materials and supports to maximize learning?**

Instructors provide materials and support in their classrooms. Institutions also provide support systems for students. Nevertheless, these supports are not usable unless we teach students what they are, explain how they work, and help them develop the ability to use these tools productively. Usability also relates to the level of difficulty involved in the resource. If a student has trouble understanding the instructor's lectures, referring them to a textbook that's equally opaque to the student is not helpful. Likewise, sending the student to the writing center the day before the paper is due will not be useful if the writing center requires making an appointment a week before the due date. Therefore, your plan for instruction should include specific directions for using these tools, including tutorials, examples, videos, or whatever else students might need, as appropriate to your course content and the disciplinary context in which it takes place.

3. **Findable: where can the student find the materials, information, or help that they need?**

Obviously, students can't use something if they can't find it. Understanding the support systems available through the institution and knowing where the things they need are located in the physical or virtual learning environment are necessary to their success. A page of links for student services or support systems should exist in the "Start Here" area of your online classroom, and you should mention these support systems as often as they're needed. The ability to find help also lies with the student, to a certain extent. I've heard faculty express their displeasure with students' poor communication skills, such as sending badly written, demanding, or rude email or failing to communicate with their instructor when they need help. Even though we'd like to hope our students have already learned how to communicate appropriately with faculty, we may have to include a lesson like this in our plan of instruction if we notice that they cannot meet our expectations.

4. **Credible: does this _____ (information, activity, requirement, etc.) make sense to the student?**

Critical thinking is an essential life skill and crucial for academic success. First, students should learn how to monitor their understanding as they read, listen to lectures, or watch an instructor's demonstration. They must be able to recognize when there are gaps in their understanding of what they've seen, heard, or read—a skill called metacognition, which means thinking about thinking. The trick is to pause and ask, "Does this make sense to me?" If the answer is no, students also need to learn how to take action until the answer becomes yes. Second, our students need to learn how to think critically about the topics we examine in our courses, asking questions like, "Is that true? How do we know this is accurate? What evidence supports this statement? Is the evidence from a credible source?" and so on. Developing a critical mindset rather than accepting every word the instructor utters as unassailable truth is a key to wisdom. It's also a hallmark of a well-educated person. Of course, critical thinking also differs by discipline and specialty. To critique a work of art is not the same as conducting literary criticism, for example, nor is it the same as evaluating the validity of scientific research, even though all are types of critical thinking. In terms of our course design, however, our goal is to deliver instruction that makes sense to the student and that they can perceive as being valid and valuable.

5. **Desirable: does the learning experience inspire the student? Does the student see how their learning will help them build a career after they graduate?**

   We need to keep the big picture in mind across everything that we ask our students to do. Learning about the Peloponnesian Wars in World History 101 doesn't exist in isolation—it informs students' understanding of how Western civilization grew and developed to become what it is today. That knowledge informs graduates' future careers since the workplace exists within a society governed by principles developed in ancient Greece. Excellent instructors help their students make these connections, but others remain committed to the notion that sole responsibility for learning rests with the student, leaving them to make connections for themselves. Furthermore, our methods of instructional delivery increase the desirability of our course. Instructors who are dynamic and engaging teachers communicate their excitement about their course content, inspiring students to learn more. Instructors who implement learning experiences beyond the walls of the classroom or studio empower students' learning. All of us can help students learn how to make connections between their prior knowledge, what we're teaching, and its application after graduation. Even more, we can teach our students how to find something of value in each class period or educational experience they encounter beyond our sphere of influence, learning how to keep themselves engaged in learning and motivated to succeed.

6. **Accessible: how can students manage the problems they face as learners?**

   About 26% of the general population has some form of disability, according to the US Centers for Disease Control,[24] and nearly all of us have areas where we're not as strong or skillful as we'd like to be. When

43

we apply UX design to learning, we think about how we can strategically adapt processes, materials, or systems to shore up these areas of weakness.

Access does not only apply to those with a documented disability. Low-income students might lack the ability to obtain the supplies or materials they need for class. Issues of diversity, equity, or inclusion can interfere with students' studies. Students cannot learn when they're hungry, cold, exhausted, unwell, or overwhelmed by other factors that negatively impact their quality of life. Therefore, we should share information on resources like the campus food pantry, options for students who have no home or transportation and therefore cannot leave campus during breaks, or problems common to specific institutions. For instance, students at a university in Florida aren't likely to struggle with being unable to obtain adequate winter clothing, but the same need could prevent students from attending classes during a "polar vortex" weather event in Wisconsin. Solutions should suit the particular challenges of the university and its specific student population.

7. **Valuable: how will the education we deliver to our students allow them to meet their goals?**

This question might be the most important of all. Most students want to earn a degree because it allows them to pursue a particular career, yet some instructors object to this pragmatic viewpoint, resisting suggestions to connect classroom learning to students' personal lives or careers. Nevertheless, it's up to us as educators to communicate the value of what we're teaching and help students persevere even when they don't feel engaged in a course or face personal hardships. Believing that their education is worthwhile overall can sustain students' motivation to complete activities and requirements that may not seem to be of value at the time. It's as simple as prefacing an activity with the statement, "This assignment will help you _____ [name of skill] so that you can _____ [career application]."

An Analogy

To better understand the conditions facing our students, let's consider the following analogy. A homeowner named Patrick decides to build a backyard gazebo. After acquiring lumber, fasteners, roofing material, and other supplies he believes will be useful, Patrick attempts to build the structure. Even if Patrick has purchased the highest-quality materials, the gazebo is unlikely to turn out well if his prior construction expertise is limited, his tools are inadequate, or he lacks a set of step-by-step instructions for the project.

Just so, we give our students the materials of an education through the courses they complete to earn a degree, but we don't always connect the knowledge they acquire in one class to their learning in another, nor do we clarify how their studies outside their major relate to the profession the student hopes to pursue after graduation. Even within a major, faculty might not explain the relationship between the knowledge imparted in the classroom and its application to professional practice. We tend to let students puzzle out the connections for themselves.

Now let's extend the metaphor. To build anything, we need a set of tools. Someone working with excellent tools is more likely to achieve a good result than someone working with inferior tools. True, we can attach boards with either a hammer or a pneumatic nail gun, but the power tool will be far more efficient. Our students come to us with vastly different tool kits—their life experiences, upbringing, and the education they received in K–12 have a pronounced impact on their ability to succeed in college. Do we shrug our shoulders and say, "That's just the way it is," or should we try to improve the odds by building up the tool kits of those students who weren't lucky enough to begin college with the same high-quality experiences?

The same is true of access to support. If our friend Patrick's next-door neighbor is a professional carpenter who's willing to help when inevitable problems arise, it will enhance his project's potential for success. However, if Patrick has no resources beyond carpentry tutorials on YouTube, the gazebo is much less likely to turn out well. Just so, our students vary in the supports available to them. Having a parent with a college degree statistically increases students' likelihood of graduation. "One-third of first-generation students dropped out of college after three years, compared to 14% of their peers whose parents had earned a college degree," according to the National Center for Education Statistics.[25] The parallel might be if Patrick's parents had previously built a gazebo in their backyard and were able to give Patrick first-hand advice about the process. Establishing a personal relationship with someone knowledgeable in the ways of higher education, such as a mentor, can make a crucial difference, too, just like Patrick's neighbor, the professional carpenter. Students trying to find their way through college alone might have to conduct a detailed investigation just to find available campus services, then schedule an appointment with a stranger in an unfamiliar office before they can begin to get the help they need. The difficult process of getting help might be more daunting than whatever problem the student was experiencing in the first place, or it might be so stressful the student simply gives up. On the other hand, students who have someone they can turn to for help, even if it's as simple as knowing where to go to fix a computer issue, are more likely to succeed.

UX design could take the gazebo project to the next level. Let's say a company consulted with users to create a gazebo kit designed to facilitate customers' do-it-yourself success. Patrick decides to purchase one of these kits instead of trying to build the structure from scratch. The kit contains clear instructions, access to video tutorials, and all the necessary materials, including pre-cut lumber. The

45

gazebo company even provides a hotline customers can call for one-on-one advice if they run into construction problems.

Similarly, UX design transforms an otherwise difficult process by ensuring that all seven criteria are met so that the users are happy with their purchase. It puts the designer in the customer's shoes, so to speak, and attempts to anticipate problems before they arise. Patrick still has to do the labor of building the gazebo—it's a kit, not a finished product. He might also want to consult with his parents or with his neighbor if he runs into trouble. Nevertheless, his experience in building the gazebo from a kit is likely to be more successful than it might otherwise have been if he'd tried to do the project from scratch.

We can do the same for our students. We're the experts in higher education. We know the ins and outs of the university. We know where to find support and how to connect students to resources. Everything we need to design a much better user experience for our students is at our fingertips. There's really no reason students should have to find their own path through our system of disparate departments and disconnected courses and navigate alone through layers of administrative complexity. Our institutions are generally anything but student-friendly, even when we publicly proclaim we're student centered. Large-scale structural changes are on the horizon at many colleges and universities, which might achieve this goal in time. For now, it's up to us as faculty to embrace our role as the "contact patch" and keep our students on track to achieving Priority One.

Design Thinking

Traditional design processes begin with a decision of what to create. Then designers figure out how to create it, and finally, they tell potential customers why they should buy it. The product comes first, the process is next, and the people who might use the product are last, seen mainly as a means of generating profit through their purchase of the product.

Like UX design, design thinking[26] comes to us through its commercial applications, but we can modify and adapt it to higher education, just as we did with UX. Design thinking and UX design both vary from standard design methods in their relationship to the user, but UX and design thinking differ from one another in their purpose. UX design maximizes the user's *experience* with a product or service. Design thinking, on the other hand, focuses on solving a human problem *beginning with the user* rather than the product, learning who they are, what they want, and what they need, usually in the context of a particular problem the user wants to solve. Then designers define the problem, ideate to find potential solutions, prototype their ideas, and test them with users to evaluate their effectiveness. Many cycles through the steps of ideate, prototype, and test may be necessary before finding a solution that works for the user.

Empathize. When used in a business context, design thinking begins by developing empathy for the user of a product or service, whereas in higher education, we're designing for our students. We try to put ourselves in the other person's place—to set aside our assumptions and see the problem through their eyes. We want to find out what causes the other person to experience frustration or other negative emotions related to the situation we're trying to rectify. We also want to find out what the other person values. The point is to gain empathy for the people who will use our solution by discovering:

- How do they feel?
- What do they want?
- What's important to them?
- What do they need?

Developing empathy requires us to set aside our assumptions. The more different we are from the user, the more we have to resist the temptation to impose our values or perceptions on them. Methods for developing empathy might include:

- Direct observation
- Participant observation
- Interviews
  - Ask "why" even if you think you know the answer.
  - Pay attention to facial expressions and body language.
  - Ask non-binary questions.
  - Encourage storytelling.

Developing empathy with someone leads to understanding what's important to them. We can observe someone's values in:

- What they say
- What they do
- What they choose
- How they live

Some observations can be conducted from a distance. In that case, we use descriptions or information other researchers have compiled. We can also look at artifacts or evidence of the others' lives:

- What have the users created or written (art, literature, music, media)?
- What can we observe in their clothing, housing, or food choices?
- What do they appear to like or dislike?

All of these offer clues about the values of the people for whom we're designing something, revealing what's important to them. However, we also have to dig below the surface and use our powers of inference to discover the meanings behind what we observe, asking ourselves, "Why . . . ?" as we consider the evidence we gather.

By choosing to apply design thinking to higher education, we reject traditional sink-or-swim attitudes toward our students and let go of insistence upon college readiness. Instead, we choose to develop care for our students, demonstrating a desire to facilitate their success and concern for their well-being both while they are students and after they earn their degrees.

Developing empathy involves setting aside our preconceptions and learning about our students at a personal level, speaking with them directly about their needs, hopes, and experiences. Just as product designers use various tools for gathering information about the project's user, we can similarly employ surveys, interviews, and direct observation to deepen our understanding of their experience. Personal interactions keep us from simply presuming our students' collegiate experiences are the same as ours or forgetting that things have changed quite a bit since we were students. It helps us remember that it's not about us. It's about them.

Our everyday first-hand observations can become powerful tools for deeper understanding. For example, I overheard a conversation between two faculty members in which one said, "I just don't understand why our students don't dress better." The faculty member who made this comment was stating an uninformed value judgment, not seeking knowledge. Nevertheless, it stopped me in my tracks. Yes, I thought, our students are often poorly clothed. Is this a fashion choice, or is something else at work here? Digging deeper, I found that many students dressed poorly because they simply had no money to buy decent clothes. They couldn't even afford food or other necessities of life because they prioritized purchasing the things they need for class, sometimes going hungry to do so because they placed such a high value on their education. I began to research support systems on campus that could alleviate some of these students' financial strain. The point is that I didn't stop on the surface (dressing poorly) but kept searching for the root of the problem (poverty), then tried to find a possible solution.

We've already spent quite a bit of time discussing who our students are, which gives us a head start on our work as course designers. However, please remember that there's no substitute for directly interacting with the people for whom you're designing the course, especially since your students are likely to be different from those at other institutions.

Key Questions for Course Designers:

- Who are my students?
- How can I learn what my students want and need from me?

48

- What are the students' greatest challenges or difficulties at our institution?
- What do students think would be most helpful in overcoming these problems?
- How will the information I've learned from students affect the course I'm developing?

Define. The next step in design thinking is to pair the data you've gathered about your users (students) with additional information so that you can form as comprehensive a picture as possible, studying existing assets, needs, and best practices. The task is to look beyond appearances and assumptions to get to the heart of the problem and then develop a clear problem statement framed in terms of the user.

It might be helpful to begin by defining the parameters of the problem. Organizing your thoughts in a format like the example in Table 2.1 can assist your analysis. The questions reflect general design terminology in their use of "user"

TABLE 2.1 Design Thinking—Problem Analysis

Question	Answer
Who is the user?	Students who are new to the university, including incoming freshmen and transfer students.
What will users gain from a solution? What do they stand to lose?	Students will have an easier time transitioning into university life; they will gain essential skills that assist their learning in other courses; they will begin to form relationships with peers and become acclimated to the university environment. They have little, if anything, to lose.
What prevents users from reaching a solution?	Left to their own devices, new students tend to flounder and are at risk of leaving college. They don't understand the systems, processes, or topography of the university. This unfamiliarity can create roadblocks to success.
What other factors contribute to the problem? (Social, financial, emotional)	The university's histories and traditions can stand in the way of offering incoming students extra help; faculty attitudes can be prohibitive; the cost of offering the courses (faculty salaries, etc.) can be steep.
What has been done so far?	Little had been done before the new program's design, but a faculty committee had conducted research into the program and generated some promising ideas.

to indicate the designed solution's intended recipients. Answers are based on the problem of creating a seminar course for incoming college students at a university with which I'm familiar.

Identify Your Assets. Your institution's Center for Teaching and Learning is a wonderful resource for course designers. Most of these employ highly knowledgeable people who are eager to help you create an outstanding course. They might be able to connect you to fellow faculty members who have developed courses similar to what you're trying to achieve, help you find some inspiration, or suggest elements you could incorporate into your course. Interviews with faculty or staff who work most closely with struggling students can be another source of valuable data. It might help to determine whether any colleagues in your college or university are particularly skilled at fostering students' success. You can also extend your investigation to courses or faculty at other institutions.

Identify Your Needs. Examining student data from the courses you've taught in the past provides a good starting point in determining areas of student need. The more specific this investigation and analysis, the more useful the data it can yield. What common threads can you identify between students who persist and those who drop your courses? Are there particular assignments or points during the course where you've noticed trouble?

As an example, I knew an instructor who had an extraordinarily high drop rate in his course. I spoke to students who had dropped and learned that the course required them to complete a large project that was so daunting they withdrew from the course. I suggested to the instructor that he break the project into smaller pieces, with opportunities for formative analysis along the way so that students could correct errors before completing the final product. He showed me that this was already part of his course, so we dug deeper, discovering that the problem lay with the instructor. He admitted that he disliked grading, so he would regularly fall behind in posting comments, which meant his students didn't receive the formative feedback they needed in time to act upon it before the next checkpoint in the project. Looking beyond our understandable tendency to ask, "What's wrong with the student, and how can I tell them to fix it?" means we must have enough courage to trace the problem back to ourselves, as this instructor did. It can also help us identify aspects of our institutional systems or processes that cause problems for our students.

Key Questions for Course Designers:

- What resources for learning more about student success are available to me?
- What could I find in these resources that would be useful in the course I'm developing?

50

- Where can I identify significant areas of need among my students?
- What support do students need?
- How can I define my course design problem in terms of my students?

Ideate and Innovate. The investigations you've conducted fuel your ideation process, informed by your knowledge of the resources available within your institution and your identification of students' needs. After taking all this information into account, we're ready to brainstorm solutions specific to the course we're creating.

Brainstorming is at its best when it follows the principles of design as practiced at IDEO—a leading design firm associated with Stanford's d.school.[27] Remember, the point is to design a solution that meets the user's needs. When you understand your user and define the problem, you'll see things differently than you would have if you'd jumped into the design process here in the middle (which, unfortunately, is the case with most design efforts). Although brainstorming is not usually a solo activity, please make the most of the following advice relative to your situation. You might also consider inviting a friend or two to brainstorm with you: an outside opinion can be quite helpful because it gives you a fresh perspective. The strategies for brainstorming presented here presume you're working with a team or partner rather than all alone. You might also find them helpful if you're working on a committee charged with solving a problem in your program, department, school, or college.

- **Defer judgment**. Negativity is the enemy of creativity. There will be time to evaluate ideas later, but during brainstorming, a philosophy of "Yes, and . . ." is much more productive than "No, but . . ." or (even worse) "That's stupid," or "That could never work," or "We tried that fifteen years ago and it was a disaster."
- **Encourage wild ideas**. Sometimes, our craziest ideas contain the seeds of something great. To jump-start divergent thinking, it can help to ask, "If you could wave a magic wand to change one thing, what would it be?" and "If we had all the money in the world to address the problem, what would you do?"
- **Build on the ideas of others**. Two heads are indeed better than one, although it's a cliché. Listening to others instead of focusing only on what we want to say draws upon this power, allowing us to generate more powerful solutions than one person is likely to come up with alone.
- **Stay focused on the topic**. Any time people get together, the tendency to go off on a tangent or engage in side conversations is strong. Staying focused and in the moment makes our discussions more productive.
- **Have one conversation at a time**. Each person deserves to be heard. Talking over one another or engaging in multiple conversations at once makes our brainstorming less effective.

51

■ **Be visual.** There is considerable power in sketching ideas, even if you can only draw stick figures. Translating a thought to an image and then coming up with a verbal explanation for that image engages multiple brain systems, allowing us to communicate effectively. Jotting ideas on colorful Post-it notes and placing them on a whiteboard where the whole group can see them establishes parameters for the process and keeps participants from being too detailed or too wordy.

■ **Go for quantity.** Our first few ideas are not always our best. The more ideas we generate, the greater the likelihood we'll eventually develop something that works.

After you've generated as many ideas as you can, it's time to sort and evaluate them. Draw, diagram, map, and label your proposed solutions. Compare them and decide which are best. Eventually, you'll come up with a workable idea ready for prototyping (planning your course). Choose the most promising and sketch out strategies for how you could bring these ideas to life in your course. Remember: brainstorming is about divergent thinking, in which we branch out in many directions. Solutions are about convergent thinking, sorting, prioritizing, merging, and refining ideas until you arrive at a plan.

As a suggestion, you might explore how you could incorporate the crucial experiences of the Big Six into your course because we know that these are essential to graduates' views about the value of the education they received. By utilizing the principles of design thinking and UX design, we can build these into our teaching to ensure that more students receive them.

By far, the majority of the time we spend designing a course occurs in the Define and Ideate phases we've just discussed. A course comprises multiple topics, learning experiences, teaching methods, resources, assessments, etc., each of which can become a mini-design project of its own.

Prototype and Test. The last steps in design thinking involve creating a prototype and testing it with the target audience. A prototype is a model of what

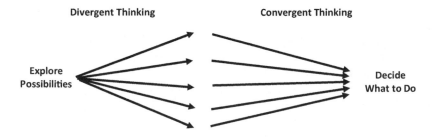

FIGURE 2.1 Divergent and Convergent Thinking

TABLE 2.2 Classroom Application of the Big Six

Big Six	Sample Classroom Application
Professors who made students feel excited about learning	Study how you can improve your instructional delivery to become more dynamic and inspiring, making students feel excited about learning.
Professors who cared about students as people	Set a personal goal to know every student by name and need from the beginning of the academic year.
A mentor who encouraged students to pursue their goals and dreams	Think of yourself as a mentor, making a direct connection with your students. It might not be possible to adopt this role with every student you teach, but certainly, those majoring in your discipline, especially those whom you've taught in more than one course, could and should receive more than cursory attention from you. Check up on those students regularly and provide academic and emotional support as needed and appropriate.
The opportunity to work on a long-term project	Utilize project-based learning to engage student interest, provide a meaningful context for acquiring academic skills and competencies, build interpersonal relationships, and acquire disciplinary knowledge related to the project.
Taking part in an internship or job where they could apply what they were learning in the classroom	Incorporate internship or practicum experiences, if appropriate, including partnerships with local businesses, organizations, or agencies. Practical experiences could also include volunteering or opportunities for community service.
Being extremely active in extracurricular activities and organizations during college	Promote engagement in co-curricular opportunities and strongly encourage students to join these organizations. Field trips, service projects, and group outings to off-campus locations or events also connect classroom learning to real-world settings.

you'd like to do in real life. One of the core tenets of design thinking is "bias toward action." Prototyping is thinking through making and exploring, transforming abstract ideas into concrete scenarios or objects. The prototyping process identifies glitches in the proposed solution, which takes us back to the Ideate phase to figure out a way to fix it. We might have to do this several times before we reach a workable solution. In commercial applications of design thinking, prototypes of products or services don't have to be elaborate or expensive. (In fact, they tend to use quite a bit of cardboard in the first stages.) Their purpose is to

53

transform something abstract (an idea) into something concrete, making it easier to see its strengths and weaknesses. In educational settings, our prototypes usually won't involve something tangible, but we can still use strategies like role playing or storyboarding, depending on the problem we're trying to solve.

The first prototyping activity in course design is to create a map of what your course will include, structured around a week-by-week plan of instruction. The course map is a work in progress, constantly subject to changes and adjustments as you think about what you'll teach, how you'll teach it, and what resources or assessments you'll need to create for your students.

The final prototype in course design occurs the first time we teach the course. Then we evaluate its success upon completion, make modifications, and then teach it again. The revised course should have detailed, specific, and measurable student learning outcomes that allow for actionable analysis.

The first iteration of the course is a prototype, and the first time we teach it is the test. Therefore, it's helpful to include specific activities for collecting data in addition to standard end-of-term surveys. We might choose to survey or interview student participants to monitor their impressions and reactions, concluding with a detailed exit survey and analysis of students' achievement of the course's objectives and outcomes. Finally, all the evidence gathered during the first time we teach the course helps identify areas for improvement, which we can then enact in the next iteration of the course. This pattern can be repeated every time we teach, maintaining a cycle of continuous improvement.

Part of the course design process, then, is to decide how you will know if your course is effective. Assessment mechanisms help you identify areas of strength and weakness, but they don't have to be overly complicated. A basic approach might look something like this:

1. Identify the desired learning outcomes.
2. Write parallel surveys to administer on the first and last day that measure students' acquisition of the desired learning outcomes. The instructor should also complete a self-assessment at the beginning and end of the course too.
3. Write a formative midterm quiz or exam to measure students' learning in-progress, identifying areas where adjustments might be necessary to support student learning before the course's conclusion.
4. Incorporate an assignment such as a one-page essay in which students reflect on their learning in the course, discussing what was most valuable to them and what they would change.

Finally, we should recognize that few courses achieve perfection the first time we teach them, underlying the benefit of adopting a mindset of continuous improvement. This approach parallels the principles of action research: identifying a problem we want to solve or asking a question we want to answer, taking steps to solve the problem or answer the question, evaluating the success of our efforts, then making necessary changes and trying again. No matter how many times we've taught a course, we can always find things to improve. Curricular development is not a one-and-done proposition. Instead, it's a cycle of teach, reflect, plan, and revise. We take action to fix flaws we notice along the way, create additional resources to support our students' learning of concepts or processes with which they struggled, rework a lecture that students didn't understand, add or change instructional components to increase student engagement. Reflective educators who care about their students' success don't stop at "good enough"— they constantly monitor what they could do better and then take action to do it.

Learning Experience Design

Yet another aspect of design we can apply to our work as educators, Instructional Design (ID) utilizes a process nicknamed ADDIE, coined by Robert Branch,[28] which stands for:

Analysis of the institution's goals, learner's goals, and the problem to be solved
Design of the course structure
Development of course content
Implementation of the new course by instructors
Evaluation of the course

ADDIE gives us a useful plan of action akin to the five steps of Design Thinking. Many universities employ instructional designers, who consult with faculty to develop courses. We should note that Instructional Design's main emphasis is on creating courses, whereas UX (as applied to instruction) focuses on the interaction between the student and the course. Elizabeth Boling and Colin Gray analyzed two mathematics learning applications to examine aspects of Instructional Design and UX present in each, concluding that each utilizes different vocabularies, pointing to different values. "ID terms address the instructional support required on behalf of learner/users, while the UX terms address the support of user/learners' actions required to benefit from the instruction on artifact, interaction, and sociocultural levels."[29] In other words, Instructional Design focuses on creating supports for learning (instruction), whereas UX focuses on the learner's actions when interacting with course content (interaction).

Learning Experience Design (LXD) combines the principles of UX, Design Thinking, and Instructional Design. The term originated with Niels Floor, who defined LXD as "the process of creating learning experiences that enable the learner to achieve the desired learning outcome in a human-centered and

55

goal-oriented way."[30] LXD differs from Instructional Design in its focus on the learner over course content, relying heavily on empathy as is common to design thinking. Floor describes LXD as being human centered and goal oriented, utilizing theories of human cognition, providing ways for students to put their learning into practice, and heavily interdisciplinary.

Our purpose in learning about these design practices is not to become experts in UX, Design Thinking, Instructional Design, or LXD. However, we can see that each one focuses on different aspects of the course design process.

- Instructional Design—designing course **structure and content**
- UX—designing learners' **interactions** with course materials and instruction
- LXD—designing the learning **experiences** within the course
- Design Thinking—developing **empathy** for the learner to drive the course **design process**

In truth, no single design method encompasses every aspect of course creation. I'm reminded of an ancient Indian parable. Six men, blind from birth, encountered an elephant for the first time. The man holding its trunk said it was like a snake. The one near the tusk thought the elephant was like a spear. The blind man touching the elephant's side disagreed, saying it was like a wall. Another blind man touched the leg and said the others were wrong; an elephant was most like a tree. The man holding its ear said it was a fan. And the one at the tail said all the others were wrong because the elephant was nothing but an old rope. None of them, of course, had a clear gestalt of what the elephant was. In the grand scheme of higher education, we've only taken a systematic approach to course design for a short time, and designing from a student-centered perspective is even more recent. Like the six blind men, each approach to course design holds part of the truth, but none encompasses everything we need to know or do.

I propose that Design Thinking could serve as a unifying methodology for the varied design approaches we've discussed. First, we develop empathy for our students. Then we use the principles of UX, ID, and LXD as we move through the steps of definition and ideation to create our course structure and content. Now let's turn our attention to how this approach could work in practice.

COURSE DESIGN FUNDAMENTALS

Historically speaking, instructors preparing to teach a new course would often begin by deciding what they wanted their course content to be. Then they would plan their instruction, choosing one or more textbooks, writing assessments, and creating assignments. Formulating the course's objectives and outcomes took place toward the end of the planning process so they could align these statements with the course they'd designed. If an instructor was teaching this new course on campus, they usually prepared their lectures and other teaching materials as needed, allowing the course to grow somewhat organically over the semester. I'd bet this process sounds quite familiar to you, but did you notice any mention of the student? No. It was entirely driven by the instructor's choices as the disciplinary expert, subject to the longstanding norms of higher education.

I propose a different approach in my book *Higher Education by Design* (2018), explaining how to plan a course by beginning with the end in mind, much as we'd plan a road trip by first deciding where we're going, then mapping out how we might reach our destination. This approach is sometimes called "backward design."[31] We might conceptualize it like this.

1. Identify the learning **outcomes** and course **objectives** your students should achieve by the end of the course, aligned with the institution's mission and vision and supportive of institutional mandates or goals. (Think back to Priority One.)[32]
2. Decide how you will use summative **assessment** to determine whether your students have achieved those outcomes.
3. Plan **instruction** that leads to students' achievement of those outcomes as measured by your planned assessments.
    a. Identify **students' needs** as they pertain to your course's purpose (empathize) and consider how you can deliver instruction that meets those needs (define).
    b. Choose **instructional strategies** that will meet students' needs while delivering disciplinary content that supports their achievement of course outcomes, including opportunities for actionable feedback and formative assessment (ideate).
    c. Create or select **instructional materials** that facilitate students' learning, including textbooks and other readings, multimedia resources, study guides, assignments, experiential learning activities, project-based or problem-based collaborative learning, and so on (ideate).
    d. Organize materials and instruction into a comprehensive, **week-by-week map** of learning activities, assignments, resources, and assessments, ending with creating the course syllabus (prototype).
4. **Create** or gather all the lectures, assignments, assessments, grading rubrics, and other resources and materials well before the first day of the new course (prototype). Evaluate the course before teaching, using the principles of **UX design, Instructional Design, and LXD** to refine your ideas so that you maximize your students' learning experience.
5. **Teach** the course, keeping track of areas where future changes will improve students' learning, gathering evidence, surveying students, and keeping anecdotal records (test).

57

6. Examine and **reflect** upon the evidence you collected as you taught the course for the first time. **Revise** the course in response to your findings, changing, adapting, or creating new materials, activities, and so on as needed.

7. Teach the course again. **Repeat** the cycle of teach, reflect, revise before each time you teach the course.

Next, let's look at each of those seven steps a bit more closely. We'll discuss them briefly here, then take a look at an example of how they come together in the design of a new course.

1. **Formulate Outcomes and Objectives**

The "end" we should keep in mind when designing a course is what we want our students to learn, which we express through the course outcomes. Every outcome should align with or support Priority One and any other relevant institution-level outcomes, the institution's mission, or applicable institution-wide mandates or initiatives such as focusing on critical thinking, writing, or engaged learning. At the same time, our course outcomes reflect the disciplinary content we will teach, which should align with relevant accreditation standards. We might think of an outcome as the goal we're reaching toward or the destination of our

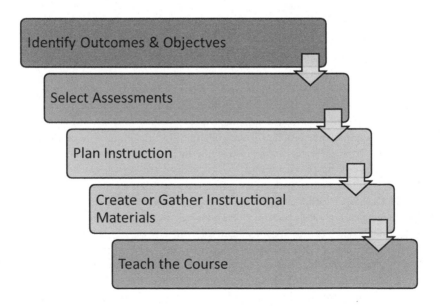

FIGURE 2.2 Course Design Flow Chart

journey. It's a concise statement of what we want our students to know or be able to do as the direct result of their learning in the course.

In general, a course should have somewhere between five and nine outcomes, but this will certainly depend on your institution and your disciplinary norms. Writing good outcomes is a bit like writing poetry or creating a tweet-size summary of a vast amount of information—every word counts. Objectives serve as a bridge between the outcomes and our assessments. Although it should still be measurable, an outcome can be quite broad, and it might apply to more than one course within an academic program or department. Objectives are specific to the course, clarifying what students must do to demonstrate their achievement of the outcomes through the course's assessments. We might think of objectives as the action steps that lead to the outcomes or the component skills and knowledge that contribute to students' achievement of the outcomes. In backward design, we plan the outcomes first; then, we write objectives that support them. Think back to the metaphor of the journey. If we're going to take a long road trip, we first choose our destination (the outcomes), but we also have to plan our route and schedule stopping points along the way. Those stopping points are the objectives.

Outcomes and objectives should use active verbs indicating higher-order thinking, usually aligned with Bloom's Taxonomy of Knowledge.[33] Basic knowledge exists at the lowest levels, but the highest levels demonstrate students' ability to use what they've learned. Undoubtedly, students ought to remember and understand what they're taught, but our instruction should provide them with knowledge and skills beyond mere facts, preparing students to apply their learning in new situations, evaluate information, and create something new. This is why our outcome and objective statements should use words from the higher end of the scale rather than the lower end whenever possible. Figure 2.3 provides some example terms we might use under each heading, but it is not an exhaustive list.

Many outcomes begin with phrases like "Students will . . ." or "Students will be able to . . ." because they point to what students will do in the future as the result of their learning. An English class, for example, might set an outcome such as "Students will be able to write a complete paragraph conforming to the norms of college-level English." This statement indicates the learned ability students should carry with them and use in their lives once the course is over.

The number of outcomes and objectives need not match, but they should correlate with each other. Every outcome should align with one or more objectives, and every objective should link to one or more outcomes. Neither should stand alone. A given outcome and objective pair

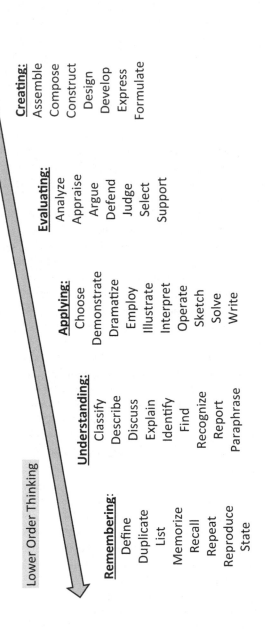

Higher Order Thinking

Creating:
Assemble
Compose
Construct
Design
Develop
Express
Formulate

Evaluating:
Analyze
Appraise
Argue
Defend
Judge
Select
Support

Applying:
Choose
Demonstrate
Dramatize
Employ
Illustrate
Interpret
Operate
Sketch
Solve
Write

Understanding:
Classify
Describe
Discuss
Explain
Identify
Find
Recognize
Report
Paraphrase

Remembering:
Define
Duplicate
List
Memorize
Recall
Repeat
Reproduce
State

Lower Order Thinking

FIGURE 2.3 Thinking Continuum

may sound rather similar, but they may differ in their purpose. To write good objectives, you'll need to consider what students must know or be able to do if they are to achieve the outcome and then break it down into smaller parts. Four objectives supporting the outcome of writing a paragraph could be "Write a clear thesis statement. Support the thesis statement with evidence and explanation. Cite sources according to MLA requirements. Compose a convincing conclusion."

We should also note that when we're designing the course, the outcomes drive our decision-making processes, but when we're teaching the course, the objectives take priority so that our students can achieve the outcomes by the end of the course. In other words, we design in reverse, but we drive forward to the destination.

The last thing we should keep in mind is that each outcome and objective should be measurable. That is, we should be able to determine whether our students have achieved the objectives and the outcomes of the course. Naturally, this leads us to the topic of assessment.

2. Decide on Assessments

Assessment should never be a surprise or a mystery to students. TILT (Transparency in Learning and Teaching)[34] promotes best practices in assessment in which the instructor sets the purpose for learning, assigns a task that allows the student to develop the requisite skills or knowledge, and finally, assesses students' work based on transparent criteria provided to the student at the beginning of the learning process. TILT is highly suitable to our design premise, in which we first tell our students why they will learn something, explain how they'll learn it, and then measure what they have learned. The better our students understand what we want, the more we empower their learning. Faculty and students both err when we fall into the trap of thinking that teaching and learning have a transactional relationship: students do the work, and instructors give them a grade in return. That misses the whole point of higher education. *Learning* is what's important, not grades. Or, to paraphrase one of my favorite professors from my undergraduate days, I like to tell my students, "You're not here for my approval. You're here to *learn*."

Assessments linked to course outcomes tend to be summative, which means they occur at the conclusion of a learning process. We're all familiar with midterm and final exams, of course, but summative assessments can be more holistic. Projects or performance tasks can measure students' learning, as can reflective essays, presentations, or creative works that demonstrate what the student knows or can do as the result of their experience in the course.

Multiple-choice exams reduce the instructor's grading burden, especially when delivered through the LMS, which—if designed properly—automatically scores the exams. Nevertheless, questions should reflect students' ability to apply the *concepts* you've taught. Unless one of your course outcomes is "Students will memorize _____ [long list of technical terms]" (a lower-order task, by the way), exams shouldn't test for memorization. Rote learning remains necessary for certain situations and in some professions, but when we have literally all the information in the world at our fingertips, we would do well to question the value of memorizing facts anybody can look up in a second or two online. Speaking only for myself, I'd prefer for my students to know how to find an answer or solve a problem independently using the tools at their disposal. No one in the world outside higher education quizzes our graduates on vocabulary words or mathematical formulae. Our responsibility as disciplinary experts is to equip our students with the knowledge, skills, and competencies necessary in our professional fields. Learning the language of our discipline is part of that process, as is being able to recognize common tools and be proficient at using them. We wouldn't want a future engineer to be unfamiliar with engineering terminology or to be incapable of making correct calculations. However, a good assessment will ask students to *apply* that knowledge in context rather than state *that* they know it. I won't lie to you: it's much more difficult to write exams this way. I wrestle with this, myself. It takes longer to grade subjective, open-ended responses than objective test questions, too. Nevertheless, I know I'm seeing a better picture of my students' learning of the course outcomes and objectives when I deliver an exam that measures their acquisition of core concepts through their ability to apply, evaluate, or create something that demonstrates their learning.

Some back and forth is necessary when planning our assessments since these must also align with instruction that we haven't yet planned. Therefore, at this early stage of the course design process, we decide *how* to assess students' learning, but we might wait to write the exams or other assessments until after mapping the rest of the course.

3. **Plan Instruction**

This stage of the course design process is where we can utilize design thinking most fully. Let's start from the premise that you've written your course outcomes and have a good idea of how you'll assess your students' learning. We'll also assume that you've formed an accurate understanding of the students you'll teach and have developed empathy for them. Please remember, though, that empathy isn't just a point on the course design checklist. Instead, we constantly need to circle back to empathy, asking ourselves questions such as these as we try to look at our course components through a student's eyes.

- Can my students complete this task/assignment/activity within the time I've allowed?
- Are the instructions I've provided clear enough for my students to understand without my help?
- Have I provided sufficient resources so that students can do what I've asked them to do? Could I add anything else like a video tutorial, link to an external website, supplementary reading, and so on that might enhance or deepen their learning?
- What do I know about my students that might make it difficult for them to do what I've asked them to do? (For instance, if you want them to complete a project, they might need to buy materials. Some students will not be able to afford these materials. How can you meet this need? Or how can you modify the assignment to allow for less-expensive materials?)
- Will students be interested in what I'm asking them to do? Will they find it engaging and motivational?
- What potential pitfalls, drawbacks, misconceptions, or common errors can I identify that may occur during this learning activity? How can I mitigate those problems?

Make the Course Map: I begin my work as a course developer by making a grid with 17 rows and four columns. The rows allow for a header, plus one row per week of the semester. Column 1 is the week number. Column 2 is the topic for the week and planned instruction. Column 3 is for readings and out-of-class activities. Column 4 indicates assignments or assessments due that week.

Choose Textbooks and Create Reading Assignments: I also decide on textbooks at this point in the design process, and I plan the weekly topics to align with the students' reading assignments. Sometimes I want students to complete their reading before we engage with the topic in class, so they're primed to understand the lectures and classroom activities. Other times, readings supplement and reinforce

TABLE 2.3 Course Map Template

Week #	Topic/Instruction	Readings or Activities	Assignments and Assessments
1	_____	_____	_____
2	_____	_____	_____
3	_____	_____	_____
4	_____	_____	_____

what we've worked on in class. I'll set due dates for these reading assignments to clarify which of these two purposes the readings serve. I'll also explain this to students before they read because knowing the purpose for reading enhances their ability to assimilate the text's information.

I try to be careful about the number of pages I expect students to read per week. We can't assume our students will read at the same rate we do, and their unfamiliarity with the genres specific to our discipline can slow them down even further. The purpose for reading makes a difference in their reading rate, too. Reading to survey a topic goes more quickly than reading to understand the text well enough to take a quiz over the material. Reading a book published for a mass-market audience will be less challenging than comprehending an article in a professional journal packed full of dense technical language.

When we plan what we want our students to do each week, we should keep credit hour definitions in mind. The US Department of Education states that one credit hour should provide "not less than one hour of class and two hours of out-of-class student work per week over a semester."[35] Therefore, a three-hour course would require three hours of class time and six hours of work out of class, per week, for a total of nine hours. Lab and studio courses sometimes alter this ratio. For instance, NASAD (the National Association of Schools of Art and Design) recommends that students spend six hours in the studio with the instructor present and three hours working independently.[36] The rules for online courses are less specific. According to the US Department of Education,

> There is no "seat time" requirement implicit in the definition of a cred-it hour. An institution that is offering asynchronous online courses would need to determine the amount of student work expected in each online course to achieve the course objectives, and assign a credit hour based on at least an equivalent amount of work as represented in the definition of credit hour.
>
> (Guidance issued 3/18/2011)[37]

Based on this information, we can conclude that nine clock hours is the outer limit we can command of our students' time for any given course, regardless of whether it takes place in the studio, online, or on campus. This standard helps us judge how much work we can reasonably expect our students to do.

To simplify course planning for instructors, Wake Forest University's Center for the Advancement of Teaching offers an online "Workload Estimator 2.0" tool that allows you to calculate the time required for reading assignments, writing, discussion posts, and more. (You can find it at https://cat.wfu.edu/resources/tools/estimator2/.)

BOX 2.1 Credit Hour Definition

Student Time Expectations

Part 600, Institutional Eligibility under the Higher Education Act of 1965, as amended, provides the following definition:

> "A credit hour is an amount of work represented in intended learning outcomes and verified by evidence of student achievement that is an institutionally established equivalency that reasonably approximates not less than—
>
> (1) One hour of classroom or direct faculty instruction and a minimum of two hours of out of class student work each week for approximately fifteen weeks for one semester or trimester hour of credit, or ten to twelve weeks for one quarter hour of credit, or the equivalent amount of work over a different amount of time; or
>
> (2) At least an equivalent amount of work as required in paragraph (1) of this definition for other academic activities as established by the institution including laboratory work, internships, practica, studio work, and other academic work leading to the award of credit hours" (34 CPR Part 600.2).

Therefore, a three-credit course should occupy nine engaged hours of learning activities per week, per course.

Correlate Assignments and Assessments: Each week's topic and readings should be accompanied by assignments or other learning activities that allow students to practice new skills, deepen their understanding of course content, and promote their acquisition of the course outcomes. I use a model of guided instruction as I plan, which I think of as "I do, we do, you do." First, I teach the lesson. (I do.) Then I give students opportunities to practice and apply what they just learned while they're still in the classroom. (We do.) Afterward, they have further opportunities to practice by doing work independently. (You do.)

A simple example could be found in a mathematics course. The instructor demonstrates and explains a mathematical concept. (I do.) She provides practice problems to do in class, which allows her to check students' understanding and correct their errors and misconceptions. (We do.) Then students complete additional problems as an out-of-class assignment. (You do.)

We could also call this model "talk through, walk through, drive through": we talk our students through our instruction and walk them through doing a process or understanding the lesson's content in the classroom where we can help them shore up their understanding, and they drive through the process or ideas outside class. The "we do" or "walk through" step of guided learning

65

can also occur outside our direct supervision. Students can complete learning activities independently, which we later review, providing feedback and allowing opportunities for correction or revision. Whether they're done in class or independently, these types of activities are *formative*: they help students improve their learning and let us know which aspects of our instruction are working and which are not. If most of my students misinterpret the same part of the activity or get the same wrong answers on a question, it tells me they need additional instruction or clarification. Formative assignments should have a low point value in the overall grading scheme because their purpose is to be part of the learning process, not serve as a final evaluation. Alternatively (or additionally), we can allow students to resubmit their work for an improved score on formative tasks, especially if the item is worth a substantial part of the final grade.

Most instructors organize their course by dividing it into modules or units, each containing instruction, discussion, learning activities, assignments, and assessments. I keep the guided learning model in mind when considering how to distribute the content I plan to teach. The first module provides instruction and practice of the foundational skills and knowledge students will need in the course. The next module or two might include group projects or exploratory activities that build and deepen students' knowledge. Then I conclude the course with an independent project or an assignment such as a research paper to serve as a summative assessment demonstrating students' acquisition of one or more course outcomes. This isn't a hard and fast rule, of course. Every instructor has personal preferences, and institutions vary in their requirements, too.

As we plan the course schedule, we also need to be aware of special events, scheduled breaks, holidays, and other potential complications. I generally enter these on my course map first, mainly because it's aggravating to have everything planned only to discover a scheduling conflict that forces me to modify my schedule. For instance, I recently designed an online eight-week summer course, but when I began to upload it to the LMS, I saw that the first week began on Wednesday, not Monday, as I'd presumed. I had to reconfigure the first and second weeks' plans so that students weren't overwhelmed by the shortened time to do their work just as the class began.

This list of questions might help you organize your thinking as you work on mapping your course.

- How can I divide the content I want to teach into modules or units?
- What will I teach each week (topics)?
- How will I teach it (lecture, demonstration, discussion, multimedia, active learning)?
- How will I provide practice or opportunities for students to engage with the topic I'm teaching (assignments or activities, in class or outside class)?
- What supplementary materials or readings will help my students learn what I'm teaching (readings, multimedia content, handouts, study guides)?

■ How will I know if students have learned what I taught in this module/unit/week (assessment: quizzes, exams, assignments, projects, presentations)?

4. Gather Materials and Apply UX Design

Each item on the course map will require writing, creating, or finding a resource of some kind. Let's say that in the second week of the course, you plan to deliver a lecture during one class period, have students complete a partner activity during the other, require students to read a section of one of the course textbooks outside class, and take a quiz through the LMS. That means you need to:

1. Create your lecture, which will vary depending on the format of the course. You might deliver the lecture live, either on campus or synchronously online, but you'll probably want to have a supporting presentation such as a PowerPoint or at least an outline to keep your remarks on track.
2. Write complete instructions for the in-class partner activity, including criteria you'll use to assess the students' work, such as a checklist or rubric, and factor the activity in the course's grading scheme.
3. Communicate which chapters of the textbook students should read and set the purpose for reading. Readings should include a means of holding students accountable, so you might ask them to write a response or post to a discussion board or tell them to bring something to contribute to the class discussion, as a few examples. Whatever you choose, you'll need to provide written directions and grading criteria as well.
4. Write the quiz, decide on its point value and grading criteria, and post it to the LMS, communicating this expectation to students.

Each of these elements is a mini design project of its own. No lecture, assignment, activity, or assessment exists for its sake alone—all share the instrumental purpose of promoting students' learning of the course outcomes. Therefore, everything you do must touch back to that central purpose. If you can't articulate that connection to your students, then you should seriously question whether it's worth asking them to do that activity. Our course components are like puzzle pieces. We have to design the pieces to fit together if we expect our students to assemble the puzzle.

UX design lets us check our work to be sure we've kept our students in mind. We'll use the phrase "learning resource" to stand in for any document or file you might build into the course: a lecture, instructions, quiz, handout, and so on.

- Useful: does the learning resource serve the purpose of supporting students' learning of the course outcomes?
- Usable: will students be able to use the learning resource effectively and efficiently by themselves?
- Findable: will students be able to find the learning resource?
- Credible: will students understand the learning resource's value within the course?
- Desirable: will students find the learning resource to be engaging, interesting, or enjoyable?
- Accessible: can students who experience learning difficulties use this learning resource successfully, and is it clear how they can access help using the item?
- Valuable: will students understand that the learning resource delivers value to their educational experience or helps them meet their career goals?

I realize it might seem incredibly cumbersome to evaluate your course's entire contents according to UX criteria. However, once you become more proficient in maintaining a student-centered mindset, these considerations will become second nature. Furthermore, uploading everything into the LMS according to standards such as Quality Matters (which we'll discuss in the next chapter) addresses issues of findability and accessibility automatically, taking those two considerations off your plate. We can clarify usefulness and credibility when introducing a learning resource or by building explanations into our written course materials. Therefore, we're just left with usability, desirability, and value: can students use the item successfully? Will students find the item to be intrinsically valuable because they will appreciate it on its merits? And will they perceive its instrumental value to their overall education?

Faculty-centered culture leads instructors to believe we can ask our students to do whatever we want, offering no more rationale than "because I'm the instructor, and I said so." Adopting a student-centered philosophy of education motivates us to aim higher: to explain *why* students should do what we ask, tell them *how* to do what we want them to do and *how* we'll evaluate their work, and finally, communicate *what* they'll achieve or receive by doing it.

An Example

Before moving on to the last three steps in the course design process, I'd like to share the course map I created for an undergraduate Design Thinking course and walk you through the design process. This course was initially offered as an eight-week summer session. First, let's look at Module 1.

The Reading Journals in this course hold students accountable for doing the assigned reading. They serve another purpose that I identified in the "empathize"

TABLE 2.4 Design Thinking Course, Module 1 Course Map

Week #	Topic	Readings	Assignments/Assessments
MODULE 1—WHAT IS DESIGN THINKING?			
1	Lecture 1A: Course Introduction: What is Design Thinking? Lecture 1B: Virtual Crash Course ("The Wallet Project")	Liedtka Ch. 1&2 Why Design Thinking?	Take the "Start Here" quiz. Post to the "Introduce Yourself" discussion and comment on two peers' posts. Reading Journal 1: 1. Post reflection and three questions to the Discussion area; comment on two peers' posts. 2. Upload the reading journal document to the Assignment area.
2	Lecture: People, Process, and Products—Steps of Design Thinking LIVE ONLINE MEETING on Thursday	Liedtka Ch. 13&14 The Four-Question Method in Action	Reading Journal 2 1. Post reflection and three questions to the Discussion area; comment on two peers' posts. 2. Upload the reading journal document to the Assignment area.

phase of design thinking, too. I've noted that students often struggle with reading assignments, sometimes just not doing the reading at all, while other times, they simply don't know how to read for comprehension. Reading Journals develop students' skills as readers by requiring structured notetaking and analysis. I explain to students that this helps improve their comprehension and retention of what they've read because paraphrasing the text demands that we understand it well enough to put an idea into our own words. Highlighting and underlining ask us to analyze and evaluate, which lifts students to a higher level of thinking, demonstrating deeper understanding. I'd originally planned to have students attach each journal to a discussion post, but due to limitations in the LMS, I had to modify the assignment by splitting it into two parts. As a result, students upload their actual notes to the assignment area and post a short reflection on their reading to the discussion area, along with three questions that occurred to them as they read. These questions give us some good material to discuss since responses will differ from one student to the next. (I've found that asking

69

TABLE 2.5 Design Thinking Course, Module 2 Course Map

MODULE 2—CASE STUDIES IN DESIGN THINKING

Case Study Intro & Instructor preview of Case 1 (Lecture 3)	Brown • Ch. 1 Getting Under Your Skin • Ch. 2 Converting Need into Demand • Ch. 9 Design Activism Read Case 1	Reading Journal 3 1. Post reflection and three questions to the Discussion area; comment on two peers' posts. 2. Upload the reading journal document to the Assignment area. Group Discussion of the case (MS Teams group meeting).
Small groups apply design thinking to Case 1 and formulate solution (meet via MS Teams) LIVE ONLINE MEETING 2—Check-In		Case 1 Presentation & Submission Midterm Exam
Instructor preview of Case 2 **Instructor will personally check with each team during their meeting this week**	Read Case 2	Initial Group Discussion of the case (MS Teams group meeting).
Small groups apply design thinking to Case 1 and formulate solution (meet via MS Teams) LIVE ONLINE MEETING 3—Debrief Case Study Unit & preview personal design problem	Roth Ch. 3 Getting Unstuck Roth Ch. 5 Doing is Everything (readings included in Reading Journal 4, due at the end of Week 7)	Case 2 Presentation & Submission

everybody to post a summary makes for a dull discussion because the responses are too similar.)

The first lecture in Week 1 introduces students to the course and the basics of design thinking. The second lecture leads students through a partner activity in design thinking. Week 1 also includes a requirement that students work through a "Start Here" area in the LMS, take a short quiz, and introduce themselves on a discussion board. We'll talk more about these first-week requirements in the next chapter.

In Week 2, there's only one lecture because we hold one of our four live online meetings this week instead. These meetings don't include scripted lectures. Instead, they allow students to interact with one another in real time, ask me questions, and receive supplementary instruction or explanation of things occurring in our online classroom.

Now let's move on to Module 2. Module 1 focused on acclimating students to the course and providing a foundation for design thinking. In Module 2, students will begin to apply this knowledge in a group project featuring case studies.

Students work on the case studies in groups of four, designing a solution for a real-world problem. The case study method of instruction has been around for many years, employed in MBA programs, healthcare, education, and more. In this module, my goal as an instructor is to facilitate students' application of design thinking. However, I also had to keep in mind that students won't be fully proficient just two weeks into the course. The case study requirement also introduces the new challenge of working as a team, potentially complicated by using an online meeting application (Microsoft Teams) that students might not have used before. I created resources to help them with these tasks, embedding multimedia into the Week 3 lecture. On the plus side, students find that working with a real-world problem is motivational, and learning by *doing* design thinking is more engaging than reading or listening to yet another lecture. Each of the two case studies lasts two weeks, concluding with groups' five-minute video presentations explaining

TABLE 2.6 Design Thinking Course, Module 3 Course Map

MODULE 3—PERSONAL APPLICATION OF DESIGN THINKING			
7	Lecture 7A: Designing Your Life Lecture 7B: Strategies: apply design thinking to your problem/ challenge	Roth Ch. 8 Self-Image by Design Roth Ch. 10 Make Achievement Your Habit	Reading Journal 4 (all of Roth) 1. Post reflection and three questions to the Discussion area; comment on two peers' posts. 2. Upload the reading journal document to the Assignment area.
8	Presentations of Individual Design Problems LIVE ONLINE MEETING 4— Debrief		Design Project Part 1: Presentations (post to discussion area by Tuesday; comment on two peers' work by Thursday). Part 2: Submit the Reflective Essay by Thursday. 2-part Final Exam due by Thursday night.

their design process and their solution, which they post to the discussion board and Case Report forms submitted to the LMS assignment area. Students receive a group grade for both the presentations and the reports, but I inform them I will deduct points from individuals' grades if they did not participate appropriately with their group.

The midterm exam occurs during Week 4. Students compare and contrast two articles about design thinking from the *Harvard Business Review*. A multiple-choice exam would be easier to grade, but I learn more about their understanding of design thinking by reading their 300-word essays.

Finally, we'll turn our attention to Module 3. This module's textbook discusses applying design thinking strategies to change one's life or solve a personal problem. Students choose a problem they'd like to solve, such as procrastination, habitually misplacing one's keys, making a major life decision, and so on. Then they will make a plan and implement it for a week, reporting on the results of their efforts.

You might have noticed the guided learning embedded in the progression of these modules. Module 1 provides required information, Module 2 leads students in guided practice, and now Module 3 gives students a chance to demonstrate what they've learned about design thinking through an independent design project. Students submit the project in two parts. Like the case studies, students create a short video presentation about the personal problem they tried to solve with design thinking, posted to the Discussion area. They also submit a reflective essay about the project to the Assignments area. The final exam has two parts. Part 1 is a multiple-choice exam with questions about all the readings and lectures. Part 2 is a performance task in which students choose from three real-life problems and create a quick solution using design thinking.

The next table shows how the activities in the course fit together with the course objectives and outcomes. I wrote the course outcomes to align with university requirements and expectations while also supporting my core ideas as the course designer. Next, I decided how students could reach those outcomes by way of the objectives and then determined how I would measure their learning through the assessments. However, the chart lists the objectives first since students must meet the objectives before they can achieve the outcomes. You might note that the objectives and outcomes express similar ideas but are grammatically distinct. The objectives tell students what they will do and how they will do it, so each sentence begins with an active verb. Outcomes describe what students will have learned by the end of the course, which is why they begin with the phrase "Students will . . ." followed by active verbs that indicate what students can do after completing the course.

The assessments column shows which of the graded items in the course will include an evaluation of students' achievement of the objective and outcome. You might notice that this is not a 1:1 correspondence. The Case Studies, for instance, touch on all five of the course objectives and outcomes, whereas the Reading

TABLE 2.7 Design Thinking Course Outcomes, Objectives, and Assessments

Learning Objectives	Course Outcomes	Assessments
1. Develop Understanding of Design Thinking		
Develop an understanding of the steps in the design process, building capacity for empathy and insight when seeking solutions to challenges, and engaging in processes of ideation, prototyping, and testing potential solutions.	Students will cultivate an understanding of the design process: developing empathy, defining a problem, ideating solutions, and creating and testing prototypes.	Reading Journals Wallet Project Assignment Case Studies Midterm Exam Final Exam
2. Formulate Solutions		
Identify opportunities, gather information, generate insights, and synthesize input to formulate potential solutions to challenges.	Students will identify and synthesize relevant opportunities, insight, and information to develop solutions to complex or ambiguous challenges.	Wallet Project Assignment Case Studies Design Project Final Exam
3. Apply Design Thinking		
Apply design thinking processes to specific challenges or problems presented in the case studies and real-world personal contexts.	Students will apply design thinking when engaging with complex or ambiguous situations.	Wallet Project Assignment Case Studies Design Project Final Exam
4. Demonstrate Critical Thinking, Creative Problem Solving, and Collaboration		
Engage with peers through group activities involving the application of design thinking to case studies, developing and refining skills in critical thinking, creative ideation, interpersonal interaction, and collaborating toward a solution.	Students will develop and refine skills in critical thinking, creative problem solving, collaboration, and teamwork, including the ability to learn from all those with whom they work.	Case Studies Design Project Final Exam
5. Communicate Effectively		
Build proficiency in written and verbal communication, including class discussion, small-group interaction, presentations, and written documentation.	Students will strengthen their skills in communication with various audiences.	Discussions Case Studies Design Project

73

Journals assess only the first objective and outcome dealing with developing students' understanding of design thinking.

To clarify this idea further, I added a header row for each set of objectives, outcomes, and assessments to show the unifying principle that binds them together.

We can also look at this matter from a different angle by matching the principle behind each outcome and objective pair with the assessments that will measure students' learning of that principle.

- Reading Journals (200 points)
  - *Develop Understanding of Design Thinking*—increasing knowledge of design thinking as shown in students' posted reflections and questions and the quality of thought expressed in their responses to peers in the discussion board
- Wallet Project Assignment (30 points)
  - *Develop Understanding of Design Thinking*—engagement in the design thinking process as students formulate a solution for their partner
  - *Formulate Solutions*—identification of opportunity through an interview with a partner
  - *Apply Design Thinking*—application of design thinking to the partner's problem
- Case Studies (200 points)
  - *Develop Understanding of Design Thinking*—engagement in the design thinking process throughout the case study activity
  - *Formulate Solutions*—identification of opportunity that supports the designed solution
  - *Apply Design Thinking*—application of design thinking in formulating a solution to the problem of the case study
  - *Demonstrate Critical Thinking, Creative Problem Solving, and Collaboration*—demonstrate capacity for collaboration and teamwork; demonstrate creativity and critical thinking
  - *Communicate Effectively*—written case report form and solution presented in the discussion board show growth of students' ability to communicate verbally and in writing
- Design Project (100 points)
  - *Develop Understanding of Design Thinking*—engagement in the design thinking process throughout the design project
  - *Formulate Solutions*—identification of opportunity that supports the designed solution
  - *Apply Design Thinking*—application of design thinking in formulating a solution to the problem selected by the student
  - *Demonstrate Critical Thinking, Creative Problem Solving, and Collaboration*—the creation of a solution to the problem demonstrating critical thinking

- *Communicate Effectively*—communication of the solution in the presentation and reflective essay
- Midterm Exam (100 points)
  - *Develop Understanding of Design Thinking*—knowledge of design thinking process
  - *Demonstrate Critical Thinking, Creative Problem Solving, and Collaboration*—critical thinking, analysis, and synthesis of information about differing views about design thinking
  - *Communicate Effectively*—communication of analysis and evaluation in the written document submitted for the Midterm Exam
- Final Exam (100 points)
  - *Develop Understanding of Design Thinking*—knowledge of design thinking process (Part 1); synthesis of differing views of the design thinking process (Part 2—Synthesis)
  - *Formulate Solutions*—identification of opportunity that supports the designed solution (Part 2—Application)
  - *Apply Design Thinking*—application of design thinking in formulating a solution to the problem selected by the student (Part 2—Application)
  - *Demonstrate Critical Thinking, Creative Problem Solving, and Collaboration*—critical thinking, analysis, and synthesis of information (Part 2—Synthesis and Part 2—Application)
  - *Communicate Effectively*—communication of the solution in the written document submitted for Part 2 of the Final Exam

Everything students must do has a corresponding set of instructions or resources on the LMS, including a checklist for each module, overviews, "to do" lists of all expectations, links to student support services, and more. I've made sure to state *why* students are completing these tasks, explain *how* they should do them and *how* I'll grade their work, and teach them *what* they can achieve with the skills and knowledge they've gained in the course.

Once I uploaded everything to the LMS before the first day of class, I applied UX design to my prototype, applying a few tweaks and adjustments until I was reasonably sure the course and the materials within it were useful, usable, findable, credible, desirable, accessible, and valuable.

5. **Teach**

   Teaching has a way of revealing the holes in our plans, no matter how prepared we believe we are or how well we think we've designed the course. In the first week of teaching Design Thinking, for instance, it became quite clear that students needed further explanation of the two parts of the reading journal, and when I graded their work on

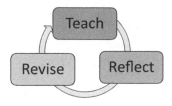

FIGURE 2.4 Reflective Teaching Cycle

this assignment, I saw that they also needed reminders of the expectations because several people did not do the required highlighting and underlining.

If we consider that our course map and the course, as uploaded to the LMS, are our prototype, then teaching serves as the testing phase of design thinking. We're interacting with our users (the students) and gathering data through these interactions and their performance on activities, assignments, and assessments. We can examine their messages and email, seeing patterns in their questions or the problems they encounter. All this provides valuable and actionable data that can help us make the course better the next time around.

Of course, there's much more to talk about regarding excellent teaching, but as our focus in this chapter is on the design process, we'll defer that discussion to a later chapter.

6. Reflect and Revise

Teaching naturally provides opportunities for reflection when we grade our students' work or analyze their scores on exams.

- Where did they make mistakes? Errors reveal areas where additional instruction could be helpful.
- Where did they all succeed with ease? We might choose to increase the rigor or difficulty here so that the activity provides a more appropriate level of challenge.

We can gather additional information through informal discussions with students or by administering a survey.

- Did your students comment on any particular aspects of the course?
- What did they like? What did they dislike?
- Was the workload appropriate? If it was too heavy, what could you reduce or eliminate? If too light, what could you add?
- What could you do differently to make the course better?

Reflecting on these answers leads to revision, refining our prototype before we teach the course again. Think about it: the word *revise* means "to look again."When we pause to look at our course again, we see opportunities to improve.

7. **Repeat**

After you've taught the course three times or so, you'll probably have worked out most of the glitches or rough spots. Nevertheless, that doesn't mean you can go on autopilot and stop paying attention. We always have opportunities to improve and refine our teaching and curriculum. For instance, I can anticipate that the textbooks I used for Design Thinking will become outdated at some point. I might want to exchange one or more of the case studies for newer examples. I especially hope the LMS will receive an upgrade that allows me to ask students to attach files to their discussion posts in a way that lets me grade their work properly, rather than making the file submission a separate grading item.

By becoming thoughtful, empathetic, and reflective educators, we demonstrate a growth mindset. Each of us can improve our teaching practice, and no curriculum is "perfect," at least, not forever. I know the Design Thinking course isn't perfect—it's a work in progress that I'll continue to revise and improve. As thoughtful, reflective, and student-centered educators, we can remain flexible in our approach to teaching, being willing to make changes even to the parts of our courses we value the most if it becomes apparent that they aren't as effective as we'd believed them to be or when external forces mandate change.

REFLECTION AND REVIEW

Adapting UX design, Instructional Design, LXD, design thinking, and backward design to our work as educators allows us to enact our student-centered, student-ready philosophies in our classrooms, labs, and studios. It also reinforces another aspect of what it means to be an educator. In Chapter 1, we compared the fields of education, medicine, and law, contemplating the fact that all are service-oriented professions. I'd like to point out that they're also *practice*-based disciplines, which means they involve doing something repeatedly *while striving to improve*. We wouldn't want to visit a doctor whose medical skills and knowledge had remained static since medical school, nor would we want to hire a lawyer who didn't maintain an awareness of and proficiency in current legal standards or processes. The very word *practice* reflects a mindset of repeating an action with the intention of improving our performance.

I've worked with some educators who simply can't envision their teaching in this way, especially when their course content deals with topics that change very little over time or in fields where pedagogical approaches haven't changed for

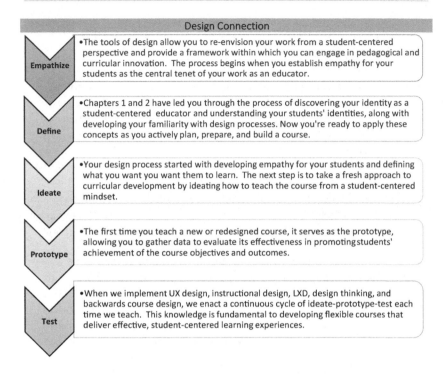

	Design Connection
Empathize	•The tools of design allow you to re-envision your work from a student-centered perspective and provide a framework within which you can engage in pedagogical and curricular innovation. The process begins when you establish empathy for your students as the central tenet of your work as an educator.
Define	•Chapters 1 and 2 have led you through the process of discovering your identity as a student-centered educator and understanding your students' identities, along with developing your familiarity with design processes. Now you're ready to apply these concepts as you actively plan, prepare, and build a course.
Ideate	•Your design process started with developing empathy for your students and defining what you want you want them to learn. The next step is to take a fresh approach to curricular development by ideating how to teach the course from a student-centered mindset.
Prototype	•The first time you teach a new or redesigned course, it serves as the prototype, allowing you to gather data to evaluate its effectiveness in promoting students' achievement of the course objectives and outcomes.
Test	•When we implement UX design, instructional design, LXD, design thinking, and backwards course design, we enact a continuous cycle of ideate-prototype-test each time we teach. This knowledge is fundamental to developing flexible courses that deliver effective, student-centered learning experiences.

FIGURE 2.5 Chapter 2 Design Connection

decades, if not centuries. They put a course together and keep teaching it from one semester to the next, as is. Some don't even bother to change dates on their syllabus. One of the first things I do as a program consultant is to ask the department chair or program director if I can look at their faculty's current syllabi. It's always eye opening to see how many of these documents are poorly written, incomplete, out of date, or clumsily formatted. A syllabus that demonstrates a lack of care and attention speaks volumes about the person who produced it and the level of professionalism they bring to their teaching.

It's not a stretch of the imagination to presume students find stale syllabi to be rather off putting. An out-of-date syllabus says, "I've been teaching this course a long time, and I think it's fine just the way it is. I don't have any interest in making changes. I didn't even proofread it before giving it to you." The course is likely to reflect the same attitude. The instructor stays on autopilot, not reflecting on their students' experiences or thinking of how they might improve the course or their teaching. We might say this attitude is about as faculty centered as it can be.

I trust you'd never want to send this message to your students. You want them to know you're excited about the course and invested in their success. The design-based process we've examined in this chapter allows us to achieve this positive, engaged mindset, putting our students first and upholding the ideal of professional practice as a commitment to continuous growth and improvement as educators. This fresh new mentality fuels the next step in our journey together: learning how to design courses that can pivot easily between online, on-campus, hybrid, and other delivery systems.

Notes

[1] McNair, T., Albertine, S., Cooper, M., McDonald, N., & Major, T. (2016). *Becoming a student-ready college. Association of American colleges and universities.* San Francisco, CA: Jossey-Bass.

[2] Vehicle Dynamics Institute. (2014, January 25). *The tire contact patch.* Retrieved from http://vehicledynamics.com/the-tire-contact-patch/

[3] Seymour, S., & Lopez, S. (2015, April 8). "Big six" college experiences linked to life preparedness. *Gallup News.* Retrieved from https://news.gallup.com/poll/182306/big-six-college-experiences-linked-life-preparedness.aspx?_ga=2.257344514.80664403.1592689990-189468891.1592689990

[4] Gallup-Purdue Index. (2014). *Great jobs, great lives: The 2014 Gallup-Purdue index report.* Retrieved from www.gallup.com/services/176768/2014-gallup-purdue-index-report.aspx

[5] Chingos, M. M. (2016). Instructional quality and student learning in higher education: Evidence from developmental algebra courses. *The Journal of Higher Education, 87*(1), 84–114. doi:10.1353/jhe.2016.0002

[6] Trolian, T., Jach, E., Hanson, J., & Pascarella, E. (2016, October). Influencing academic motivation: The effects of student-faculty interaction. Project muse. *Journal of College Student Development, 57*(7), 810–826. Retrieved from https://muse.jhu.edu/article/636338/pdf

[7] Carrell, S., & Kurlaender, M. (2020). *My professor cares: Experimental evidence on the role of faculty engagement* (National Bureau of Economic Research Working Paper No. 27312). doi:10.3386/w27312; see also Miller, A., & Mills, B. (2019). 'If they don't care, I don't care': Millennial and generation Z students and the impact of faculty caring. *Journal of the Scholarship of Teaching and learning, 19*(4), 78–89. doi:10.14434/josotlv19i4.24167

[8] Trolian, T., Jach, E., Hanson, J., & Pascarella, E. (2016, October). Influencing academic motivation: The effects of student-faculty interaction. Project muse. *Journal of College Student Development, 57*(7), 810–826. Retrieved from https://muse.jhu.edu/article/636338/pdf

See also:

Pascarella E. T., & Terenzini, T. P. (1978). Student—faculty informal relationships and freshman year educational outcomes. *Journal of Educational Research, 71*, 183–189.

Pascarella, E. T., Terenzini, T. P., & Hibel, J. (1978). Student-faculty interactional settings and their relationship to predicted academic performance. *Journal of Higher Education, 49*, 450–463.

Endo J. J., & Harpel, R. L. (1982). The effect of student-faculty interaction on students' educational outcomes. *Research in Higher Education, 16*, 115–138.

Woodside, B. M., Wong, E. H., & Wiest, D. J. (1999). The effect of student-faculty interaction on college students' academic achievement and self concept. *Education, 119*, 730–733.

Umbach, P. D., & Wawrzynski, M. R. (2005). Faculty do matter: The role of college faculty in student learning and engagement. *Research in Higher Education, 46*, 153–184.

Cho, M., & Auger, G. A. (2013). Exploring determinants of relationship quality between students and their academic department: Perceived relationship investment, student empowerment, and student-faculty interaction. *Journalism and Mass Communication Educator, 68*, 266–268.

 [9] Gartner, T., Thomas, C., Geedey, K., Bjorgo-Thorne, K., Simmons, J., Shea, K., . . . Zimmerman, C. (2020). Strategies for incorporating long-term, distributed network projects into the undergraduate curriculum: Lessons from the ecological research as education network's decomposition project. *The American Biology Teacher, 82*(3). doi:10.1525/abt.2020.82.3.142

[10] Strauss, V. (2017, December 20). The surprising thing Google learned about its employees—and what it means for today's students. Answer sheet, analysis. *The Washington Post*. Retrieved from www.washingtonpost.com/news/answer-sheet/wp/2017/12/20/the-surprising-thing-google-learned-about-its-employees-and-what-it-means-for-todays-students/

[11] Nunley, J., Pugh, A., Romero, N., & Seals, R. (2016). College major, internship experience, and employment opportunities: Estimates from a resume audit. *Labor Economics, 38*, 37–46. doi:10.1016/j.labeco.2015.11.002

[12] To improve the readability of this book, I've attempted to de-clutter the text as much as possible. Endnotes contain complete citations, limiting in-text references to sources I've quoted verbatim or paraphrased at length.

[13] Shea, H. (2018, January 16). *Tracking co-curricular contributions to student success at MSU*. Michigan State University Hub for Innovation in Learning and Technology. Retrieved from https://hub.msu.edu/tracking-co-curricular-contributions-to-student-success-at-msu/ See also:

Astin, A. (1993). *What matters in college? Four critical years revisited*. San Francisco, CA: Jossey-Bass.

Cress, C. M., Astin, H. S., Zimmerman-Oster, K., & Burkhardt, J. C. (2001). Developmental outcomes of college students' involvement in leadership activities. *Journal of College Student Development, 42*(1), 15–27.

Kuh, G. (1995). The other curriculum: Out-of-class experiences associated with student learning and personal development. *The Journal of Higher Education, 66*(2), 123–155.

Kuh, G. (2003). *High-impact educational practices: What they are, who has access to them, and why they matter*. Washington, DC: Association of American Colleges and Universities.

Kuh, G. (2011). What educators and administrators need to know about college student engagement. In S. R. Harper & F. L. Jackson (Eds.), *Introduction to American higher education* (pp. 189–212). New York: Routledge.

Wolf-Wendel, L., Ward, K., & Kinzie, J. (2009). A tangled web of terms: The overlap and unique contribution of involvement, engagement, and integration to understanding college student success. *Journal of College Student Development, 50*(4), 407–428.

[14] Gallup-Purdue Index. (2014). *Great jobs, great lives: The 2014 Gallup-Purdue index report*. Retrieved from www.gallup.com/services/176768/2014-gallup-purdue-index-report.aspx

[15] McNair, T., Albertine, S., Cooper, M., McDonald, N., & Major, T. (2016). *Becoming a student-ready college. Association of American colleges and universities* (p. 75). San Francisco, CA: Jossey-Bass.

[16] Harvey, V. S. (2007). Schoolwide methods for fostering resiliency. *National Association of Secondary School Principals.* Retrieved from https://nanopdf.com/download/schoolwide-methods-for-fostering-resiliency-student-services-b_pdf

See also:

Kramer, G. L., & Gardner, J. N. (2007). Fostering student success in the campus community. San Francisco, CA: Jossey-Bass.

Lerner, G. L., & Brand., B. (2006). The college ladder: Linking secondary and postsecondary education for success for all students. Washington, DC: American Youth Policy Forum. Retrieved from https://eric.ed.gov/?id=ED494929

McClure L., Yonezawa, S., & Jones, M. (June 2010). *Personalization and caring relationships with adults in urban high school: Is there a relationship with academic achievement?* California Education Supports Project Brief #5. Retrieved from https://create.ucsd.edu/_files/publications/CESP_policybrief5_UCSD.pdf

[17] McClure, L. V., Yonezawa, S., & Jones, M. (2010). Can school structures improve teacher-student relationships? The relationship between advisory programs, personalization and students academic achievement. *Education Policy Analysis Archives, 18*, 83.

[18] See also Kuh, G. (2008). *High-impact educational practices: What they are, who has access to them, and why they matter* (p. 92). Washington, DC: Association of American Colleges and Universities; Kuh, G. D., & O'Donnell, K. (2013). *Ensuring quality and taking high-impact practices to scale.* Washington, DC: Association of American Colleges and Universities; Finley, A., & McNair, T. (2013). *Assessing underserved students' engagement in high-impact practices. With an assessing equity in high-impact practices toolkit.* Washington, DC: Association of American Colleges and Universities.

[19] Miller, L. (2015). *The practitioner's guide to user experience.* New York: Grand Central Publishing.

[20] Ive, J. (2016). *Designed by Apple in California.* Self-published. Cupertino, CA: Apple.

[21] Ford, H., and Crowther, S. (1922). *My life and my work* (p. 72). New York: Doubleday, Page, & Company.

[22] Nichols, N. (2018, April 22). Cupholders are everywhere. *The Atlantic.* Retrieved from www.theatlantic.com/technology/archive/2018/04/cupholders-are-everywhere/558545/

[23] Interaction Design Foundation. (2018, January). *The 7 factors that influence user experience.* Retrieved from www.interaction-design.org/literature/article/the-7-factors-that-influence-user-experience

[24] Center for Disease Control. (2019, September 9). *Disability impacts all of us.* Retrieved from www.cdc.gov/ncbddd/disabilityandhealth/infographic-disability-impacts-all.html#:~:text=61%20million%20adults%20in%20the,is%20highest%20in%20the%20South

81

[25] www.insidehighered.com/news/2018/02/08/students-postsecondary-education-arcs-affected-parents-college-backgrounds-study

[26] As used in this book, *design thinking* is based on ideas developed at Stanford University's d.school; the writings of Tim Brown (*Change by Design*, 2019), Tom Kelley (*The Art of Innovation*, 2001), and Bernard Roth (*The Achievement Habit*, 2015); and resources made available through the design firm IDEO at https://designthinking.ideo.com/resources and Design Kit: The Human-Centered Design Toolkit (2015) at www.ideo.com/post/design-kit

[27] See Brown and Kelley for additional information brainstorming and design thinking.

[28] Branch, R. (2009). *Instructional design: The ADDIE approach.* New York: Springer.

[29] Boling, E., & Gray, C. (2019). Instructional design and user experience design: Values and perspectives examined through artifact analysis. *Research Gate.* Retrieved from www.researchgate.net/profile/Colin_Gray3/publication/340654686_Instructional_design_and_user_experience_design_Values_and_perspectives_examined_through_artifact_analysis/links/5e9720f7299bf130799c2bc3/Instructional-design-and-user-experience-design-Values-and-perspectives-examined-through-artifact-analysis.pdf

[30] Floor, N. https://lxd.org/ cited in Correia, A.-P. (Ed.). (2018). *Driving educational change: Innovations in action.* eBook. Retrieved from https://ohiostate.pressbooks.pub/drivechange/

[31] Wiggins, G., & McTighe, G. (1998). *Understanding by design.* Alexandria, VA: ASCD.

[32] Priority One: to prepare students for the kinds of challenges they will confront in work, in life, and as citizens, both US and global, and to help them integrate and apply their knowledge and skills to complex and unscripted problems.

[33] Anderson, L., & Kranthwohl, D. (2000). *A taxonomy for learning, teaching and assessing: A revision of bloom's taxonomy and educational objectives, complete edition.* London: Pearson.

[34] TILT Higher Ed. (2020). Retrieved from https://tilthighered.com/

[35] US Department of Education. (2009). *Program integrity questions and answers.* Credit Hour. Retrieved from www2.ed.gov/policy/highered/reg/hearulemaking/2009/credit.html

[36] NASAD Handbook (2019–2020). Section III.A.2.a.(1).

[37] NASAD Handbook (2019–2020). Section III.A.2.a.(1).

Chapter 3

Building a Course Online

CHAPTER 3 SUMMARY

- Design Brief for Online Course Development
- Using the Learning Management System
- Online Course Quality Standards
- Quality Recommendation Synthesis Explanation
- Putting It All Together
- Moving Forward
- Quality Recommendation Checklist

****

The tools and strategies of design can help both experienced and inexperienced instructors alike as we approach the task of establishing a course online. In professional contexts, designers often begin a project with a design brief—a written description of the problem to be solved, an explanation of what the project will achieve, and parameters for how this will occur and when it must be accomplished. How might we adapt this practice and apply it to our efforts as educators?

DESIGN BRIEF FOR ONLINE COURSE DEVELOPMENT

- *The Problem*
  The COVID-19 pandemic is probably not the first emergency we have faced, nor will it be the last. Natural disasters, political upheavals, and other emergencies also force campus closures. When Hurricane Katrina devastated the city of New Orleans in 2005, Tulane University made the difficult and costly decision to cancel its entire fall semester. In contrast,

the University of New Orleans took the unprecedented step of moving many of its classes online.[1] Despite UNO's leadership, emergency preparedness measures in higher education were slow to embrace online learning as a strategy for ensuring academic continuity before 2020. For instance, Meyer and Wilson (2011) examined each state's public flagship university's emergency plans as the H1N1 flu threatened to become a pandemic, finding that just one-third offered non-specific suggestions that faculty identify alternative ways of delivering courses, and none provided clear guidance for moving courses online in case of a disaster.[2] Very few faculty, administrators, or institutions were ready for the sudden move to online education in March 2020. Nevertheless, we learned some valuable lessons that we can now employ to be prepared for future emergencies.

■ *The Goal*

If our academic leaders have learned from the experiences of the pandemic, every college and university would implement a policy requiring all courses to be housed on their institution's learning management systems (LMS), regardless of the actual format of instructional delivery, effectively serving as a universal online back-up plan. Each instructor would then be prepared to pivot flexibly from one mode of instructional delivery to another, eliminating the stress and frustration accompanying unforeseen format changes. Perhaps this will occur in time, but higher education is not known for its cohesion or decisiveness. For the present, each instructor can make this change for themselves. Many of us already use the LMS for part of our course organization even when we teach entirely on campus, and others among us are experienced online instructors. Our purpose in this chapter is to explain how every instructor can translate existing course materials into a student-centered online format with the potential to improve both teaching and learning.

■ *Design Constraints*

   ■ **Technological**: The LMS each of our institutions adopts is the most influential constraint on our work as course designers. Perhaps the three best-known providers are Blackboard, Brightspace/D2L,[3] and Canvas, although many others exist. The functionality of the LMS will dictate how instructors put their course materials online and how students interact with those materials throughout the course. Neither the instructor nor the student has a choice in this matter, but we can remain alert for places where our students may need extra support or guidance as we work within this constraint.

   ■ **Disciplinary**: Our disciplines have always affected the way we develop our courses and the tools we use for teaching. Some disciplines can move quite easily between on-campus and online instruction with little loss of quality, if any. However, disciplines that rely most heavily

BOX 3.1 Author's Note

Having used several LMS in my career, I must confess that I like Canvas the best. In my opinion, it's the most intuitive and user friendly of the systems I've used. I am not receiving any compensation for this statement—I'm merely expressing an informed personal preference.

on face-to-face interactions between faculty and students experienced significant hardship when forced to move online, as did those dependent on specialized technologies and equipment unavailable outside the campus environment. Our task as designers is to find workable solutions to challenges such as these, creating a viable back-up plan even as we hold on to the fervent hope never to be in such a situation again. Furthermore, whether in-person or online, our disciplinary expectations and assumptions can constrain us unconsciously or implicitly.

- **Personal**: Each instructor may face personal constraints regarding time, energy, experience, or understanding.
  - Instructors who taught the same set of on-campus courses for many years, with curricular materials that were highly refined and as comfortable as a favorite pair of shoes, found the leap into online learning somewhat of an emotional hurdle. Even before our dive into Emergency Remote Teaching, I spoke to many educators whose plaintive cry of, "But that's the way I've always . . ." was a constant refrain when told they might have to change their ways. It's hard to shake ourselves loose from the grip of habit and familiarity. I feel the same myself, sometimes. Nevertheless, just because we've done something the same way for a very long time does not mean it is the best way to do it, nor does it justify clinging to past practice when changing circumstances render it untenable.
  - Lack of time and energy is nearly epidemic among faculty, who are legitimately overworked. For those of us who perform both administrative and faculty duties, the strain can be intense. Undertaking a course revision or developing a new course is often the last thing any faculty member wants to do, especially if we won't receive additional compensation for our efforts.
  - Even faculty who are blessed with sufficient time, energy, and motivation to undertake course revision or development may still lack the necessary knowledge and experience, making the task of building a course online quite challenging.
- These constraints exist singly or in varied combinations, affecting our efforts despite our best intentions. Nevertheless, constraints aren't all

bad. We might think of them as the edges of our design space, within which we're free to exercise our imagination, ingenuity, and creativity— to empathize, define, ideate, prototype, and test until we've created a multipurpose online course that will see us through whatever fate throws our way.

APOLLO 13 MOMENTS

In the following sections, we'll explore recommendations for using a learning management system, compare and contrast two quality review systems, and synthesize these standards into a list of recommendations for best practices in online course design. Then we will put these ideas together to show an example of a completed course, and we'll consider how building our courses online helps us move toward becoming more adaptable as instructors.

One of the most important aspects of intentional course design is that it helps us avoid what I call "Apollo 13 moments." Whether because you're of a certain age, you're a NASA enthusiast, or you're familiar with Ron Howard and Tom Hanks's cinematic masterpiece *Apollo 13* (1995), you may recall that there was a tense moment when the astronauts and the ground crew scrambled to find a solution to a completely unexpected problem. They had to find a way to fit the square lithium hydroxide canisters from the command module into the round openings of the lunar module—the proverbial square peg in a round hole. As the clock ticked, the air quality grew steadily worse until the ground crew designed a solution using cardboard, tape, and plastic bags, relaying the instructions to the astronauts, who replicated the procedure in space.[4] It was far from a pretty solution, but it saved the astronauts from suffocating on their own exhalations.

We can find another (albeit fictional) example in the Ridley Scott and Matt Damon film *The Martian* (2015). Damon plays an astronaut who's stranded on Mars and must figure out how to grow four years of food "on a planet where nothing grows." Damon's character in *The Martian* kept his good humor, noting in his video journal, "Luckily, I'm a botanist. Mars will come to fear my botany powers."[5]

The real astronauts of Apollo 13—Jim Lovell, Fred Haise, and Jack Swigert— and the fictional astronaut played by Matt Damon were exceptionally gritty and growth-minded individuals. Indeed, these traits were likely the key to their survival. We stand amazed at their fortitude, courage, and ingenuity. Like these astronauts, those of us who found ourselves teaching during an unprecedented emergency had to come up with a solution, and fast. It wasn't pretty in many cases—more like the contraption made of plastic bags, cardboard, and tape on Apollo 13. But, just as those astronauts returned to Earth safely, we completed our semesters.

Lovell noted that he saw several red flags preceding his mission's launch: "Looking back, I realize I should have been alerted by several omens that occurred in the final stages of the Apollo 13 preparation." Their command module pilot was grounded, a helium tank had a problem, and an oxygen tank wasn't working properly.

> With the wisdom of hindsight, I should have said, "Hold it. Wait a second. I'm riding on this spacecraft. Just go out and replace that tank." But the truth is, I went along, and I must share the responsibility with many, many others for the $375 million failure of Apollo 13. On just about every spaceflight, we have had some sort of failure, but in this case, it was an accumulation of human errors and technical anomalies that doomed Apollo 13.[6]

As educators, we now know beyond a doubt that circumstances may occur that prevent us from teaching as normal. Universities have always been prone to disruption from natural disasters, political upheaval, civil unrest, and disease outbreaks but never before on as grand a scale. We have ample reason to plan and prepare for these disruptions so that we need never experience an Apollo 13 moment again. The solution is to build every course into the LMS, no matter which form (or forms) of instructional delivery we use.

USING THE LEARNING MANAGEMENT SYSTEM

Building a course online depends on the LMS each institution has selected. Every system has distinctive quirks, and the process of online course development is not necessarily intuitive, even if you've built a website or have taught online using a different LMS. I cannot overemphasize the importance of completing any tutorials or helpful videos your institution's technology services or Center for Teaching and Learning might have to offer before beginning your work in the LMS. Informing yourself up front can save hours of frustration later.

Terminology and processes for common tasks can differ between systems, which can be confusing for faculty members who have worked with a different LMS or an older iteration of the present LMS. For example, I had worked with Canvas on many courses in the past, which I found to be relatively easy to use. To add a page to a module in Canvas, all I had to do was click a plus sign next to the module's title, and a window opened containing a dropdown menu for "Add _____," which included the option for "Page." In the version of Brightspace I was using to build the Design Thinking course, however, the Course Builder tool options for "Add Content" were limited to creating a link, HTML file, discussion, assignment, quiz, new grade item, or new learning objective. I wanted to make a page of instructions for the Start Here module, so I was frustrated that there was no option to add a page. Given the limited choices, I decided to create a link, uploading the Word document containing the information and creating a link to it in the module. I continued building course content, using this method in each module. When I was finished, I clicked through the student workflow and found that my linked documents looked awful. So I did what I should have done in the first place: I searched my institution's e-learning website, where I discovered the option I needed wasn't "Create a Link" but "Create an HTML file." Then I had to go back and remove all those Word docs from the LMS, copy the text from each one, and paste it into a new HTML page. The results were much better, but I still encountered several other bumps in the road before I finished creating the course.

Furthermore, technologies evolve. If an institution installs an upgraded version of the LMS its faculty members have become accustomed to, it can be just as frustrating as using an entirely new system. My heartfelt advice—whether you're using an LMS that's new to you, it's your first time building a course online in any system, or the version of the LMS you've used for years has received an upgrade— is to use the tutorials and supports your institution makes available to you. Even if you think you don't have time, you'll save yourself quite a bit of aggravation.

Course Content

In a traditional on-campus class, instructors convey information by simply speaking to our students, distributing printed copies of documents, and using physical equipment and materials (depending on the course and the discipline). Although we can't do most of that online in the same manner we're used to, the basic elements are the same in both settings.

- We deliver direct instruction, which can include lectures or demonstrations.
- We facilitate activities such as discussion, small-group work, individual or collaborative projects, problem-based learning, and guided practice.
- We give students assignments to complete outside class, usually accompanied by handouts containing directions, performance expectations, and grading criteria.
- We administer quizzes and exams to assess students' learning.
- We grade students' work, provide feedback, and post final grades.

One of the most significant differences between teaching on campus and teaching online is the level of preparation required before the first day of class. On campus, it's not unusual to begin teaching with little more than a syllabus, creating, finding, and delivering course content as we go along throughout the semester. Teaching from week to week like this works with face-to-face courses because we directly control the flow of information and instructional resources in real time. Students don't have access to anything until we choose to provide it.

In contrast, online courses are normally fully prepared and uploaded to the LMS before the first day of class. Students typically make their way through the course without the instructor's direct intervention, although this may be subject to selective delivery options that enable instructors to choose what we make available to certain students.

I'd like to suggest that our habit of releasing information to students only as we think they need it (or as we create it) is a faculty-centered practice. In contrast, preparing everything in advance and making it available online from the first day of class is far more student centered. It lets anxious students look ahead to see what's coming up, allaying their fears. It lets students look back at lectures from previous lessons, using them to review for exams or reinforce their learning. It lets us embed supports like study guides, demonstration videos, glossaries, writing guides, and links to helpful websites or tutorials. Students with documented disabilities should have access to course materials as early as possible so they can work with the disabilities services office to modify these materials per their legal accommodations. Perhaps most importantly, a fully prepared course that allows access to all our materials from the outset frees us to focus on teaching because the work of course development is complete. We can devote more attention to our students' learning needs when we don't have to spend time racing to keep up with the course's demands.

Our attitudes and implicit biases are present in every aspect of our work as educators, including our choices as instructional designers. Controlling the release of course content as a deliberate instructional strategy might be appropriate and effective in cases in which we must scaffold students' learning of a sequential process in which each step must be mastered before learning about the next. Conversely, limiting access to course materials because we prioritized personal convenience over devoting sufficient time to preparing the course up front sends an implicit message that our time is more valuable than the students' need for the learning resources.

In truth, course design touches on issues of social justice. One of the best definitions I've found for social justice comes from the Counseling Center at the University of South Florida: social justice is "a process of building individual and community capacity for collaborative action with the purpose of empowering all people, including disadvantaged and marginalized persons, to exercise self-determination and realize their full potential."[7] Does creating and releasing your course content one week at a time empower students or disempower them? Does limiting students' access by developing learning resources according to your personal schedule allow students to exercise self-determination in using these resources? Or does it limit students' choices and decrease their capacity for action?

I admit I sometimes find that my desire to maintain a student-centered perspective clashes with my implicit personal interests. Time is a precious resource, and comprehensive course design requires vast quantities of it. It's much easier to think, "This assignment doesn't come up until Week 10 of the course, so I'll create those resources later on" than to press forward and make sure I've written everything students will need for success with that assignment before the course launches. However, I choose the harder path because I know I'll be just as busy and just as short of time in Week 10 as I am at this moment, but my students deserve the opportunity to look ahead and plan for that assignment well in advance. Their needs and success are my priority because I am deeply committed to creating an environment that fosters empowerment, respect, and opportunity.

Some readers might be thinking, "But, Bruce, my students *always* do things at the last minute. Nobody's going to look at that Week 10 assignment until it's actually Week 10." I'd respond, you may be right. I've seen the same thing, myself. But what if one of your students knows they have a personal event scheduled for that week and wants to plan ahead so they can do the assignment successfully? What if another student sees that the assignment will require them to purchase supplies and materials that they cannot afford and needs time to figure out how to get help or talk to you about an alternative? When we do not give students what they need from the beginning, we deprive them of the ability to be proactive and thereby disempower them, implicitly disrespect them, and prioritize our convenience over their achievement. Our common objection, "I don't have time!" is truthful and accurate. Nevertheless, it reflects a faculty-centered mentality that we hope to change.

Throughout this chapter, I will continue to write from the standpoint that we are striving to achieve Comprehensive Instructional Design, by which I mean fully preparing every course in the LMS regardless of whether we will teach fully face to face on campus, fully asynchronously online, or any combination of the two. As you read, however, please know I understand that what I'm suggesting is very challenging. Just as we maintain empathy for our students, I also empathize with you because I'm a faculty member with conflicting personal and professional responsibilities, just like you. I *recommend* this as a best practice but am certainly not saying that it is a mandate. Each of us can only do our best, especially under difficult circumstances. Our hands are more than full. I uphold the idea of a fully prepared course as an aspiration toward which I believe we should all strive, even though I realize it will not always be possible. Sometimes, a good-faith effort to prepare as much as we can before the first day of class is all that is within our power.

I'd like to add one more caveat. This chapter is very detailed, breaking the online course creation process into small steps, with checklists for each stage. I also provide a point-by-point comparison of two major systems for online course quality review. Not every reader will need this much information or this level of support, but I've worked with many faculty members who do. If you're comfortable working in your institution's LMS and familiar with the fundamentals of course quality review, I invite you to skim the following sections and then apply the Quality Recommendations Checklist (located at the end of the chapter) to the course you've built in your institution's LMS. However, if you're new to course design or online teaching, then this chapter was specially designed with you in mind! I hope you find it to be useful.

With that said, we will now turn our attention to organizing our course content in the LMS.

Modules

The basic organizational unit used in learning management systems such as Blackboard, Brightspace, or Canvas is called a "module." The Canvas Instructional Guide[8] topic "What Is a Module?" explains:

> Modules allow instructors to organize content to help control the flow of the course.
>
> Modules are used to organize course content by weeks, units, or a different organizational structure. Modules essentially create a one-directional linear flow of what students should do in a course.
>
> Each module can contain files, discussions, assignments, quizzes, and other learning materials.

Therefore, a module is simply a tool for organizing the elements of your course. We might as easily use terms such as *group*, *unit*, *chapter*, *topic*, or *segment*. I used to teach in a program that used the term *milestones* instead of modules and *benchmarks* instead of weeks. The point is not what we call our organizational system but to create logical content groups that support students' learning. It might help to think of the module as a container into which we place components of our course linked by a common topic, theme, concept, or learning objective. Modules provide scaffolding for students' learning and convey the course's narrative: just as a book is divided into chapters, an online course is divided into modules.[9]

If you're most comfortable teaching from week to week, you could organize your content into weekly modules. If you prefer to use instructional units in your face-to-face courses, you could create modules that group your instruction accordingly, preserving the organizational structure you've already established.

Furthermore, modules represent an advantageous curricular and pedagogical strategy. When students understand how we've organized the online classroom, they spend less time trying to guess what we expect them to do or searching for what they need, enabling them to focus on learning. Modules assist in the presentation and application of teaching and learning by creating a "road map" that keeps students on track.[10] Modular design also benefits the instructor. Creating an online course is a daunting proposition, but breaking the task into smaller pieces by creating distinct modules gives us room to be more thoughtful in our selection and design of each learning component. Furthermore, a module-based structure helps instructors discern the relationship between each activity on the course syllabus and the course's learning outcomes and objectives.[11]

Therefore, the first step in building your course online is to decide how you'll organize your content, determining the order and sequence of the instructional components you've planned. Content should follow a logical progression, creating a learning path or workflow that leads students from one activity to the next.

Content Types

Several types of online course content are available to us as course designers, each of which normally has a section in the online classroom:

- Information about the course and the LMS
- Announcements
- Assignments and activities
- Assessments
- Discussions
- Gradebook

Each type of content requires different choices and actions as we build the course. Posting an announcement, for example, is similar to sending an email or updating a social media account:

- Choose "new announcement." A content window will open.
- Type your message in the window.
- Insert images or multimedia and attach files using the toolbar in the content window.
- If desired, select the option to send the announcement as an email to all students.
- Click "submit," and the announcement immediately appears in the course's announcements area.

The processes for adding activities, discussions, assignments, and assessments share some common features. One of the first things you'll encounter is a space for introductory text, such as written directions or explanations. This introduction need not be lengthy, but it should provide an immediate answer to these questions:

- What is it? (Identify the activity, assignment, assessment, discussion, instructions, etc.)
- What must students do with it?
- How should they do it?
- When must they complete it?
- What's next?

For example, if you want to post a lecture you've prerecorded, the introductory text could say something like this: "Please click the 'play' icon in the video below to watch Lecture 3 no later than Friday of Week 3. After you have finished watching the lecture, click 'next' to make your post to the Week 3 discussion board." It's concise yet informative. All the answers are contained in just 39 words. What is it? A lecture. What must students do with it? Watch it. How should they do it? Click play. When must they complete it? By Friday of Week 3. What comes next? The discussion.

Opponents might say that the page's title, "Lecture 3," is self-explanatory. Others might insist that students should be able to infer that the "play" icon means they should watch the lecture and should similarly presume they should click "next" when they're done. They grumble that writing out the instructions feels unnecessarily redundant, or they say they "shouldn't have to cater to" their students this much. I hear you. I share your frustrations.

However, what if we turn this around and consider the matter from the students' viewpoint? First, leaving a big blank space where the instructions should go looks to students as though the instructor forgot something, or it might even appear that the course site is not working correctly. Including short explanatory text creates a feeling of intentionality on the page and makes it immediately clear what students should do rather than leaving it up to them to figure it out for themselves. Taking a few minutes to set up the page for the lecture with these brief directions is a student-centered gesture that increases the likelihood they will succeed.

Activities like watching the lecture don't lead directly to a grade, even though they contribute to students' learning. However, everything that *does* result in a grade, whether an activity, assignment, or assessment, should provide answers to these same questions, along with a bit more text that explains:

- What must students do to meet the requirement?
- How and where should students post their work?
- How will the instructor assess students' work?

The amount of detail that goes along with an assignment or activity will vary. For assignments or activities requiring a page or more of instructions, I recommend attaching them as a PDF document, using the textbox on the LMS page to note something like, "Please read the attached directions for Assignment 4." Include the grading criteria and the rubric, checklist, or explanation of how you will assess their work. The full post might sound like this example from the Design Thinking course, which I formatted with bullet points to increase readability. Underlined items indicate hyperlinks to areas or files in the course.

- Case Study 1 is due by 11:59 p.m. on Sunday of Week 4.
- Please embed your group's project video into the Case 1 Discussion.
- Then upload your group's completed Case Report Form into the Case 1 Assignment area.
- Click to access the Case Study instructions, a blank Case Report Form, the Case Study Rubric, and instructions for posting a video to the discussion board.

To set students up for success, we engage in a metacognitive process as we analyze our expectations. The more thorough we can be, the fewer student questions we'll receive. I've learned that directions cannot be too explicit, nor is any information too basic. If I want students to put their names on their work, I say so in the instructions. When I only accept certain types of file formats, I state this clearly. Even though my syllabus says students should use standard college-level English and format their documents a certain way, each assignment's instructions repeat those expectations. I also try to anticipate common questions, errors, or misconceptions as I create directions to accompany the online content. Students constantly ask, "When is this due?" and "How long does this paper have to be?" so I always include that information in the directions for any assignment or activity.

If you've taught the course on campus several times, you're probably already aware of sticking points for students. How might you build supports into the online course to help them navigate those difficulties? You won't have this prior knowledge if the course is new to you, but it's worthwhile to predict which places in the course ask students to do something they might not know how to do. For instance, if you want students to use the tools in the LMS to create a video post to a discussion, they'll be more successful if you provide step-by-step directions for how to do this. A course I recently taught asked students to convert a PowerPoint presentation into an MP4 and post the video to a discussion board. I'd embedded a link to a video tutorial from Microsoft in the instructions, but students still did not understand what to do. I made a quick PowerPoint explaining the process, attached it to the assignment, and sent it out as an email. When I revised the course for the next semester, I put that instructional PowerPoint in the course stream right after the assignment was first introduced.

Once you've written the explanations and instructions, your next steps might include any of the following:

- Upload files or embed multimedia elements, if any, using the content tools on the page.
- Set conditions or properties for the course element you're creating, such as its due date and point value in the course gradebook.
- Create a grading rubric using the tools in the LMS, which makes subsequent scoring easier.
- If desired, select a date range limiting students' access to the content. For example, you might want to release a quiz or exam after a particular date or close an item after a deadline has passed. (However, I recommend you use this feature sparingly. Our goal should be to provide open access whenever possible.)
- Mark the item as "published" or "available."

Tools for Instruction

Lectures or demonstrations are our primary means of delivering direct instruction. When we put our course online, we have several options for this task:

1. **Synchronous instruction via live video conferencing software** such as Zoom, WebEx, Microsoft Teams, Google Hangouts, GoToMeeting, etc., most closely replicates on-campus teaching. Instructors teach as they normally would, using screen sharing and the computer's built-in webcam, or in a classroom equipped with broadcasting capabilities that allow the presentation to appear more like a regular classroom experience. Instructors may choose to record the lecture live and upload it to the LMS so that students who were unable to attend the live session can view it later. Students also find these recordings useful when they study for exams. (Be sure to know and follow your institution's rules for recording class sessions.)
2. **Asynchronous instruction via prerecorded multimedia** allows students greater flexibility in viewing course instruction because it is not time dependent like an on-campus class session or video conference. It also helps keep instructors on point because students don't interrupt with questions or pull us into interesting yet tangential discussions. We can utilize video capture software built into the LMS or use an external program

such as Screencastify, Camtasia, or many other options if we record using our computer's integrated webcam and microphone. These apps allow us to share our computer screen, toggle to the webcam view so students can see our faces, or use a picture-in-picture view so both remain visible. Students' attention naturally shifts between your face, the whiteboard or screen behind you, and things within the physical classroom environment. In a video, however, we control what they see the entire time they're looking at their computer. Varying what your students can look at during your presentation helps keep them engaged—their view shouldn't be only on your face or your computer screen for the whole lecture.

It's possible to record instruction using only the tools built into your computer, but we can expand our options and improve the quality of our recordings with external webcams and microphones. Given the right equipment, you can focus on your hands to show students how to work with materials or demonstrate something like a mathematical algorithm, creative process, or the details of a model or specimen.

If your planned lecture would take an hour or more to deliver face to face, consider dividing it into several shorter videos (no more than 10–15 minutes each) presenting a single topic or process. Shorter videos with breaks in between help students focus on your teaching. You may want to consider reducing your course's lecture components and increasing engaged learning activities by adding supportive content through external videos, process tutorials, independent investigations, partner discussions, and so on. You can also set up your course's learning path to require that students answer a couple of quiz questions before moving on to the next video in the series. This strategy not only holds them accountable for watching—it gives you quick formative feedback you can use to judge how well students understand your instruction. No matter how you modify or update your planned lectures, keep the time equivalencies in mind. Replacing an hour of lecture with two 10-minute videos gives you 40 minutes to fill with supplementary content. Even online, we need to remain mindful of our duty to fulfill clock-hour parameters.

3. **Asynchronous instruction via written text and images** is the least engaging method of delivering online content, but it's also well established and widely accepted. PowerPoint and other slideshow programs tend to be the vehicle we use for this purpose, with or without audio narration of each slide. Many of us use slideshows in our regular on-campus teaching, so this familiar option shouldn't pose a high degree of difficulty for instructors who might not be very comfortable with online instruction.

Whatever format we choose for instruction, we should be mindful of the Americans with Disabilities Act (ADA), which requires us to provide all individuals with equal access to instruction.[12] You'll save time and headaches if you design your online materials in compliance with these rules up front, rather than having to retrofit your course after everything is in place. I say this from experience: several years ago, I designed an online course as part of a consultancy and was subsequently invited to teach it as a part-time online faculty member. After I'd finished uploading the course to Canvas, I learned it would be reviewed using the Quality Matters rubric, which was new to me at that time. Lo and behold, I had not met ADA standards in a handful of the lectures I'd created, which meant I had to remove the files from the course, reformat the parts of the lectures that were not in compliance, and upload them again. Then I had to go back and redo all the hyperlinks to those lectures in the module instructions and discussions. Had I known about the quality check, I could have designed the materials correctly in the first place. To help you avoid the same problem, here are a few considerations you might want to bear in mind as you build your course.

1. Text Design (applies to the course site design and all documents, slide-shows, assignments, assessments, etc. included in the course)

   a. Use a sans serif font such as Arial, Calibri, or Helvetica to maximize readability.
   b. Use a design template with dark text on a light background. Avoid red-green or blue-yellow combinations because individuals with color blindness cannot distinguish the text from the background.
   c. Use font sizes of 12 points or greater.
   d. Use bold and italics sparingly. Do not use underlining for emphasis because it can be confused with hyperlinked text.
   e. Keep slides uncrowded and uncluttered.
   f. Hyperlinks should appear as descriptive words. Avoid "click here" or copying and pasting the entire URL into a page or document, neither of which is intelligible to someone using a screen reader.
   g. All documents should be searchable. A PDF created by converting a Word doc or PowerPoint is searchable, but a PDF created by taking a screenshot is not searchable without additional document processing. If the text is not searchable, ensure that a plain text version is also available.
   h. Tables and charts should have headers, labels, and in-text summaries because screen reader devices do not always handle these visuals very well or will skip over them entirely.

2. Images or graphics

   a. Visual elements should be purposeful, not merely decorative.
   b. Avoid animated or blinking images.

    c. Add alt-tags or alt-text to all visual elements: photographs, illustrations, charts, graphs, etc.

3. Multimedia

    a. Audio and video should have minimal background noise, clear pronunciation of words, and consistent volume.

    b. Written transcripts and closed captioning should be available for every video.

    c. Videos should be less than ten minutes long, when possible.

    d. Select mp3 (audio) and mp4 (video) formats for maximum accessibility.

Meeting ADA compliance standards protects our institutions from adverse legal actions brought by or on behalf of individuals with disabilities who do not have an equal opportunity to learn in our online classrooms. However, these standards also result in excellent course design that helps all learners, which is among the benefits of Universal Design: "the design and composition of an environment that can be accessed, understood, and used to the greatest extent possible by all people regardless of their age, size, ability, or disability."[13] Universal Design relies on seven basic principles.[14]

Good design:

1. Is useful to people with diverse abilities
2. Accommodates individual preference and abilities
3. Is simple and intuitive to use
4. Effectively communicates needed information to the user regardless of their sensory abilities
5. Tolerates user error
6. Requires minimal physical effort
7. Allows sufficient size and space

These conditions make a design better for everyone and not just online. All of us take advantage of one of the first triumphs of Universal Design that's become ubiquitous in the built environment: curb cuts, or lowered sections of curbs that allow wheelchair users greater mobility, also provide easier access for everyone.[15] ADA-compliant online design is no different. The adaptations we build into our courses can help all students, not just those with vision or hearing differences. For instance, my vision and hearing are fine, but I'll often download the transcript for a video I want to use for research so I can more easily return to the speaker's important points. I'll use a screen reader app when I want to listen to a document while I'm doing something else at the same time, like making dinner. What's good for one is often good for many.

Assessment

In Chapter 2, we talked about the purpose of assessment: to measure students' achievement of our course objectives and outcomes. All of us are probably familiar with courses that assess students' learning primarily through a midterm and final exam, but assessment shouldn't stop there. The more opportunities we provide for students to demonstrate their learning through varied assessments, the more accurate a picture we can form of their true learning. Anything and everything receiving a grade or score is an assessment. Furthermore, our evaluation of the level to which students have met the course objectives and outcomes generates useful data for determining our instruction's effectiveness, contributing to the periodic assessment of our programs, departments, colleges, schools, and universities. In other words, the assessments you build into your course do more than contribute to your students' final grades. They also generate meaningful data about your students' learning and your effectiveness as an instructor while providing evidence of your program's and department's quality, all of which reflect on the institution as a whole.

The assessments you choose should align with your disciplinary norms, practices, or standards. Fields such as the visual and performing arts or creative writing lend themselves to skills-based evaluations of students' performances or creative output, while others rely on objective[16] exams measuring mastery of content-area knowledge. The question only you can answer is how to translate your on-campus assessments into an online environment.

In many cases, online assessments represent a clear advantage for the instructor. An objective exam in the LMS can automatically score students' work and export the results to the gradebook. Other times, we must find creative alternatives to our usual assessment practices, especially for creative fields such as visual and performing arts that rely upon group and individual critique or those like laboratory sciences that utilize practical or skills-based assessments. Even then, the online format can be advantageous. An instructor could assess a live performance in the moment, but when students upload a recording of their performance to the LMS, the instructor can view it multiple times and achieve a more comprehensive evaluation of their students' achievement.

It might help to consider the functions of different aspects of the LMS. The assignment and discussion areas can be used for assessment when the instructor assigns a paper, report, or another artifact that attests to their ability to synthesize their learning. Assignment areas are open only to the instructor and student, which ensures privacy. Discussion boards can be useful if you want students to create something such as a presentation, performance, or creative work to share with their classmates and receive feedback or critique, much as we would have students conduct a presentation in a face-to-face class. And, of course, we can input quizzes and exams in the appropriate area. (Brightspace and Canvas label all of these "quizzes," but Blackboard calls them "tests.")[17]

Instructors who rely on objective exams for the majority of students' grades tend to be especially concerned about the problem of cheating. Learning management systems may offer options such as a lockdown browser that disallows students from opening new windows to research test questions, but as we all know, that doesn't stop students from looking for answers on their phones or texting their classmates for answers when they're completing the exam away from the instructor's watchful eyes. One way to avoid the problem, at least somewhat, is to use assessments such as performance tasks or reflective essays rather than objective exams, making it more difficult for students to cheat. Of course, objective exams are far easier to grade, and open-ended questions or performance tasks undoubtedly increase the instructor's grading burden. Nevertheless, authentic assessments generate a more accurate and nuanced picture of students' learning since lucky guesses or cheating rarely influence their work.

When setting up a quiz or exam, you'll need to provide brief introductory text and a title just as you would for an assignment or discussion. Then you'll select the question type and begin keying in your questions. Unfortunately, we can't just upload a Word document containing our questions and expect it to populate the assessment tool online automatically—every question and answer must be keyed in by hand. To help minimize cheating, we can sometimes choose to randomize the order of answer choices or randomize the order of the questions for each student who takes the exam.[18]

Most learning management systems offer many question types like true/false, matching, short answer, extended answer, and more. Good test questions assess students' mastery of concepts rather than facts and measure students' higher-order thinking such as application, analysis, evaluation, and synthesis. The following question stems[19] might help spark your thinking as you write your assessments.

Application:

- Which action would we take to _____?
- Which is an example of _____?
- What other way could we _____?
- What would be the result if _____ occurred?
- Why does _____?
- How could we change ____?
- Solve: _____.

Analysis:

- Which is a benefit of _____?/Which is a drawback of _____?
- Classify the following . . .
- Which explanation connects _____ and _____?
- List the advantages and disadvantages of _____.
- What can we infer if _____?
- Which evidence supports _____?
- Which of the following ideas validate _____?/Which of the following ideas refute _____?
- Identify the problem in the paragraph below.
- Which offers the best analysis of _____?
- Which of the following statements best expresses the _____ point of view?
- Identify the connection between _____ and _____?

Evaluation:

- Which reason best supports the premise that _____?
- Which plan has the greatest likelihood of success?
- How could _____ improve _____?
- What is the most likely outcome if _____?
- Which change would be the most effective in achieving _____?
- How would _____ be detrimental to _____?
- What could happen if _____?
- Which facts can be discerned in the following scenario?

Creation/Synthesis

- What data was used to evaluate _____? How do you know?
- What is the most important _____? Explain.
- What criteria would you use to assess _____? Explain.
- What would you recommend if _____? Why?
- What is your opinion of _____? Explain.
- What is likely to occur if _____?
- Devise a way to _____.
- Elaborate on the reason for _____.

My priority for the Design Thinking course was to teach students what design thinking is and how to use it to solve problems. Objective quizzes or exams didn't seem to be a good match for this purpose, so for the midterm, I asked students to write a 200-word essay comparing and contrasting two articles from the *Harvard Business Review*, one of which presented a favorable opinion of design thinking and one that took a more critical standpoint. I began to set up the exam in the Quizzes area of Brightspace but quickly discovered that there was no option allowing students to attach a file. So I modified the instructions to warn students they would need to type or paste their response into a text box in the single essay question on the quiz. I could have set this up in the Assignments area instead of using the Quiz option, which would have allowed students to upload a document, but I decided that placing it in Quizzes was advantageous in maintaining the organization of the gradebook and would make more sense to students.

The final exam in the Design Thinking course has two parts, allowing me to form a more thorough picture of students' achievement. Part 1 is built into the Quiz area, with 30 multiple-choice questions about the course's readings and lectures. Because I had never asked students to memorize their readings, I allowed them to refer to their journals and notes during the exam. Part 2 contains two performance tasks. The first task asks students to create a one-page drawing, diagram, or other visual representation synthesizing the two approaches to design thinking presented in our textbooks. The second part of Part 2 asks students to use design thinking to create a potential solution to one of three hypothetical scenarios when given a brief description of the problem and a short list of constraints. Due to the aforementioned limitations in the LMS's functionality, I built Part 2 of the exam into the Assignments area so that students could attach documents or other types of files of their work. Combining objective and subjective sections in the same exam allowed me to measure students' achievement of the course objectives and outcomes more effectively than an objective exam alone.

Exams with open-ended questions like these also minimize cheating. The synthesis and application questions, for instance, aren't something students can answer from Google. I suppose they could conceivably cheat on Part 1, but when I tell them they're welcome to refer to their course materials for help, it takes away the forbidden nature of looking for answers, making it much less appealing. My instructional goal was for students to access and use the information in our textbooks and lectures, not to memorize it. This reason also supports my rationale for allocating just 30 points to Part 1 of the exam, whereas the synthesis and application sections of Part 2 are worth 30 and 40 points, respectively. By placing a higher value on the part of the exam that measures skills associated with higher-order thinking, I'm sending a clear message to students that it's not about what you remember; it's about how well you're able to use what you learned.

Your assessment strategies will be different from mine, of course. Before we leave the topic of assessments, though, I'd like to mention that delivering assessments through the LMS gives instructors a great deal of flexibility and control. We can set conditions applicable only to certain students, such as providing a wider date window to complete the exam or extended time for students with documented learning disabilities.[20] We never have to bother with making copies or spend time processing old-fashioned Scantron cards. We don't have to transport stacks of exams home to grade, nor do we have to pass them back to students. In my opinion, the LMS offers a significant improvement over past strategies for testing.

The explanations I've provided here cannot substitute for your own exploration of your LMS, nor can I replace the excellent tutorials and supports your college or university assuredly offers. Take the time to learn how the system works, and don't hesitate to reach out to the "tech-sperts" available to you. I acknowledge again that moving your course online requires a substantial investment of your time, even when you have everything from the syllabus to the final exam ready to go when you begin the process. Of faculty surveyed by Lee Freeman of the University of Michigan at Dearborn (2015), 29% said online course development required more than 100 hours of work, and 85% said content development was more time consuming than face-to-face courses.[21] It takes me at least three weeks of full-time work (about 120–160 hours) to create a course from the ground up, and at least another 40 hours to upload everything to the LMS. The most time-consuming part for me is developing the course map, followed by creating the lectures. Be patient with yourself and allow sufficient time to manage the technological and pedagogical learning curve you'll experience when building your first completely online course. It's not something you can do over a weekend, but it *is* well within your abilities as an instructor and disciplinary expert. Furthermore, please reach out to your institution's Center for Teaching and Learning, information technologies, or other support services if you need help. You do not have to struggle alone.

ONLINE COURSE QUALITY STANDARDS

Each online course will be as unique as the person who designed it, just as is true of the courses we teach on campus. Nevertheless, we would do well to ensure our courses meet quality standards and adhere to disciplinary norms as we strive to give our students the best possible learning experience.

Although qualitative judgments are inherently subjective, efforts to develop quality standards emerged as online learning grew in popularity over the 1990s and 2000s. Baldwin, Ching, and Hsu (2017)[22] conducted a comparison of online course design standards in higher education, noting that they "could not identify a clear set of 'best practices' for online courses through [their] literature review." The authors searched for similarities and differences between six quality review instruments, updated by Baldwin and Ching (2019) with the addition of a seventh instrument.[23] Three of the seven sources are specific to individual states (two

103

in California and one in Illinois), and two pertain to particular LMS platforms (Blackboard and Canvas).

- Blackboard's Exemplary Course Program Rubric
- California Community College's Online Education Initiative
- California State University Quality Online Learning and Teaching
- Canvas Course Evaluation Checklist
- Illinois Online Network's Quality Online Course Initiative
- Quality Matters Higher Education Rubric
- The Open SUNY Course Quality Review Rubric (OSCQR)

Based on their comparison, the authors identified a set of standards common across all or most (at least five) of the seven instruments.

- Objectives are available.
- Navigation is intuitive.
- Technology is used to promote learner engagement/facilitate learning.
- Student-to-student interaction is supported.
- Communication and activities are used to build community.
- Instructor contact information is stated.
- Expectations regarding the quality of communication/participation are provided.
- Assessment rubrics for graded assignments are provided.
- Assessments align with objectives.
- Links to institutional services are provided.
- The course has accommodations for disabilities.
- Course policies for behavior expectations are stated.
- Learners can give feedback on the course for improvement.
- Course activities promote students' achievement of objectives.
- Instructor response time is stated.
- Collaborative activities support content and active learning.
- Self-assessment options are provided.
- Assessments frequently occur throughout the course.
- Instructions are written clearly.
- Guidelines for multimedia are available.
- Guidelines for technology are available.

Only the course review rubrics from Quality Matters and the Online Learning Consortium were developed for a national audience and applicable to any LMS. The Quality Matters organization was founded in 2003 by Maryland Online, Inc.—a small group of colleges that wanted to create a system for sharing available courses. Funded by a grant from the US Department of

Education, participants developed a rubric of course design standards intended to train faculty, guide course improvement, and assure the quality of online and blended college courses. Today, Quality Matters serves over 60,000 members.[24]

The Online Learning Consortium began in 1992 as the Alfred P. Sloan Foundation's Anytime, Anyplace Learning program. Its continuing purpose is to help institutions "create high-quality educational experiences, improving the U.S./international field of online education, contributing to the creation of an educated workforce, and creating mutually beneficial partnerships with like-minded organizations."[25] One such partnership has been with the State University of New York (SUNY), developing the OLC OSCQR Course Design Review Scorecard.[26]

Table 3.1 compares the OSCQR to QM standards and criteria. Although descriptors don't match exactly, we can see many areas of similarity. OSCQR has 50 criteria across six categories, whereas QM has 43 criteria over eight categories.

TABLE 3.1 Quality Matters and OSCQR Comparison

QUALITY MATTERS	OSCQR Note: italics indicate the second or subsequent time an OSCQR criterion is mentioned in comparison to Quality Matters.
Course Overview and Introduction	Course Overview and Information
1.1 Instructions make clear how to Start Here area and where to find various course components.	1. Course includes Welcome and Getting Started content.
1.2 Learners are introduced to the purpose and structure of the course.	2. An orientation or overview is provided for the course overall, as well as in each module. Learners know how to navigate and what tasks are due. 3. Course includes a Course Information area that deconstructs the syllabus for learners in a clear and navigable way. 4. A printable syllabus is available to all learners (PDF, HTML). 7. Course information states whether the course is fully online, blended, or web enhanced.

(*Continued*)

105

TABLE 3.1 (Continued)

QUALITY MATTERS	OSCQR Note: italics indicate the second or subsequent time an OSCQR criterion is mentioned in comparison to Quality Matters.
1.3 Communication expectations for online discussions, email, and other forms of interaction are clearly stated.	39. Expectations for interaction are clearly stated (netiquette, grade weighting, models/examples, and timing and frequency of contributions. 41. Course contains resources or activities intended to build a sense of class community, support open communication, and establish trust (at least one of the following: ice breaker, Bulletin Board, Meet Your Classmates, Ask a Question discussion forums).
1.4 Course and institutional policies with which the learner is expected to comply are clearly stated within the course, or a link to current policies is provided.	5. Course includes links to relevant campus policies on plagiarism, computer use, filing grievances, accommodating disabilities, etc.
1.5 Minimum technology requirements for the course are clearly stated, and information on obtaining the technologies is provided.	8. Appropriate methods and devices for accessing and participating in the course are communicated (mobile, publisher websites, secure content, pop-ups, browser issue, microphone, webcam).
1.6 Computer skills and digital information literacy skills expected of the learner are clearly stated.	11. Requisite skills for technology tools (websites, software, and hardware) are stated and supported with resources.
1.7 Expectations for prerequisite knowledge in the discipline and/or any required competencies are clearly stated.	No match
1.8 The self-introduction by the instructor is professional and is available online.	10. Course provides information for instructor, department, and program. 40. Learners have an opportunity to get to know the instructor.
1.9 Learners are asked to introduce themselves to the class.	*41. Course contains resources or activities intended to build a sense of class community, support open communication, and establish trust (at least one of the following: ice breaker, Bulletin Board, Meet Your Classmates, Ask a Question discussion forums).*

QUALITY MATTERS	OSCQR Note: italics indicate the second or subsequent time an OSCQR criterion is mentioned in comparison to Quality Matters.
Learning Objectives (Competencies)	(No Match)
2.1 The course learning objectives, or course/program competencies, describe measurable outcomes.	9. Course objectives/outcomes are clearly defined, measurable, and aligned to learning activities and assessments.
2.2 The module/unit-level learning objectives or competencies describe measurable and consistent outcomes with the course-level objectives or competencies.	
2.3 Learning objectives or competencies are stated clearly, are written from the learner's perspective, and are prominently located in the course.	
2.4 The relationship between learning objectives or competencies and learning activities is clearly stated.	
2.5 The learning objectives or competencies are suited to the level of the course.	
Assessment and Measurement	**Assessment and Feedback**
3.1 The assessments measure the achievement of the stated learning objectives or competencies.	45. Course includes frequent and appropriate methods to assess learners' mastery of content.
3.2 The course grading policy is stated clearly at the beginning of the course.	44. Course grading policies, including consequences of late submissions, are clearly stated in the course information area or syllabus.
3.3 Specific and descriptive criteria are provided for evaluating learners' work, and their connection to the course grading policy is clearly explained.	*45. Course includes frequent and appropriate methods to assess learners' mastery of content.*

(Continued)

107

TABLE 3.1 (Continued)

QUALITY MATTERS	OSCQR Note: italics indicate the second or subsequent time an OSCQR criterion is mentioned in comparison to Quality Matters.
3.4 The assessments used are sequenced, varied, and suited to the level of the course.	46. Criteria for assessing a graded assignment are clearly articulated (rubrics, exemplary work).
3.5 The course provides learners with multiple opportunities to track their learning progress with timely feedback.	38. Expectations for timely and regular feedback from the instructor are clearly stated (questions, email, assignments). 47. Learners have opportunities to review their performance and assess their learning throughout the course (pretests, automated self-tests, reflective assignments, etc.).
No match	49. Learners have easy access to a well-designed and up-to-date gradebook.
No match	50. Learners have multiple opportunities to provide descriptive feedback on course design, course content, course experience, and ease of online technology.
Instructional Materials	**Content and Activities**
4.1 The instructional materials contribute to the achievement of the stated learning objectives or competencies.	30. Course provides activities for learners to develop higher-order thinking and problem solving skills, such as critical reflection and analysis. 31. Course provides activities that emulate real-world applications of the discipline, such as experiential learning, case studies, and problem-based activities.
4.2 The relationship between the use of instructional materials in the course and completing learning activities is clearly explained.	29. Course offers access to a variety of engaging resources that facilitate communication and collaboration, deliver content, and support learning and engagement.
4.3 The course models the academic integrity expected of learners by providing both source references and permissions for the use of instructional materials.	33. Course materials and resources include copyright and licensing status, clearly stating permission to share where applicable.

QUALITY MATTERS	OSCQR Note: italics indicate the second or subsequent time an OSCQR criterion is mentioned in comparison to Quality Matters.
4.4 The instructional materials represent up-to-date theory and practice in the discipline.	*31. Course provides activities that emulate real-world applications of the discipline, such as experiential learning, case studies, and problem-based activities.*
4.5 A variety of instructional materials are used in the course.	32. Where available, Open Educational Resources, free or low-cost materials are used.
Learning Activities and Learner Interaction	Content and Activities; Interaction
5.1 The learning activities promote the achievement of the stated learning objectives or competencies.	*30. Course provides activities for learners to develop higher-order thinking and problem-solving skills, such as critical reflection and analysis.*
5.2 Learning activities provide opportunities for interaction that support active learning.	42. Course offers opportunities for learner-to-learner interaction and constructive collaboration. 43. Learners are encouraged to share resources and inject knowledge from diverse information sources in their course interactions.
5.3 The instructor's plan for interacting with learners during the course is clearly stated.	*38. Expectations for timely and regular feedback from the instructor are clearly stated (questions, email, assignments).*
5.4 The requirements for learner interaction are clearly stated.	*39. Expectations for interaction are clearly stated (netiquette, grade weighting, models/examples, timing, and frequency of contributions).*
Course Technology	Course Technology and Tools
6.1 The tools used in the course support the learning objectives or competencies.	*30. Course provides activities for learners to develop higher-order thinking and problem-solving skills, such as critical reflection and analysis.*

(*Continued*)

109

TABLE 3.1 (Continued)

QUALITY MATTERS	OSCQR Note: italics indicate the second or subsequent time an OSCQR criterion is mentioned in comparison to Quality Matters.
6.2 Course tools promote learner engagement and active learning. 6.3 A variety of technology is used in the course.	29. Course offers access to a variety of engaging resources that facilitate communication and collaboration, deliver content, and support learning and engagement.
6.4 The course provides learners with information on protecting their data and privacy.	14. Course includes links to privacy policies for technology tools.
Learner Support	No match
7.1 The course instructions articulate or link to a clear description of the technical support offered and how to obtain it.	6. Course provides access to learner success resources (technical help, orientation, tutoring).
7.2 Course instructions articulate or link to the institution's accessibility policies and services.	15. Any technology tools meet accessibility standards.
7.3 Course instructions articulate or link to the institution's academic support services and resources to help learners succeed in the course.	6. Course provides access to learner success resources (technical help, orientation, tutoring).
7.4 Course instructions articulate or link to the institution's student services and resources to help learners succeed.	
8.1 Course navigation facilitates ease of use.	13. Frequently used technology tools are easily accessed. Any tools not being utilized are removed from the course menu. 16. A logical, consistent, and uncluttered layout is established. The course is easy to navigate (consistent color scheme and icon layout, related content organized together, self-evident titles).

QUALITY MATTERS	OSCQR Note: italics indicate the second or subsequent time an OSCQR criterion is mentioned in comparison to Quality Matters.
Accessibility and Usability	Design and Layout
	17. Large blocks of information are divided into manageable sections with ample white space around and between the blocks. 19. Instructions are provided and well written. 20. Course is free of grammatical and spelling errors.
8.2 The course design facilitates readability.	18. There is enough contrast between text and background for the content to be easily viewed. 21. Text is formatted with titles, headings, and other styles to enhance readability and improve the document's structure. 23. A sans-serif font with a standard size of at least 12 points is used.
8.3 The course provides accessible text and images in files, documents, LMS pages, and web pages to meet diverse learners' needs. 8.4 The course provides alternative means of access to multimedia content in formats that meet diverse learners' needs.	22. Flashing and blinking text are avoided. 24. When possible, information is displayed in a linear format instead of as a table. 25. Tables are accompanied by a title and summary description. 26. Table header rows and columns are assigned. 34. Text content is available in an easily accessed format, preferably HTML. All text content is readable by assistive technology, including PDF or any text contained in an image. 35. A text equivalent for every non-text element is provided ("alt" tags, captions, transcripts, etc.). 36. Text, graphics, and images are understandable when viewed without color. Text should be used as a primary method for delivering information. 37. Hyperlink text is descriptive and makes sense when out of context (avoid using "click here"). 48. Learners are informed when a timed response is required. Proper lead-time is provided to ensure there is an opportunity to prepare an accommodation.

(Continued)

111

TABLE 3.1 (Continued)

QUALITY MATTERS	OSCQR Note: italics indicate the second or subsequent time an OSCQR criterion is mentioned in comparison to Quality Matters.
8.5 Course multimedia facilitate ease of use.	27. Slideshows use a predefined slide layout and include unique slide titles. 28. For all slideshows, there are simple, non-automatic transitions between slides.
8.6 Vendor accessibility statements are provided for all technologies required in the course.	14. Course includes links to privacy policies for technology tools. *15. Any technology tools meet accessibility standards.*

Synthesis of Quality Standards

Looking more closely, we see the biggest differences in Quality Matters' emphasis on aligning instruction and course materials with learning outcomes, compared to OSCQR's specific criteria for design and formatting to ensure accessibility. We can also observe that Quality Matters tends toward broad, general statements, whereas OSCQR is more detailed. What might it look like if we took the best of both instruments and synthesized them into a simple checklist that any faculty member or course designer could use when building a course online? The next section presents a combined version of these standards aligned with the two sources, resulting in a set of recommendations faculty at any institution could use to create a high-quality online course. We'll call this new version "Quality Recommendation Synthesis."

Quality Recommendation Synthesis

1. Welcome
The course includes a welcome from the instructor and instructions for completing the Start Here module. This message:

- Extends a warm welcome to students and communicates excitement about the course (video preferred).
- Includes instructions to read the entire "Start Here" module, post to the "Meet and Greet" discussion and take the short quiz at the end of the Start Here module.

Quality Matters
(No specific recommendation)

OSCQR
1. Course includes Welcome and Getting Started content.

Quality Recommendation Synthesis

2. Meet and Greet Discussion
The course includes a discussion area intended to build community, establish trust, and foster communication.

- Students post a brief introduction of themselves (video preferred; inset photo if video is unavailable).
- Students post comments on one or more peers' posts (video or audio preferred).

Quality Matters
1.9 Learners are asked to introduce themselves to the class.

OSCQR
41.Course contains resources or activities intended to build a sense of class community, support open communication, and establish trust (at least one of the following: ice breaker, Bulletin Board, Meet Your Classmates, Ask a Question discussion forums).

Quality Recommendation Synthesis

3. About the Instructor
The course provides a self-introduction by the instructor, including:

- Preferred name and pronouns
- Contact information (also provided in writing)
  - Email
  - Phone
  - Alternative contact (text, Skype)
  - Preferences and hours of availability
- Short academic biography
- Short philosophy of teaching

Quality Matters
1.8 The self-introduction by the instructor is professional and is available online.

113

OSCQR
10. Course provides information for instructor, department, and program.
40. Learners have an opportunity to get to know the instructor.

Quality Recommendation Synthesis

4. Course Orientation
The course provides an orientation to the online classroom, including the following:

- Explanation of how to navigate the online classroom (video preferred). Statement about course prerequisites, if any.
- Textbooks and required materials (include links for purchase or download), using free or low-cost materials where possible.
- A printable copy of the course syllabus.
- Course calendar.

Quality Matters
1.1 Instructions make clear how to complete the Start Here area and where to find various course components.
1.2 Learners are introduced to the purpose and structure of the course.
1.7 Expectations for prerequisite knowledge in the discipline and/or any required competencies are clearly stated.

OSCQR
2. An orientation or overview is provided for the course overall, as well as in each module. Learners know how to navigate and what tasks are due.
3. Course includes a Course Information area that deconstructs the syllabus for learners in a clear and navigable way.
4. A printable syllabus is available to all learners (PDF, HTML).
32. Where available, Open Educational Resources, free or low-cost materials are used.

Quality Recommendation Synthesis

5. Objectives and Outcomes
The course includes learning objectives and outcomes that are:

- Suited to the level of the course
- Clearly stated

- Measurable
- Written from the student's point of view
- Present in each module and aligned with those for the course as a whole

Quality Matters

2.1 The course learning objectives, or course/program competencies, describe measurable outcomes.

2.2 The module/unit-level learning objectives or competencies describe measurable and consistent outcomes with the course-level objectives or competencies.

2.3 Learning objectives or competencies are stated clearly, are written from the learner's perspective, and are prominently located in the course.

2.5 The learning objectives or competencies are suited to the level of the course.

OSCQR

9. Course objectives/outcomes are clearly defined, measurable, and aligned to learning activities and assessments.

Quality Recommendation Synthesis

6. Overview of Activities, Assignments, and Assessments

The course includes an overview of the activities, assignments, and assessments that will be utilized. This overview includes:

- An explanation of how each assignment, assessment, or learning activity aligns with course and module objectives and outcomes.
- A clear explanation of the weight or value of each graded item in the course.
- A description of how the varied assessments provide multiple opportunities for students to demonstrate learning.
- An explanation of opportunities for students to review their performance and assess their learning (self-graded tests, reflective assignments, etc.).
- Gradebook is present, well organized, and kept up to date.

Quality Matters

3.1 The assessments measure the achievement of the stated learning objectives or competencies.

3.4 The assessments used are sequenced, varied, and suited to the level of the course.

OSCQR

45. Course includes frequent and appropriate methods to assess learners' mastery of content.
47. Learners have opportunities to review their performance and assess their own learning throughout the course (pre-tests, automated self-tests, reflective assignments, etc.).
49. Learners have easy access to a well-designed and up-to-date gradebook.

Quality Recommendation Synthesis

7. Policies and Expectations

The course provides an explanation of all policies and expectations for the instructor and students, including, but not limited to, the following:

- Instructor's expectations for students:
  - Late work, make-up work, re-submission of work
  - Grading policy
  - Attendance and participation
  - Communication
  - How students can provide feedback about the course
  - Netiquette and classroom civility
- Students' expectations for the instructor:
  - Where and how the instructor will provide feedback
  - When grades will be posted
  - Where they will receive feedback
- Links to relevant or required university policies such as academic honesty, grievances, accommodations for students with disabilities, etc.

Quality Matters

3.2 The course grading policy is stated clearly at the beginning of the course.
1.3 Communication expectations for online discussions, email, and other forms of interaction are clearly stated.
1.4 Course and institutional policies with which the learner is expected to comply are clearly stated within the course, or a link to current policies is provided.
3.5 The course provides learners with multiple opportunities to track their learning progress with timely feedback.
5.3 The instructor's plan for interacting with learners during the course is clearly stated.

5.4 The requirements for learner interaction are clearly
   stated.

OSCQR
5. Course includes links to relevant campus policies on plagiarism,
   computer use, filing grievances, accommodating disabilities, etc.
38. Expectations for timely and regular feedback from the instructor
   are clearly stated (questions, email, assignments).
39. Expectations for interaction are clearly stated (netiquette,
   grade weighting, models/examples, timing, and frequency of
   contributions.
44. Course grading policies, including consequences of late sub-
   missions, are clearly stated in the course information area or
   syllabus.
50. Learners have multiple opportunities to provide descriptive
   feedback on course design, course content, course experience,
   and ease of online technology.

Quality Recommendation Synthesis

8. Student Support
The course provides a description, contact information, and links to student
   support services, including, but not limited to:

- Technology help
- LMS support
- Tutoring services or online tutorials
- Writing center or academic support services
- Library
- Health, wellness, and mental health services
- Office of Disabilities Services (include a link to university's accessibil-
  ity policy)

Quality Matters
7.1 The course instructions articulate or link to a clear description
   of the technical support offered and how to obtain it.
7.2 Course instructions articulate or link to the institution's accessibility policies and services.
7.3 Course instructions articulate or link to the institution's academic support services and resources to help learners succeed
   in the course.
7.4 Course instructions articulate or link to the institution's student
   services and resources to help learners succeed.

OSCQR
6. Course provides access to learner success resources (technical help, orientation, tutoring).

Quality Recommendation Synthesis

9. Technology
The course provides information about all technologies to be utilized, including:

- A statement of the course format (all online, hybrid, hyflex, blended, on campus, etc.)
- Minimum hardware, software, and equipment requirements, including information on how to obtain required hardware and software
- Explanation of how the varied technologies used in the course support students' achievement of course objectives and outcomes, deliver content, and facilitate active learning, communication, engagement, and collaboration
- List of technological skills and knowledge required for students' success in the course, along with resources such as video tutorials of required skills
- Links to privacy policies and vendor accessibility statements for all technology tools used in the course

The instructor will:
- Ensure students can easily access all tools.
- Remove any unused tools from the course menu.

Quality Matters
1.5 Minimum technology requirements for the course are clearly stated, and information on obtaining the technologies is provided.
1.6 Computer skills and digital information literacy skills expected of the learner are clearly stated.
6.1 The tools used in the course support the learning objectives or competencies.
6.3 A variety of technology is used in the course.
6.2 Course tools promote learner engagement and active learning.
6.4 The course provides learners with information on protecting their data and privacy.
8.6 Vendor accessibility statements are provided for all technologies required in the course.

118

OSCQR

7. Course information states whether the course is fully online, blended, or web enhanced.

8. Appropriate methods and devices for accessing and participating in the course are communicated (mobile, publisher websites, secure content, pop-ups, browser issue, microphone, webcam).

11. Requisite skills for technology tools (websites, software, and hardware) are stated and supported with resources.

13. Frequently used technology tools are easily accessed. Any tools not being utilized are removed from the course menu.

15. Any technology tools meet accessibility standards.

29. Course offers access to a variety of engaging resources that facilitate communication and collaboration, deliver content, and support learning and engagement.

Quality Recommendation Synthesis

10. Instructional Materials

Instructional materials used in the course demonstrate the following characteristics:

- Support students' achievement of the course's stated learning objectives and outcomes.
- Demonstrate up-to-date theory and practice in the discipline.
- Correlate with student learning activities.
- Integrate a variety of engaging resources.
- Facilitate communication and collaboration.
- Model expectations for academic integrity by clearly stating copyright or licensing status, permission to share (where applicable), and correct citations or references.
- Minimize students' expenditures for materials associated with learning activities.

Quality Matters

4.1 The instructional materials contribute to the achievement of the stated learning objectives or competencies.

4.4 The instructional materials represent up-to-date theory and practice in the discipline.

4.2 The relationship between the use of instructional materials in the course and completing learning activities is clearly explained.

4.3 The course models the academic integrity expected of learners by providing both source references and permissions for the use of instructional materials.

4.5 A variety of instructional materials is used in the course.

OSCQR

29. Course offers access to a variety of engaging resources that facilitate communication and collaboration, deliver content, and support learning and engagement.

31. Course provides activities that emulate real-world applications of the discipline, such as experiential learning, case studies, and problem-based activities.

33. Course materials and resources include copyright and licensing status, clearly stating permission to share where applicable.

Quality Recommendation Synthesis

11. Course Content, Activities, and Interaction

The course content, including learning activities and interaction, demonstrates the following characteristics:

- Promotes students' achievement of the course's stated learning objectives and outcomes.
- Develops students' higher-order thinking and core competencies such as critical thinking, problem solving, reflection, and analysis.
- Includes activities that link to real-world applications of the discipline (examples: experiential learning, case studies, problem-based activities)
- Provides opportunities for interaction:
  - Peer-to-peer
  - Student-to-instructor
  - Student-to-content
- Incorporates active learning, collaboration, and peer-to-peer sharing of knowledge and resources.
- Demonstrates logical organization and follows a clear progression from the beginning to the end of the course.
- Provides instructions that clarify where to find necessary resources and how to use them to complete assignments, activities, or assessments.
- Associates every graded item with clear written directions and includes a rubric, checklist, or other transparent grading criteria.

■ States all due dates and submission requirements clearly and makes these evident in the instructions for each graded item.

Quality Matters

2.4 The relationship between learning objectives or competencies and learning activities is clearly stated.

3.3 Specific and descriptive criteria are provided for evaluating learners' work, and their connection to the course grading policy is clearly explained.

5.1 The learning activities promote the achievement of the stated learning objectives or competencies.

5.2 Learning activities provide opportunities for interaction that support active learning.

OSCQR

30. Course provides activities for learners to develop higher-order thinking and problem-solving skills, such as critical reflection and analysis.

42. Course offers opportunities for learner-to-learner interaction and constructive collaboration.

43. Learners are encouraged to share resources and inject knowledge from diverse information sources in their course interactions.

46. Criteria for assessing a graded assignment are clearly articulated (rubrics, exemplary work).

Quality Recommendation Synthesis

12. Online Environment Design

The online environment of the course is well designed and demonstrates the following characteristics:

■ Frequently used tools are apparent and convenient.
■ Navigation and learning paths are evident and intuitive.
■ Page layouts are consistent and uncluttered.
■ Color scheme and icons are consistent on all pages.
■ Related content is organized together.
■ Large blocks of information are divided into manageable sections.
■ All instructions are clear, well-written, and free from grammatical and spelling errors.

Quality Matters

8.1 Course navigation facilitates ease of use.

OSCQR

16. A logical, consistent, and uncluttered layout is established. The course is easy to navigate (consistent color scheme and icon layout, related content organized together, self-evident titles).

17. Large blocks of information are divided into manageable sections with ample white space around and between the blocks.

19. Instructions are provided and well written.

20. Course is free of grammatical and spelling errors.

Quality Recommendation Synthesis

13. Readability

All text-based materials in the course fulfill standards for readability, including:

- Sufficient contrast between text and background
- Formatting uses titles, headings, and other visual organization
- Sans-serif font of no less than 12 points
- Absence of flashing or blinking text
- Slideshow formatting also ensures readability:
  - Slides use a predefined slide layout.
  - Slides have unique titles.
  - Transitions between slides are simple and non-automatic.
  - Slides adhere to readability requirements.

Quality Matters

8.2 The course design facilitates readability.

OSCQR

18. There is enough contrast between text and background for the content to be easily viewed.

21. Text is formatted with titles, headings, and other styles to enhance readability and improve the document's structure.

23. A sans-serif font with a standard size of at least 12 pt. is used.

27. Slideshows use a predefined slide layout and include unique slide titles.

28. For all slideshows, there are simple, non-automatic transitions between slides.

Quality Recommendation Synthesis

14. Access for Diverse Learners

The course ensures access for diverse learners consistent with the requirements of the Americans with Disabilities Act:

- Text is the primary means of conveying information. All text is:
  - Available in easily accessed format (HTML preferred).
  - Readable by assistive technology, including PDF files and text contained in images.
  - Information is displayed as in-line text rather than tables whenever possible.
  - Tables are accompanied by a title, header rows, and a summary description.
- All visual elements in the course are understandable when viewed without color.
- A text equivalent for every non-text element is provided (alt-text tags, captions, transcripts, etc.) in all documents, files, LMS pages, multimedia, and web pages.
- Visual presentations include audio narration (recommended).
- Hyperlinks are descriptive and make sense out of context (avoid "click here").
- Students are informed of assessments with time limits and provided sufficient lead time to arrange accommodations.

Quality Matters

8.3 The course provides accessible text and images in files, documents, LMS pages, and web pages to meet diverse learners' needs.

8.4 The course provides alternative means of access to multimedia content in formats that meet diverse learners' needs.

8.5 Course multimedia facilitate ease of use.

OSCQR

22. Flashing and blinking text are avoided.

24. When possible, information is displayed in a linear format instead of as a table.

25. Tables are accompanied by a title and summary description.

26. Table header rows and columns are assigned.

34. Text content is available in an easily accessed format, preferably HTML. All text content is readable by assistive technology, including PDF or any text contained in an image.

35. A text equivalent for every non-text element is provided ("alt" tags, captions, transcripts, etc.).
36. Text, graphics, and images are understandable when viewed without color. Text should be used as a primary method for delivering information.
37. Hyperlink text is descriptive and makes sense when out of context (avoid using "click here").
48. Learners are informed when a timed response is required. Proper lead time is provided to ensure there is an opportunity to prepare an accommodation.

QUALITY RECOMMENDATION SYNTHESIS EXPLANATION

Next, we'll examine each of the 14 Quality Recommendations to see why they represent best practice and how we can incorporate them into the courses we build online. This list is admittedly much more instructor centric than student centric because it describes what we must do as educators. However, establishing a common understanding of what a high-quality online course looks like gives us a set of design constraints within which we can work to meet our students' needs.

First Impressions

Students sometimes refer to the first day of an on-campus course as "Syllabus Day." Instructors introduce themselves to their new students, distribute printed copies of the syllabus, explain their policies and procedures, and provide an overview of what students will do in the course. Some of us include an ice-breaker activity or casual discussion so students can get to know one another, too. Students are eager to see what their instructors are like, and they want to know how difficult the course will be and how much work they'll need to do. They want to know if the course will be interesting, enjoyable, and help them achieve their goals and dreams. Therefore, the first impression we make is crucial because it sets the tone for the rest of the semester. I'm sure most readers are already familiar with these ideas. After all, we've probably gone through this experience many times in the past as students and as faculty members.

Online, we cannot command students' attention in quite the same way as we would on campus. There's often no teacher-led, synchronous "Syllabus Day" as there is in a face-to-face course. Basic course information tends to be rather dry, but just like the syllabus review we'd conduct on the first day of a face-to-face course, it generates a set of common understandings between the instructor and the students. Therefore, our design challenge is to convey this information clearly and persuade students to read it all the way through so they know what to expect, understand what to do, and are prepared for success.

The first impression we make begins to establish rapport between students and instructors—an essential task when we remember that one of the Big Six is having professors who cared about students as people. Rapport is the foundation of successful human relationships. Please don't confuse rapport with friendship, however. Friends can and do develop rapport, but we can also develop a rapport with colleagues, casual acquaintances, and many other people. We can maintain an appropriate professional distance even as we allow our students to see that we are approachable, warm, and caring. Demonstrating these characteristics has nothing to do with lowering our standards or diluting rigor, but it has everything to do with being student centered. Sadly, far too many faculty members fail to perceive the difference. As evidence, a faculty discussion group on Facebook with the partial title "Instruction in the Age of Social Distancing"[27] hosted a rather enlightening conversation about this topic. The following is an exchange between three of the participants in a larger discussion thread. (I have identified them as Professors 1, 2, and 3.)

Professor 1: *I do not try to make friends with my students. I am not interested in their personal lives and have no interest in them knowing about mine. I feel that professional distance is important. I am not teaching because I want a bunch of 18–25-year-old friends. They are my students. It is my job to teach them in my area of expertise.*
Professor 2: *We are being forced to engage with our students more personally. . . . I expect it will continue, but I am very concerned about how to limit their contact with me. They are used to their parents tending to them, and I am not interested in being a substitute parent. . . . Maintaining professional distance is difficult.*
Professor 1: *I did all asynchronous instruction. That helped me.*
Professor 3: *We are not their parents or therapists, nor should we be. But we are their mentors, and some look to us for cues about how to conduct adulthood, including collegial friendships with boundaries.*

The statements made by Professors 1 and 2 reflect attitudes I've often encountered among faculty, yet Professor 3 makes an insightful point. We're not called upon to become surrogate parents or amateur therapists—it's up to us to establish the boundaries of our relationships with students. We mentor all our students to some degree, even if only while they're on our class list. The point of building rapport is not to initiate lasting relationships, although these can develop over time, nor should we presume that establishing rapport means we have to become our students' friends. Rather, it's about demonstrating that we're human beings, showing students that we care about them personally, and communicating our desire to facilitate their success while enrolled in our courses.

Quirk and Young (2016), in "Lost (and Found) in Translation: What Online Students Want," found that "More than any other goals, students want connections and a sense of community in their online courses."[28] That sense of community begins with the first communication from the instructor. Instructors establish

125

a presence quite naturally in an on-campus course, but online we need to be more deliberate. Hajbayova (2016),[29] Kropp (2018),[30] Cicco (2018),[31] and Glazier (2016),[32] among many others, emphasize the impact that a positive online presence and appropriate rapport can have on student success. These actions are rooted in our core philosophy of teaching. If we genuinely care about our students and hold a student-centered mindset, why wouldn't we want to welcome our students warmly and begin to build a positive relationship with them from the first day of class? It's a simple, straightforward, and effective method of enhancing students' retention, establishing favorable perceptions of their experiences in our courses, and supporting their academic achievement.

The need to establish rapport is why the first three items in the Quality Recommendations Synthesis are both personal and structural. The following sections explain each recommendation and provide a list of Action Steps to help you evaluate the quality of the course you've designed.

---

1. Welcome

The course includes a welcome from the instructor and instructions for completing the Start Here module. This message:

> Extends a warm welcome to students and communicates excitement about the course (video preferred).
>
> Includes instructions to read the entire "Start Here" module, post to the "Meet and Greet" discussion and take the short quiz at the end of the Start Here module.

Because our first communication with students sets the tone for what will follow, your initial welcome message should be concise yet upbeat, encouraging, and convey your enthusiasm for the course. As students have not heard from you before, it's helpful to begin by introducing yourself. "Hello, Students—I'm Bruce Mackh, and I'll be your instructor for Design Thinking." Briefly summarize what the course will include and charge students with their first task: reading the online classroom's entire "Start Here" area. Let students know they'll be held accountable with a short quiz at the end of their reading since assessment should never come as a surprise, not even a low-value quiz. Tell students to post their self-introduction to the "Meet and Greet" discussion and invite them to learn more about you in the "About the Instructor" section of the course. Ideally, we should provide this message three ways: (1) record a video and post it to the online classroom, (2) write and send the message as an email a week before the first day of class, and (3) post the same written message as a course announcement. This way, students won't be as likely to overlook what you're trying to tell them.

Action Steps

1. Write out your welcome message according to the instructions here, thinking about how to spark positivity and excitement in your students.
2. Record your message and post to your online classroom as the first item in the Start Here section of the course.
3. Compose an email of the message and send it to all students one week before the first day of class.
4. Post the written message as a course announcement.

---

2. Meet and Greet Discussion
The course includes a discussion area intended to build community, establish trust, and foster communication.

Students post a brief introduction of themselves (video preferred; inset photo if video is unavailable).
Students post comments on one or more peers' posts (video or audio preferred).

The Meet and Greet discussion serves as students' first contact with one another, beginning to establish peer-to-peer relationships. Such discussions remain a standard feature of online courses, but students who've had some prior online learning experience don't always see them as particularly enjoyable or engaging. I've even had students tell me they keep the text for their initial post on a document and just copy and paste it into each new course. Therefore, I try to mix things up a little and stray from the usual directions to state their name, hometown, major, and reason for taking the course or expectation of what they'll get out of the course. Some of this identity information is helpful since that's the purpose of the activity, but I'll also ask a question related to the course that requires a personal response. For the Design Thinking course, I asked students to share a novel solution they'd come up with to a problem. The most innovative response was from a student who shared that she eats crunchy snacks with chopsticks to avoid getting her computer keyboard messy, which generated quite a few comments from her peers. As another example, I designed and taught a course called "The Art of Math," which aimed to help art students meet their math requirement. Knowing this audience was uncomfortable with the topic, I asked them to share their feelings about math so that we could address their anxieties from the beginning. Alternatively, you could include a quick ice breaker in this discussion such as "Two Truths and a Lie"—students tell two things that are true about themselves and one that is a lie, and classmates comment with a guess about which statement is the lie. I might say, "I've been within arm's reach of a mountain goat on a 14,000-foot peak in Colorado, I've stood at the top of the Eiffel Tower in Paris, and my summer job in grad school was driving a street sweeper in the French Quarter of New Orleans."

Video tends to be the most engaging format for this discussion. Some LMS have built-in recording tools in their discussion forums, which is a real asset. Others will allow a video to be uploaded to a post. If built-in recording capability isn't present, we can use a free app like Screencastify, FreeCam, ShareX, CamStudio, EZVid, or TinyTake, among many others. Sometimes the recording or multimedia tools in the LMS are present but somewhat difficult to find or use. For instance, I once found a student tutorial for using the recording tools in Brightspace with 16 steps from start to finish (fortunately, this is no longer available and the process is simpler than was portrayed in the deleted resource). If video isn't an option for you, consider asking students to upload a photo of themselves along with their initial post, and be sure to do the same yourself. Knowing what someone looks like helps us visualize the person with whom we're communicating, which builds connections and fosters engagement. Students could post comments as video clips, too—a function built into many discussion boards.

Even though you'll also create an "About the Instructor" page, posting your own entry to this discussion starts things off on the right foot and models what a good response should look like. Furthermore, it's very important to respond to every student in the Meet and Greet discussion. Welcome them to the class and comment on something they said about themselves. Students need to know you're interested in them and you're glad they're part of the group. I admit this is more challenging for those teaching very high-enrollment courses, but we shouldn't start the course off on the wrong foot by failing to greet our students by name.

Action Steps

1. Open a new discussion in the LMS and title it "Meet and Greet" or a similar title.
2. Write instructions for the students specifying what they should share about themselves and how many peers they should respond to.
3. Post your own contribution to the discussion.
4. Publish the discussion or mark it as "available" to students.

3. About the Instructor

The course provides a self-introduction by the instructor including:

Preferred name and pronouns
Contact information (also provide in writing)
    Email
    Phone
    Alternative contact (text, Skype)
    Preferences and hours of availability
Short academic biography
Short philosophy of teaching

The instructor biography is standard in most online classrooms. Posting this as a video helps replicate the experience of being in a face-to-face classroom, where students can both see and hear us. The most important advice I can give you for this video is to smile! Look directly into the camera, which makes it appear as though you're making eye contact with the student. Compose your face into a friendly expression. Your face reveals volumes about the kind of person you are, so even if you dislike making videos, this one is important. As with any time we make a video of ourselves, pay attention to your background, removing any distractions or things you'd rather your students not see. Make sure there's enough light on your face and your volume is set for a normal speaking level. Dress as you normally would for a face-to-face class.

I generally begin by telling my students, "Hi, I'm Dr. Bruce Mackh, but please just call me Bruce." If you prefer to be more formal, introduce yourself differently: "I'm Dr. Zaharamay, and I'll be your instructor for World History 102." You don't need to mention your contact information in the video if it also appears in writing on the "About the Instructor" or "About the Professor" page, but it's a good idea to explain your contact preferences, hours of availability, or office hours.

The biographical information you choose to share should be about your professional background. Of course, whatever personal information you include is up to you, but I don't recommend telling students about your family or pets, religious or political views, or leisure pursuits unless they're directly relevant to the course. Likewise, you don't need to share your entire CV, but students like to know why you're an expert who's qualified to teach the course. Mentioning where and when you earned your degrees, books you've published, or other professional achievements reassures students that you're someone who can be trusted to teach them valid information.

Your philosophy of teaching statement doesn't need to be lengthy, but it should convey to students that you hold a student-centered perspective and care very much about their success in your course. You might also want to invite students to contact you if they're having any problems or questions about the course, assuring them that you're happy to help.

Action Steps

1. Add a page to the "Start Here" area and title it "About the Instructor" or "About the Professor" or "About [your name]."
2. Compose a message that includes your preferred name and pronouns, a short professional biography, and a brief version of your teaching philosophy.
3. Include your phone number, email address, and alternative contact information, such as your Skype address.
4. Create a video of yourself warmly introducing yourself to the students, including the information in point 2, and letting them know you are happy to help them when they run into problems in the course.
5. Post the video to the page using the tools in the LMS.
6. Make the page visible to students. (Click "publish" or "make available to students.)

Set Expectations and Provide Resources

The next six Quality Recommendations involve pages in the Start Here module, informing students of the instructor's expectations and providing quick access to resources and information that will help them in the course. Without a doubt, these pages contain a large amount of content that exists primarily for reference rather than facilitating active learning. It's hard to avoid it being dry and dull. Nevertheless, most of this content is similar to (or even an exact copy of) our usual course syllabi. It exists in the Start Here module so students can find it when they need it.

---

4. Course Orientation
The course provides an orientation to the online classroom including the following:

Explanation of how to navigate the online classroom (video preferred).
Statement about course prerequisites, if any.
Textbooks and required materials (include links for purchase or download). Where possible, free, or low-cost materials are used.

Printable copy of course syllabus.
Course calendar.

Once students know who will be teaching them, they should know how to use the online classroom and where they can find what they need. The Course Orientation area organizes the course's basic facts and makes them accessible to students on one convenient page. The course syllabus should be available through a hyperlink on this page with the option to download a PDF copy of this document for reference, just as we would distribute a paper copy of the syllabus in a face-to-face course. I won't elaborate upon the process of building a syllabus here[33] because the pages in the Start Here module of your course cover most of the same information. However, I recommend that you include a disclaimer such as "The syllabus is subject to change at the discretion of the instructor," which offers a certain degree of protection if students object to any changes you may make midway through the course. Contrary to common belief, a syllabus is not a legal contract, yet it can become evidence in legal actions. Martha Rumore, in "The Course Syllabus: Legal Contract or Operator's Manual" (2016),[34] explains:

> Syllabi are learning tools that memorialize the course requirements, serving as both a permanent record for the benefit of accrediting bodies and faculty reviews. Despite the long-standing precedent of court noninterference with an academician's professional judgment, and lack of legality, syllabi often represent the triggering agent of instructional dissent by students. Although courts do not view syllabi as contracts, they may lead to student grade appeals and grievances. They also may be used as evidence in grievance and judicial hearings, especially with regard to various performance assessment methods or issues such as academic integrity/plagiarism, copyright, class recording, and syllabus change policy.

Syllabi are generally accepted as good-faith agreements and considered reliable sources of information about a course. Changes to course content are permissible if the syllabus includes a disclaimer to this effect, but the instructor must still follow the stated objectives and outcomes and ensure the course aligns with its catalog description. A course seldom exists unless it has received approval from a curriculum committee and the Office of Academic Affairs (or the equivalent). Thereafter, the instructor is responsible for adhering to the objectives and outcomes as written. Academic freedom is certainly an important principle, but it does not give us license to teach whatever we want. Therefore, instructors should proceed with caution when making changes to the course after the syllabus is in the students' hands.

Instructors of face-to-face courses can usually presume students understand how college works, but even experienced on-campus students may be new to online learning and require additional support. Therefore, the Start Here area of the course should include links to orientation videos or supports provided through the LMS or your institution's technology services department. Consider making a video walking students through the online classroom and showing them where to begin and what to do first. Offer encouragement about beginning the course, communicating your enthusiasm for its content and your discipline. Preview students' next steps, such as completing the Start Here area, and include a short description of any synchronous meetings you plan to hold.

Information about prerequisites, textbooks, and required materials is standard in all courses. However, a student-centered approach would include providing links to places where students can obtain these at a low or reduced cost whenever possible. A survey by the US Public Interest Research Group (2014) reported that 65% of students chose not to purchase a required textbook due to the high cost, even though 94% of those who made this decision worried about its impact on their course grade. Nearly half of student respondents said the cost of textbooks was a factor in deciding which or how many courses they took each semester.[35] Consider allowing students to purchase earlier editions or used copies of required books if it would not adversely affect their learning experience. Furthermore, you might be able to find free resources through your library or Open Educational Resources instead of requiring purchased textbooks. A student in the first section of my Design Thinking course alerted me that an electronic version of the course's first textbook was available free through the university's JSTOR account, for example. If your institution offers a textbook assistance program for low-income students or if you are willing to problem solve with individual students who have trouble obtaining what they need, this is the place to say so.

Our demonstration of compassion toward students' financial and logical difficulties means a great deal to them. For example, when I was speaking on this topic, a colleague told me about an incident during her senior year when she could not afford a key textbook for a course in her major. She reluctantly confessed the problem to the professor, who stood up from her desk, took a copy of the previous edition from her bookshelf, and handed it to my colleague. This caring gesture made such a lasting impression that she remembers the incident clearly, even though it occurred more than 35 years ago (and, as she admitted, she recalls little else about the course).

The course orientation page should also include a link to the calendar built into the LMS, a schedule of due dates, a calendar you've created, or any combination of these options. I began using Microsoft Word to make calendars[36] for my online classes years ago because it helped keep me on track as an instructor, saving the document to my computer's desktop for quick reference. I share this with my students as a Word document so they can modify it to suit their needs, such as entering due dates for their concurrent courses—a strategy I used when I was a student myself. I also recommend that students print a copy and hang it up in their workspace. I know this seems redundant since most learning management systems have a calendar function; many of us use calendar apps on our phones or computers or use something like Google Calendar. Nevertheless, if a low-tech resource like a printed calendar helps me, I believe it might help my students, too.

The Course Orientation page allows students to know what to expect in the course, just as "Syllabus Day" does on campus. Furthermore, it sets a student-centered tone for the course from the very beginning, to facilitate our students' success.

Action Steps

1. Add a page to the "Start Here" area and title it "Course Orientation" or a similar title.
2. Embed a video explaining how to navigate the course.
3. Provide links to supports in the LMS explaining general course functions and navigation.
4. Write a statement about any prerequisites, just as you'd usually include in your syllabus.
5. Insert a link to your syllabus, and make sure a printable copy of the syllabus is also available.
6. List any textbooks and required materials, providing links to sites where students can purchase what they need. Choose free or low-cost options whenever possible. Include a note stating that you will help students experiencing financial hardship.
7. Link or attach the course calendar.
8. Publish the page or mark it as "available" to students.

5. Objectives and Outcomes

The course includes learning objectives and outcomes that are:

Suited to the level of the course
Clearly stated
Measurable
Written from the student's point of view
Present in each module and aligned with those for the course as a whole

133

We discussed objectives and outcomes in Chapter 2. Now your task is to convey these crucial statements to your students in a manner that clarifies the purpose behind your course activities. To review: outcomes are what we want students to achieve by the end of the course. Objectives are the checkpoints or benchmarks that lead to the outcomes. In settings outside higher education, we might refer to these as goals (outcomes) and action steps (objectives). Outcomes are not always unique to a particular course. For instance, all courses offered in a degree program might share the same outcomes, with objectives customized for each course to support those outcomes but appropriate to the course's level and topic. We shouldn't expect first-year students to meet a senior seminar's objectives, nor should we ask advanced students to produce work only at a beginning level.

All objectives and outcomes must be measurable and tied to the course's assessments. Every objective should be associated with an outcome, and every outcome and objective should be associated with an assessment. Your task in this section of the Start Here module is to make those connections very clear to your students. Depending on requirements from your program, department, school, college, or university, your syllabus probably already includes a formalized statement of this information, which you could simply copy and paste into this page on the LMS.

However, an even better strategy might be to integrate and simplify these statements using a formula like this:

Students will _____ [objective] so that they can _____ [outcome].

Here are two examples with the blanks filled in:

> **Students will** use design thinking to solve a personal problem or challenge **so that they can** apply this strategy to situations outside the classroom upon completion of the course.
>
> **Students will** apply design thinking to a personal problem **so that they can** develop their capacity to use design thinking in situations outside the classroom.

This approach presents the objectives and outcomes in student-friendly language, making it easy to understand what they will learn and why they will learn it.

Objectives and outcomes apply to the entire course, but each module should have objectives that build toward and support those at the course level. The Design Thinking course has three modules—a structure that worked well with the three textbooks I chose and the guided instruction model I used—and each module had an objective. I also noted the course-level objectives that each module objective supports.

Module 1 Objective

Students will develop their knowledge of design thinking as they engage in a design thinking activity with a peer (Wallet Project assignment) and learn about design thinking through reading and discussion (Reading Journals 1 and 2).

—Course Objectives 1 and 3

Module 2 Objective

Students will deepen their knowledge of design thinking as they work in small groups to conduct two case studies, developing their ability to formulate solutions to complex challenges, apply design thinking methods to real-world problems, collaborate with peers, think critically, and communicate clearly and effectively.

—Course Objectives 1, 2, 3, 4, and 5

Module 3 Objective

Students will apply design thinking to their own lives in a project that provides the opportunity to solve a personal problem. They will continue to build their communication skills through discussions and in their Design Project's written components.

—Course Objectives 1, 2, 3, and 5

The number of modules you create may depend on personal preference, but it might also be subject to your program's requirements. For instance, the program for which I designed and taught the Art of Math course was quite rigid. All courses were eight weeks long, and each week was its own module containing a lecture, a discussion, an assignment, and a quiz. Discussion posts were always due on Wednesdays, assignments were due on Fridays, and quizzes were due on Sundays, the last day of the instructional week.

Therefore, even if your objectives and outcomes merely need to be copied onto this page straight from your syllabus, it's wise to decide how to organize your course content and write specific objectives for each of those organizational units, weeks, or modules. This structure will inform our next steps as we set up the course in the LMS.

Action Steps

1. Add a page to the "Start Here" area and title it "Objectives and Outcomes."

2. State the course's objectives and outcomes from the student's perspective.
3. List the objectives for each module.
4. Publish the page or mark it as "available" to students.

---

6. Overview of Activities, Assignments, and Assessments

The course includes an overview of the activities, assignments, and assessments that will be utilized. This overview includes:

An explanation of how each assignment, assessment, or learning activity aligns with course and module objectives and outcomes.

A clear explanation of the weight or value of each graded item in the course.

A description of how the varied assessments provide multiple opportunities for students to demonstrate learning.

An explanation of opportunities for students to review own performance and assess own learning (self-graded tests, reflective assignments, etc.).

Gradebook is present, well organized, and kept up to date.

Objectives and outcomes don't exist in isolation. They are the purpose toward which all the learning activities, assignments, and assessments that comprise the course content are directed. This page of the Start Here module summarizes what students will do and how the instructor will value their work. Everything that contributes to students' final grades should be included.

I've always favored tables for presenting information in an appealing and organized manner, but this choice can be troublesome for students who use assistive technologies. Text formatted with bullet points and tabs is a better alternative because it ensures equitable access. Here's the re-formatted example from the Design Thinking course.

- Reading Journals (200 points)
  - Objective 1—increasing knowledge of design thinking as shown in students' posted reflections and questions and in the quality of thought expressed in their responses to peers in the discussion board.
- Wallet Project Assignment (30 points)
  - Objective 1—engagement in the design thinking process as students formulate a solution for their partner.
  - Objective 2—identification of opportunity through an interview with a partner.
  - Objective 3—application of design thinking to the partner's problem.

- Case Studies (200 points)
    - Objective 1—engagement in the design thinking process throughout the case study activity.
    - Objective 2—identification of opportunity that supports the designed solution.
    - Objective 3—application of design thinking in formulating a solution to the problem of the case study.
    - Objective 4—demonstrate capacity for collaboration and teamwork; demonstrate creativity and critical thinking.
    - Objective 5—written case report form and solution presented in the discussion board show growth of students' ability to communicate verbally and in writing.
- Design Project (100 points)
    - Objective 1—engagement in the design thinking process throughout the design project.
    - Objective 2—identification of opportunity that supports the designed solution.
    - Objective 3—application of design thinking in formulating a solution to the problem selected by the student.
    - Objective 4—creation of a solution to the problem demonstrating critical thinking.
    - Objective 5—communication of the solution in the presentation and reflective essay.
- Midterm Exam (100 points)
    - Objective 1—knowledge of the design thinking process.
    - Objective 4—critical thinking, analysis, and synthesis of information about differing views about design thinking.
    - Objective 5—communication of analysis and evaluation in the written document submitted for the Midterm Exam.
- Final Exam (100 points)
    - Objective 1—knowledge of design thinking process (Part 1); synthesis of differing views of the design thinking process (Part 2—Synthesis).
    - Objective 2—identification of opportunity that supports the designed solution (Part 2—Application).
    - Objective 3—application of design thinking in formulating a solution to the problem selected by the student (Part 2—Application).
    - Objective 4—critical thinking, analysis, and synthesis of information (Part 2—Synthesis and Part 2—Application).
    - Objective 5—communication of the solution in the written document submitted for Part 2 of the Final Exam.

Grading and Assessment Structure

Points Possible
- Week 1 Tasks
  - Introduce Yourself discussion (15)
  - Start Here Quiz (5)
  - Wallet Project (30)   50
- Reading Journals (4 journals @ 50 points each)   200
- Case Studies (100 each)   200
- Design Problem
  - Presentation (50)
  - Reflective Essay (50)   100
- Attendance and Participation 50
- Exams
  - Midterm Exam   100
  - Final Exam   <u>100</u>
  - TOTAL   800

Your task is to consider how to explain the relationship between your course's objectives, outcomes, and assessments simply and effectively. This page should make it easy for students to understand how all graded items fit into the course plan and which objectives each will measure.

Be sure you review and organize the gradebook, creating categories that allow students to find what they're looking for. You might place graded items into groups by type, by module, or in another configuration that makes sense to you. It should perhaps go without saying that the instructor will grade students' work promptly and keep the gradebook up to date once the course is in session.

Action Steps

1. Add a page to the "Start Here" area and title it "Overview of Activities, Assignments, and Assessments."
2. Compose text that allows students to understand how their work in the course aligns with the objectives and outcomes.
3. Ensure that the points or weight for each graded item is evident.
4. Explain how students will be able to review their own performance and monitor their progress.
5. Review and organize the gradebook and keep it up to date throughout the course.
6. Publish or mark the page as "available" to students.

7. Policies and Expectations

The course provides an explanation of all policies and expectations for the
instructor and students including, but not limited to, the following:

- Instructor expectations for students
    - Late work, make-up work, re-submission of work
    - Grading policy
    - Attendance and participation
    - Communication
    - How students can provide feedback about the course
    - Netiquette and classroom civility
- Students' expectations for the instructor
    - Where and how the instructor will provide feedback
    - When grades will be posted
    - Where they will receive feedback
- Links to relevant or required university policies such as academic honesty,
  grievances, accommodations for students with disabilities, etc.

This section might be the least surprising and most straightforward in the Start
Here area because the same information is included in most course syllabi. The
point is to state all your policies as simply and clearly as possible. Nothing about
the course should be a mystery, nor should anything students could do to earn a
penalty or negative consequence come as a surprise.

Many instructors simply copy and paste much of this information from an
existing syllabus because it often remains the same across all the courses we teach.
However, we should still double-check to ensure that any dates are current and
the verbiage is appropriate to an online classroom. For example, your syllabus
might have a provision that "all work must be handed to the instructor at the
beginning of class on the stated due date." This statement doesn't work as well
online, so you'd need to edit the text accordingly. Knowing that most online
learning takes place asynchronously, timed deadlines are common, such as, "work
must be submitted online by 11:59 p.m. on the stated due date."

We should also check to make sure our course policies are applicable to online
learning. For example, civil behavior in a face-to-face course might include refraining from eating or drinking in class, whereas this does not matter in an asynchronous online course. Attendance policies differ, as well. On campus, we track the
days a student has been absent or tardy and impose penalties in accordance with

university regulations. Online attendance is a matter of how much time the student spends in the LMS. I usually tell students I expect them to log in at least four days a week, but as long as they keep up with their work, it seldom becomes an issue.

Publishing your policies has a twofold purpose. First, it provides a single point of reference when students have a question about what you expect from them, what they can expect from you, or what a particular university policy might say. Second, it creates a set of shared understandings that hold all stakeholders accountable. If you tell students that you'll respond to their email within 24 hours, you're responsible for meeting the standard you've set. Likewise, if you tell students that any work they submit more than 48 hours after the due date will be marked down by one letter grade, they should expect to receive a penalty if they fail to meet their responsibility for punctuality.

Policies should be clear, concise, and phrased positively. In other words, tell students what they *should* do rather than what they must not do. For example, your classroom civility policy might look something like this:

> Our classroom is a respectful place where all ideas receive equal consideration. Comments to discussions should build upon or react to what a peer has said and provide evidence or a rationale supporting your opinion.

Colleges and universities frequently require that syllabi include common policies such as academic honesty, procedures for adding or dropping a course, information about filing a grievance, and so on. This information should appear on the policy page along with an explanatory sentence and a link to each policy on the institution's web page.

I acknowledge that creating a policy page in your online classroom is not exactly the most engaging task, nor will it be especially interesting for your students, but clear policies and expectations are necessary to a well-run classroom. I've had conversations with faculty in which they frequently insist students "should just know" what they're expected to do or how to behave. That would be marvelous if it were true. However, what's common sense to us might be alien to our students. Their parents and teachers might not have imparted the same standards for manners, civility, self-discipline, or respectful communication that we received in our youth. Students might not know that using "text speak" (idk, lol, l8r, omg, and so on) or emojis is inappropriate in written work or email to their professor. We cannot expect students to live up to our standards unless we communicate those standards intentionally, intelligibly, and accessibly. Students cannot read our minds. They do not know what we want unless we tell them point blank.

We should also bear in mind that stating our expectations once in the Start Here area may not be enough. Directions for discussion boards, for example, should reiterate the communication expectations from the Start Here area. Assignments should link to or repeat the late work policy and feedback expectations. In a sense, we're not doing this for our students, even though this is a student-centered practice. We're also doing it for ourselves because the more clearly and frequently we communicate our expectations, the more likely it is that students will step up and meet them.

Action Steps

1. Add a page to the "Start Here" area and title it "Policies and Expectations."
2. Each of the following topics should be included under its own heading. Use bullet points to improve readability for the student.
   - Instructor's policies for late work, make-up work, and re-submission of work
   - Grading policies
   - Feedback expectations
     - When grades will be posted
     - Where they will receive feedback
   - Expectations for
     - Attendance and participation
     - Communication
     - What the instructor expects from students
     - What students can expect from the instructor
     - How students can provide feedback about the course
     - Netiquette and classroom civility
   - Links to relevant or required university policies
3. Publish the page or mark it as "available" to students.

8. Student Support

The course provides a description, contact information, and links to student support services, including, but not limited to:

- Technology help
- LMS support
- Tutoring services or online tutorials
- Writing center or academic support services
- Library
- Health, wellness, and mental health services
- Office of Disabilities Services (include link to university's accessibility policy)

Colleges and universities offer many services and resources to help students navigate their way through their educational experience. The list of supports in the textbox is only a sample of what might be available at your institution. If more options exist or if you know of external resources that would be helpful, please include them.

This page serves as a one-stop portal for any services students might need. Compose a brief one- or two-sentence description of each service. Include its contact information (phone number, physical location, email address) and a hyperlink to its page on the institution's website. Inserting an image from the resource's web page (such as a photograph of the campus library, for example) is a nice touch, but that's entirely up to you.

I used to take screenshots of each resource's contact information and upload the images to this page. However, after learning more about accessibility requirements, I chose to copy and paste the information instead. Assistive technologies cannot read text embedded in an image, such as a phone number or address, which means we have to type it into the alt-text window accompanying the image. Instead of being a time saver, my former screenshot method made things more difficult, which is why I discontinued that practice.

I usually provide information about how to contact the university's information technologies, help desk, and other available tech support as a downloadable document in addition to the information on this page, and I advise students to print it out and keep it somewhere safe. After all, if the student is having a tech problem, but the only way to find tech help is through the tech that's not working, they're stuck. A paper copy can be a lifesaver if your computer crashes or the LMS is down.

All these supports ought to be readily available on the institution's website. As you build this page, you'll probably need to do a little bit of searching to find these pages, make a note of their contact information, and copy the hyperlinks onto your page. Test each link to be sure it works.

In a perfect world, students would know how to find these things on their own. Some possess this level of self-efficacy, but many do not. Compiling useful information and providing it on an easily accessible page in your course is a student-centered practice that promotes their success. It takes only a few minutes of your time to set up the page initially, but you can then copy the page across any online course you teach. I recommend testing the links periodically to make sure they still work, but otherwise, this is a low-demand strategy with a high-impact benefit for students in need of these services.

Action Steps

1. Add a page to the "Start Here" area and title it "Student Support."
2. Search your institution's website for each of the following, adding more if available.

- Technology help
- LMS support
- Tutoring services or online tutorials
- Writing center or academic support services
- Library
- Health, wellness, and mental health services
- Office of Disabilities Services (also include a link to university's accessibility policy)
- Any other offices or organizations offering student support on or off your campus

3. For each resource you share on this page, create a bullet point or heading with the name of the resource and add the following:
   - Write a one- or two-sentence description of the resource.
   - Include its phone number, physical address or location, and a hyperlink to its web page. The hyperlink could be embedded in the name of the resource or could be placed in a sentence such as, "For more information, visit Student Services," with the link embedded in the words "Student Services."

4. Publish the page or mark it as "available" to students.

9. Technology

The course provides information about all technologies to be utilized, including:

- A clear statement of the course format (all online, hybrid, hyflex, blended, on campus, etc.)
- Minimum hardware, software, and equipment requirements including information on how to obtain required hardware and software
- Explanation of how the varied technologies used in the course support students' achievement of course objectives and outcomes, deliver content, and facilitate active learning, communication, engagement, and collaboration
- List of technological skills and knowledge required for students' success in the course, along with resources such as video tutorials of required skills
- Links to privacy policies and vendor accessibility statements for all technology tools used in the course

Instructor Actions When Setting Up the Page:

- Ensure that students can easily access all tools.
- Remove any unused tools from the course menu.

Online learning is heavily dependent on access to up-to-date technologies. The technology page in the Start Here area lets students know what is required for success.

Course Format: Establishing a course on the LMS doesn't necessarily mean teaching the course entirely online, as we'll discuss in Chapter 4. Students should know the instructor's plans for using this online classroom, including a short explanation of what this means and how it works.

Required Hardware and Software: If either the instructor or the students lack high-speed internet access or don't possess hardware and software sufficient for the course's needs, they cannot participate in the online classroom as intended. Nevertheless, the required minimum technologies for participation should be realistic. Not everyone will be able to upgrade to the latest model computer, but as long as they can use the course website, an older computer is likely to be acceptable. Not all computers have a built-in webcam or microphone for video conferencing, but most students have a smartphone that can do the job. Software requirements should be reasonable, with priority given to free, low-cost, or commonly available programs.

Sometimes an expense is unavoidable, but students will need sufficient advance notice to obtain a required item. For example, I formerly taught an online course with the sole purpose of introducing students to Adobe Creative Cloud software. The college had informed students of purchase requirements for every course upon enrollment, yet it always seemed to come as a shock. I'd inevitably have to send out multiple reminders and provide links to the free trial version of Adobe Creative Cloud that students could download as a stopgap until the low-income students could obtain a voucher from the college to purchase the necessary software. Find out if your institution has any programs that help low-income students obtain necessary technologies, then provide links and explanations to that information on this page. The university may offer software available for free download, such as Microsoft Office 365, as well. Any help we can provide our students in need is worthwhile.

We cannot underestimate the hardships posed by students' inadequate access to the required technologies. I've been in many video conferences where certain participants could not hear or see properly due to spotty Wi-Fi or low bandwidth or where the student was attempting to connect from a noisy or chaotic environment, negatively affecting their ability to learn and participate appropriately. Sadly, this problem affects our non-traditional, low-income, first-generation, and diverse students more acutely than their more affluent and traditionally aged peers. Our institutions proudly say they support access, diversity, equity, and inclusion, but we must hold them accountable to this ideal when it comes to providing for these same students' technology needs. Failing to do so is nothing less than a social justice issue, and it reveals some disturbing implicit biases against our most vulnerable students.

Purpose of Technologies: Whatever technologies we require in our courses should support students' achievement of the course objectives and outcomes, and they should facilitate students' learning by delivering instructional content, promoting active engagement, and fostering communication and collaboration. Fortunately, each of these features is available in the LMS:

- We deliver instructional content through lectures, both synchronous and asynchronous.
- We promote active learning through course activities such as partner discussions or group projects.
- We facilitate engagement through multimedia and discussion.
- We foster communication and collaboration in our discussion boards and group activities.

The technology page of the course's Start Here area should offer a brief explanation of this information.

Literacies and Competencies: Just because students own the necessary technologies doesn't necessarily mean they know how to use them. The technology page should inform students what they should already know and be able to do with regard to technologies used in the course.

Don't assume any technological competency, fluency, literacy, or skill is too basic to mention. I taught an introductory online course in which a few students had never worked with a computer before, which created some interesting dilemmas. For instance, the formatting of a couple of students' discussion posts looked very strange. I couldn't figure out why the text didn't realign properly when I resized the computer window, but then I had a revelation: these students were older adults, so they had learned to type on a typewriter, not a computer. They were hitting the "enter" key at the end of every line of type because they didn't know it was possible to keep typing and let the computer manage the line breaks on its own. Each time I ran into a misunderstanding or missing skill like this, I'd create a quick instructional PowerPoint titled "How to . . ." (convert a document to PDF, insert an image in a document, cite sources in a paper, etc.) and post it for all students. If one student needed the tutorial, I reasoned, more than one other student might benefit from it, too.

Tools: Course tools in the LMS usually work properly, but it's wise to test them just to be certain. Furthermore, many tools or features may be available,

145

but we probably won't use them all. For example, I don't use the "lock-down browser" feature for administering exams. Your ability to remove or hide tools will vary, but if you can do so, it's best to keep the tools menu uncluttered by eliminating irrelevant or unneeded tools.

Links to Privacy and Accessibility Policies: The technology page should also include links to accessibility and privacy policies for all the technologies required in your course. The list begins with the LMS itself and includes things like Zoom, Microsoft Office, YouTube, TurnItIn, Grammarly, or any other websites, programs, or providers you'll use in the course. Students may well ignore these resources, but those concerned with privacy issues and those who have learning difficulties should have access to them.

As with other pages in the Start Here module, bullet points with clear, straightforward text, hyperlinks, and headings or subheadings will help students use this page effectively and understand what they need to have, use, and do in the course.

Action Steps

1. Add a page to the "Start Here" area and title it "Technology."
2. Explain the format the course will use (all online, hybrid, hyflex, blended, on campus, etc.).
3. State the minimum hardware, software, and equipment requirements and include information on obtaining required hardware and software.
4. Explain how the varied technologies used in the course will:
   a. Support students' achievement of course objectives and outcomes.
   b. Deliver content.
   c. Facilitate active learning, communication, engagement, and collaboration.
5. List any technological literacies and competencies required in the course. Attach or link to resources such as video tutorials of required skills.
6. Check the course to make sure all the required tools are easily accessible. Remove or hide any unused tools that might be present in the course menu.
7. Provide links to privacy policies and vendor accessibility statements for all technology tools used in the course.
8. Publish the page or mark it as "available" to students.

Quality Review

The last four Quality Recommendations describe the characteristics and features of a well-designed online course that meets all learners' needs and provides an optimized educational experience. As with previous sections, these descriptions may seem to be quite instructor centered. After all, the instructor is charged with the responsibility of creating a productive and student-centered learning environment. We could think of these Quality Recommendations as a prerequisite activity that facilitates our ability to be student centered as we teach.

---

10. Instructional Materials

Instructional materials used in the course demonstrate the following characteristics:

- Support students' achievement of the course's stated learning objectives and outcomes.
- Demonstrate up-to-date theory and practice in the discipline.
- Correlate with student learning activities.
- Integrate a variety of engaging resources.
- Facilitate communication and collaboration.
- Model expectations for academic integrity by clearly stating copyright or licensing status, permission to share (where applicable), and correct citations or references.
- Minimize students' expenditures for materials associated with learning activities.

We've finally arrived at something that's not part of the Start Here module! We will presume you've already developed all the resources for your course, and they are ready to upload: lectures (slideshows or videos), written instructions for assignments, study guides, supplementary readings, rubrics, checklists, supplementary instructions, and so on. Most learning management systems have organization tools that help you manage all these files. I prefer to organize with folders labeled by types such as lectures, assignments and activities, assessments, and resources. You might just as easily choose to organize your files by module, by week, or in whatever way makes sense to you.

Most learning management systems also have a helpful course builder or developer tool, which usually has an option to upload files. However, keep in mind that there may not be an option to modify or edit files once they're uploaded. If you later decide to change something in one of these files, you may have to delete it from the LMS, upload the edited version, and replace any links you've made to the file within the students' workflow.

Student Achievement and Professional Practice: Double-check your files against the criteria in the textbox earlier in this chapter before you upload them to the LMS. The first question is, "Does this item support students' achievement of the course objectives and outcomes?" If so, the next question is, "Does it reflect up-to-date theory and practice in the discipline?" In academic fields where keeping pace with rapid developments is a basic expectation of professional practice, that may be a rhetorical question. Other fields, however, change more slowly, so practitioners might not stay as current. Furthermore, new information or resources may become available, prompting us to change our plans. When I was creating the Design Thinking course, I learned that a recent update to one of the books I wanted to use, Tim Brown's *Change by Design*, had become available. I updated the syllabus to use the newer edition and rewrote my planned discussion questions to align with the new book.

Correlation with Learning Activities: Next, the relationship between our teaching materials and the course's learning activities should be evident. Nothing in the course should remain unconnected to students' learning. Providing a short explanation or a copy of the course map helps clarify these connections. The purpose behind everything you ask students to do should be obvious and should clearly support the course objectives and outcomes.

Variety and Engagement: Our instructional materials don't just encompass files—they include everything that's included in the LMS: discussion boards, group workspaces, links to external content providers, and more. A well-built course will incorporate a variety of options to promote learning through interpersonal interaction and interesting content.

The quality of our courses exists, in part, in their capacity to engage students in the learning experience beyond listening to lectures, reading textbooks, writing discussion posts, and taking exams. What materials or resources could you incorporate to achieve this goal? Options include synchronous meetings with the whole class, small groups, or one-on-one conversations between students and instructors; virtual field trips and multimedia content; partner or small-group activities; problem-based or project-based learning, experiential learning, and case studies, among others.

Online learning has come a long, long way in the last decade, with more options for engagement than ever before. There's very little reason to limit ourselves to nothing more than text-based asynchronous engagement. Our learning management systems have built-in options for small groups to work together, or students can work with peers via video conferencing technologies. Students can conduct experiential learning in their own neighborhoods or hometowns and share their work with their peers through video posts to a discussion board. Of course, your choices should be suited to your course's topic and your disciplinary norms, but we can adapt almost any strategy for engaged learning in a face-to-face classroom to the online learning environment.

Academic Honesty: When we're teaching face to face, many of us adopt a somewhat casual attitude toward providing proper attributions for the images or references we insert into our slideshows because no one is likely to examine our instructional materials very closely. Online, our content is more accessible to external audiences, so we should exercise due diligence in following the norms of academic honesty. Just because something exists online does not make it fair game. Check for permissions before you use something you find online and follow the rules appropriate to your discipline and in accordance with US copyright laws and the Fair Use Doctrine. Your adherence to the standards of academic integrity sets a good example for your students.

Associated Expenses: Lastly, be sensitive to the costs associated with any materials or equipment students will be required to use or actions they must perform. As we said earlier, many students experience financial hardships and may not be able to afford pricey supplies. It's perfectly fine to recommend a preferred brand of something students must purchase for your course, but you should also invite students to contact you if they cannot obtain the item. For example, a photojournalism course I taught years ago required students to shoot a photo essay about a community event. One of the students found a county fair to use as his subject, but because he had no money for the modest entry fee, he chose to shoot his photos over the fence surrounding the fairgrounds, with predictably disappointing results. I offered him a chance to redo the project, suggesting options with no associated fees. Eventually, he was able to resubmit successful work and achieve a better grade. Our willingness to work with students to find a reasonable solution when one of our requirements is beyond their reach demonstrates empathy and models a student-centered teaching philosophy. Furthermore, it exhibits our commitment to ensuring access, diversity, equity, and inclusion.

Action Steps

1. Check all your files to ensure you have proper citations, have received permission, or have provided the correct attributions for anything you've quoted, paraphrased, or borrowed.
2. Verify that all the materials you use in the course directly support students' achievement of the course objectives and outcomes. If something does not contribute to this purpose, consider removing it from the course.
3. Upload and organize your course files in the LMS.
4. Check to be sure your course contains varied activities and resources to support student engagement, collaboration, and communication.

5. I recommend that you note how you have met the criteria and where your course provides evidence of these quality indicators. These notes are quite helpful when discussing your course with your director, chair, or dean.

---

11. Course Content, Activities, and Interaction

The course content, including learning activities, and interaction, demonstrates the following characteristics:

- Promotes students' achievement of the course's stated learning objectives and outcomes.
- Develops students' higher-order thinking and core competencies such as critical thinking, problem solving, reflection, and analysis.
- Includes activities that link to real-world application of the discipline (e.g., experiential learning, case studies, problem-based activities).
- Provides opportunities for interaction:
  - Peer to peer.
  - Student to instructor.
  - Student to content.
- Incorporates active learning, collaboration, and peer-to-peer sharing of knowledge and resources.
- Demonstrates logical organization and follows a clear progression from the beginning to the end of the course.
- Provides instructions that clarify where to find necessary resources and how to use them to complete assignments, activities, or assessments.
- Associates every graded item with clear written directions and includes a rubric, checklist, or other transparent grading criteria.
- States all due dates and submission requirements clearly and makes these evident in the instructions for each graded item.

Your course's quality is reflected in the activities, assignments, and assessments you expect your students to complete, not just in the content of your direct instruction. It's possible (but not advisable) to teach a course in which all instruction is conveyed through lecture, the only activities are reading and studying, and the only assessments are a midterm and a final exam. Perhaps you sat through a course or two like this when you were a student. Do you remember anything about these courses other than the fact that they were dull? Do you recall anything about the course content? Did you learn anything of lasting value? My guess is, probably not.

Active Learning: Best practice in curricular and pedagogical design sets the bar higher. Our classrooms should be rich environments for discovery and engagement where students are active participants in the learning process, not passive recipients of transmitted knowledge. Lectures continue to have their place, but so do discussions, small-group interactions, project-based and problem-based learning, and teamwork. Students should have both voice and choice, selecting learning options that best suit their preferences or goals. As we build our courses online, we might consider the work of educational researcher M. David Merrill, a leader in Instructional Design theory and practice. Merrill explains two dimensions of instructional design: content and performance. Our courses' content includes the facts, processes, procedures, and principles present in the course that we want to convey to our students. Performance occurs when our students engage with that content and respond by using, finding, or remembering a concept. Merrill also emphasizes that sound instructional design should include demonstration of what students must learn or do, application of course content to the student's life, and problem-centered tasks that are relevant and meaningful, engaging students in active learning.[57] (We will examine some of these ideas in our discussion of High-Impact Practices.)

Module Content: Use the Course Builder tool to create an introductory page for each module listing the module objectives and their relationship to the course objectives and outcomes. This page should provide an overview of the module in the order that students must complete each component. I hyperlink the title of every item to the course area where it exists or to necessary files. Students can navigate by clicking on those links or following the regular workflow path by clicking the arrows (or other navigation tools, depending on the LMS) on each page.

Minimally, a module will include one or more items in each of the following categories:

- **Direct instruction**—examples: synchronous or asynchronous lectures, readings, videos, multimedia links
- **Active learning components**—examples: projects, group or partner activities, case studies
- **Interaction**—examples: whole-class, partner, or small-group discussions, either synchronous or asynchronous
- **Assignments**—examples: practice problems, reading responses, essays, research papers, précis, analyses
- **Assessment**—examples: quiz, exam, reflective essay

The examples in the preceding categories are not exhaustive. Furthermore, a single item can exist across multiple categories. Students might complete an

151

assignment and then post it to a discussion board where they critique one another's work, and the assignment's grade could assess the quality of their work on the assignment, their peer interactions, and the quality of their analysis of their peers' work. Thus, one assignment fulfills three categories while also providing a way to meet the module's objective.

Higher-Order Thinking: If our course objectives and outcomes use active verbs for higher-order thinking, our course content should support this goal as well. Just so, we should forge intentional connections between our course and applications to our discipline outside the classroom. Tasks involving critical thinking, analysis, problem solving, reflection, evaluation, synthesis, creativity, and application of learning to real-world contexts are more engaging for students and provide instructors with a more complete picture of their learning.

Interaction: The online classroom should foster peer-to-peer interaction, which helps build connections and a feeling of community that students value highly. Discussion boards contribute to this goal, as do activities involving partners or small groups. We should encourage students to share resources and information and to help each other when problems arise. Each module of the Design Thinking course includes a "Questions and Answers" discussion where students can solve problems together. I built a collaborative workspace for each case study group to use as well. Student-to-instructor interaction takes place through course announcements, email, messaging technologies, and feedback on assignments. Student-to-content interaction occurs through lectures, assignments, and activities. In a sense, we could see everything about the online classroom as a form of interaction.

Instructions: As you're building each module, remember that every learning activity should be accompanied by a set of clear instructions that tell students what they must do, how they should do it, where they can find the necessary resources, when it is due, how it will be assessed, and how much it is worth in the course's grading scheme. I recommend placing this information in a document that students can download when it's time to do the assignment or activity, besides typing it into the page where the assignment or activity exists within the course.

Organization: Arrange all the items you add to each module in a clear and logical order so that students can proceed through them without having to jump forward or double back when they need something. Whenever I mention a resource, document, or area of the course, I hyperlink its name or title with its location in the LMS. My goal is to make course navigation as simple and easy for the students as possible. I don't like to hunt for the things I need, so I can't imagine my students enjoy it, either. It's another instance of using design thinking in support of a student-centered mindset.

Action Steps

1. Use this checklist to determine whether your course meets the quality recommendations for course activities.
   - All learning activities promote students' achievement of the course objectives and outcomes.
   - Course activities develop students' higher-order thinking and core competencies, such as critical thinking, problem solving, reflection, and analysis.
   - The course includes activities that link to real-world applications of the discipline.
   - Activities promote peer-to-peer, student-to-instructor, and student-to-content interaction.
   - The course incorporates active learning, collaboration, and peer-to-peer sharing of knowledge and resources.
   - Content is organized logically and follows a clear progression.
   - Instructions clarify where to find the necessary resources and how to use them.
   - Every graded item is associated with clear instructions and transparent grading criteria.
   - Due dates and submission requirements are clear and evident.
2. Take note of examples in the course that demonstrate how you have met these recommendations. These notes don't have to be uploaded to the course, but they're useful when speaking about the course with your program director, chair, or dean.
3. If you cannot check off any of these recommendations, consider what changes you could make to the course to optimize your students' online learning experience.

---

12. Online Environment Design
The online environment of the course is well designed and demonstrates the following characteristics:

- Frequently used tools are apparent and convenient.
- Navigation and learning paths are evident and intuitive.
- Page layouts are consistent and uncluttered.
- Color schemes and icons are consistent on all pages.
- Related content is organized together.
- Large blocks of information are divided into manageable sections.

■ All instructions are clear, well written, and free from grammatical and spelling errors.

A well-designed online environment creates a more pleasant experience for every user. Conversely, poor design can make users miserable. During my research, I've accessed several hundred college and university websites, so I believe I'm somewhat qualified to offer an educated opinion on the impact of poor website design. For instance, nearly all institutions of higher learning provide a search tool, usually at the top of the home page, which is also standard practice across many fields beyond higher education. However, some sites hide this tool or bury it in a menu somewhere, which can be very frustrating for the user. Cluttered or visually chaotic pages also confuse or annoy users. (I particularly dislike sites that use atypical scrolling, such as a background that scrolls at a different rate than the text.) Just because the site developer believes that a feature "looks really cool" doesn't mean it makes a good impression on visitors.

Instructors don't have complete authority over the LMS, but we can usually control the appearance and content of the pages in our online classrooms. A visitor's first impression should be of an organized, appealing, and interesting place where students feel comfortable and expect to have a successful learning experience. This description might be especially true of the course home page because it is the first thing students see. For the Design Thinking course's home page, I wanted to include an image of some kind to enhance the page's visual appeal. However, I did not want to use one of my own photographs, nor did I want to purchase a stock photo. I considered using a well-known visual representation of the five steps of design thinking from Stanford University's d.school, but I was unsure about its copyright status. Therefore, I created a graphic element using the "smart art" tools in Microsoft Word, adjusting it to match the color scheme I'd selected for the online classroom.

As you create the pages in your online classroom, choose one design template, and stick to it on every page. Use the same layout, same font, same colors, same size of text, and the same tools in the same places. One page shouldn't have bright blue 16-point text in Ariel and the next have 24-point dark orange text in Times New Roman. Break large blocks of text into smaller pieces. Use headings and subheadings to facilitate understanding.

Like the previous section's recommendations, consider the flow of information from one page of the course to the next. Information should be grouped logically, preferably in modules. The students' learning path or workflow should be effortless and intuitive. We want our students to focus on learning, not struggle to find what they need or where to go within the course.

Last, be sure to proofread all the content and pages in your course. We notice our students' errors and are quick to mention them. We set a poor example when we don't adhere to the same standards ourselves.

Action Steps

1. Use this checklist to determine whether your course meets the quality recommendations for the online environment's design.
   - Frequently used tools are apparent and convenient.
   - Navigation and learning paths are evident and intuitive.
   - Page layouts are consistent and uncluttered.
   - The color scheme and icons are consistent on all pages.
   - Related content is organized together.
   - Large blocks of information are divided into manageable sections.
   - All instructions are clear, well written, and free from grammatical and spelling errors.
2. Take note of examples in the course that demonstrate how you have met these recommendations. These notes don't have to be uploaded to the course, but they're useful when speaking about the course with your program director, chair, or dean.
3. If you cannot check off one or more of these recommendations, consider what changes you could make to the course to create an optimized online learning experience for your students.

---

13. Readability
All text-based materials in the course fulfill standards for readability, including:

- Sufficient contrast between text and background.
- Formatting uses titles, headings, and other visual organization.
- Sans-serif font of no less than 12 points.
- Absence of flashing or blinking text.
- Slideshow formatting also ensures readability:
  - Slides use a predefined slide layout.
  - Slides have unique titles.
  - Transitions between slides are simple and non-automatic.
  - Slides adhere to readability requirements.

Readability standards are part of the online environment's design, but they also apply to any written materials such as documents or slideshows you've included in your course. Many of us enjoy exercising our creativity when making pages of all types: electronic, printed, and projected; however, the online classroom might not afford as much freedom of expression as some of us prefer—that is, if we're keeping our students' needs in mind.

As we discussed earlier concerning ADA requirements, all text should offer high contrast, with a preference for dark type on a light background. Formatting that uses titles, headings, or other means of visually organizing the content helps the reader, too. Sans-serif fonts such as Arial, Calibri, Verdana, or Tahoma are the easiest to read, and we should avoid embellished fonts (script, handwriting, calligraphy, curls, etc.) except as small accent elements. As much as we might enjoy jazzing up our presentations or web pages with animations, flashing or blinking elements, or showy transitions between slides, these elements don't serve our students' online learning needs very well.

Slideshows should adhere to the same readability requirements as web pages or documents, just as they should follow the concepts of good design we discussed in the previous section. Use a consistent slide layout and design template across all the slideshows in the course. Ensure that every slide has a unique title to facilitate navigation and ease of use with screen-reading devices. Use manual transitions between slides so that individuals with faster or slower reading rates don't become frustrated by the pace you set.

Most of the criteria on the following checklist are quite basic and evident. Perhaps the main takeaway for this standard is just to keep everything in your online course clean and simple.

Action Steps

1. Use this checklist to determine whether your course meets the quality recommendations for readability.
   - Is there sufficient contrast between text and background?
   - Have you used titles, headings, and other visual organization methods?
   - Did you choose a sans-serif font of no less than 12 points?
   - Is there any flashing or blinking text?
   - Do all the slideshows:
     - Use a predefined slide layout?
     - Include unique titles on all slides?
     - Use simple, non-automatic transitions between slides?
     - Adhere to the same readability requirements as documents and web pages in the course?

2. Take note of examples in the course that demonstrate how you have met these recommendations. These notes don't have to be uploaded to the course, but they're useful when speaking about the course with your program director, chair, or dean.

3. If you cannot check off one or more of these recommendations, consider what changes you could make to the course to create an optimized online learning experience for your students.

14. Access for Diverse Learners

The course ensures access for diverse learners consistent with the requirements of the Americans with Disabilities Act:

- Text is the primary means of conveying information. All text is:
    - Available in easily accessed format (HTML preferred).
    - Readable by assistive technology, including PDF files and text contained in images.
- Information is displayed as in-line text rather than tables whenever possible.
- Tables are accompanied by a title, header rows, and a summary description.
- All visual elements in the course are understandable when viewed without color.
- A text equivalent for every non-text element is provided (alt-text tags, captions, transcripts, etc.) in all documents, files, LMS pages, multimedia, and web pages.
- Visual presentations include audio narration (recommended).
- Hyperlinks are descriptive and make sense out of context (avoid "click here").
- Students are informed of assessments with time limits and provided sufficient lead time to arrange accommodations.

If a student in a face-to-face course were visually impaired, hearing impaired, or used a wheelchair, the instructor would be required to make accommodations to provide the student with equal access to the learning taking place in the classroom. Nevertheless, few instructors plan every on-campus course around future students with special needs. We make adjustments only after enrolling a student with special needs, consistent with the common practice of managing face-to-face courses using a just-in-time model.

On the other hand, we've all seen how our campus buildings include features such as wheelchair ramps, doors with push-button operation, elevators, and Braille markings on signage to provide equitable access to everyone regardless of their physical limitations, even when there are few such members of our campus community. Likewise, our online classrooms must anticipate future students' needs before a special-needs student appears on our course roster.

In theory, modifications are easy to understand. Visually impaired students learn by hearing, so any of our courses' visual components must be compatible with screen reading devices that turn text into speech. Deaf and hard-of-hearing students learn by seeing, so any audio files (such as videos) should also have a written transcript, turning speech to text. We might look at it this way: students should hear what they can see and see what they can hear—both audio and visual versions of the same content must be present.

Our first steps toward accessibility are things we've already covered—making our documents, presentations, and course pages clean, easy to read, and consistent. One additional consideration is to embed as much of our content in HTML (web pages) as possible instead of (or in addition to) attaching files. We should also check to be sure that our documents are understandable with or without color. It's not difficult to check to see if a visual element remains legible when converted to grayscale. This recommendation applies mainly to pie charts, bar graphs, or other visual elements with color-coded data. A few small adjustments may be all that's necessary to meet this standard.

Screen-reader software and devices are a boon for visually impaired students, but they have certain limitations that require tweaks to our course components. First, screen readers can't interpret images. Editing tools in the software we use to create documents and slideshows (Microsoft Office, Google Docs, Google Slides, Apple Pages, etc.) allow us to attach an "alt-tag" or "alt-text" to any visual element, including charts, graphs, drawings, photographs, and screenshots. Alt-tags are simply a brief written description of what is portrayed by the image. Tables are generally made of text, but the screen reader can't always make sense of them. Therefore, tables should include a title, a header row, and a description of what's in the table either before or after the table itself. Next, some visual elements look like text but function as images. For example, screenshots may visually portray text but can't be read by assistive technologies, and the same is true of photographs of signs, memes, and some PDF documents. Each of these elements needs a text-based alternative for students using screen reader technologies. Finally, hyperlinks pose another problem for visually impaired students. Instead of pasting the full URL onto the page, take a moment to hyperlink an understandable portion of the text. For instance, if I want to direct students to a particular file contained within the course, I'll hyperlink the name of the file because a phrase like "Design Project Instructions" is more understandable than "click here."

Deaf and hard-of-hearing students benefit from visual presentations, but they also require a transcript or text-based version of the presentation. If you've made a slideshow and simply recorded yourself reading the slides aloud, then a transcript isn't necessary because you already have both words and text. Audio, video, and multimedia files such as video comments to a discussion board can prove somewhat more complicated.

In a video of your course lecture in which you used your slides only as a reference, you would deliver the bulk of your instruction by speaking to your students. Therefore, you should provide a transcript of your spoken words. There are many ways to do this, but we'll mention three here.

Option 1 is to upload the video to YouTube, where you can use the website's features to create a transcript somewhat automatically.[38] This method is not foolproof. The software does not always understand what you've said, so you'll need to read and edit the transcript to be sure it's accurate. The process is also somewhat time consuming, depending on the speed of your internet connection. The transcript may take several hours to appear.

Option 2 is Google Docs's option for "Voice Typing" in the "Tools" menu.[39] This feature works best if you stay in a very quiet room and speak directly to your computer using a headset. It's also possible to play your lecture audio through the computer's speakers and have Voice Typing create the transcript.

1. Open Google Docs.
2. Start a new document.
3. Select Voice Typing in the Tools drop-down menu.
4. Play the lecture video with sound and click on the microphone icon ("click to speak") on Google Docs.

As with YouTube transcription, this will not automatically yield a perfect replication of your words. You'll need to monitor the process as it happens because Google Docs is known to stop working for no particular reason, so you have to restart the voice-typing function.[40] If there is any noise in the background, the software will not produce an accurate transcription. As with YouTube, you'll need to edit the transcript before sharing it with students.

Option 3 is Microsoft Translator,[41] which appears to be the most comprehensive solution at present. This app will provide closed captioning for Power-Point presentations, class discussions, and other interactive components of the online classroom. It functions like a speech-to-text equivalent of a screen reader, but instead of converting text to speech, it converts speech to text.

159

Finally, students come to us with more than physical disabilities. Many students have Individual Education Plans (IEPs) due to anxiety or learning disabilities, providing documented accommodations such as extended time for assignments or an oral reader for exams. Instructors cannot provide accommodations to all students, but it's important to know how to make these arrangements when students inform you that their IEP gives them these rights. Be sure to inform students of the dates for major exams, especially those with time limits, so they can self-advocate and work with you to meet their legal accommodations.

Like you, I'm still learning about these options, but given the exponential growth of technology, spurred by the necessity for alternatives to traditional face-to-face instruction, I have to imagine that new assistive technologies will continue to emerge. Until then, each of us must make a good-faith effort to help our students with learning challenges and take the steps that are within our power to demonstrate our student-centered mindset.

Action Steps

1. Use this checklist to determine whether your course meets the quality recommendations for accessibility.
   - Is text the primary means of conveying information?
   - Is all text available in an easily accessed format (HTML preferred)?
   - Is all text readable by assistive technology, including PDF files and text contained in images?
   - Is information displayed as in-line text rather than tables whenever possible?
   - Are all tables accompanied by a title and summary description?
   - Are all visual elements in the course understandable when viewed without color?
   - Have you provided a text equivalent for every non-text element in your course (alt-text tags, captions, transcripts, etc.) across all documents, files, LMS pages, multimedia, and web pages?
   - Do all visual presentations include audio narration (recommended)?
   - Are hyperlinks descriptive, and do they make sense when read out of context (avoid "click here")?
   - Have you informed students of assessments, particularly those with time limits, and provided sufficient lead time to arrange accommodations?
2. Take note of examples in the course that demonstrate how you have met these recommendations. These notes don't have to be uploaded to the course, but they're useful when speaking about the course with your program director, chair, or dean.

3. If you cannot check off one or more of these recommendations, consider how you might change the course to meet all learners' needs, regardless of ability.

PUTTING IT ALL TOGETHER

Now that we know what a high-quality online course entails, we're prepared to build it in the LMS. Every system is different, and each of us is subject to the requirements of our various programs, departments, schools, colleges, and universities. Nevertheless, we can apply what we've learned in this chapter, adapting it to our particular circumstances to design and build the best course possible.

Step 1: Upload Files

I started building the Design Thinking course from a folder containing all the files and documents I had already developed. I opened the "manage files" feature in the Course Builder menu and created folders into which I placed my content. I put the lecture PowerPoints in the Lectures folder; student resources, grading rubrics, instructions for assignments, and all other Word docs or PDFs in the Documents folder; and I set up a folder for HTML files (called "pages" in Canvas).

Step 2: Create Modules and Build Content

Then I opened a new module in the course builder tool and titled it "Start Here" so I could create all the required content we discussed earlier in this chapter, including:

- Welcome from the Instructor
- Meet & Greet Discussion
- About the Instructor
- Course Orientation
- Objectives and Outcomes
- Overview of Activities, Assignments, and Assessments
- Policies and Expectations
- Student Support
- Technology
- Start Here Quiz

Most of the content for these pages was already present in my syllabus and course outline, but some areas needed additional explanation to make sure I'd covered everything. I also modified the order and content of the pages in the Start Here module so the course would conform to my institution's requirements. (This is why you may observe some differences in terminology as you view the tables that follow.)

Then I opened three new modules for my course content, adding the pages, assignments, discussions, and quizzes as needed. The following tables show what all the modules looked like when I was finished building my content.

Start Here

Content Type	Content Title
Course page	Start Here To-Do List
Course page	About the Course
Course page	About the Instructor
Course page	How to Navigate the Course
Link to Course File	Syllabus
Course page	Course Outline
Course page	Outcomes, Objectives, and Assessments
Course page	Policies and Expectations
Course page	Grading Policy
Link to Course File	Course Calendar
Course page	Exams Overview
Course page	Student Support
Course page	Technology
Discussion	Start Here Comments, Questions, and Answers
Quiz	Start Here Quiz
Checklist	Start Here Checklist

Module 1—What Is Design Thinking?

Content Type	Content Title
Course page	Module 1 Introduction and To-Do List

Content Type	Content Title
Discussion	Module 1 Comments, Questions, and Answers
Link to Course File	Lecture 1A-Introduction to Design Thinking
Discussion	Introduce Yourself Discussion
Link to Course File	Lecture 1B-The Wallet Project
Assignment	Wallet Project Assignment
Link to Course File	Reading Journal Instructions
Discussion	Reading Journal 1 Discussion
Assignment	Reading Journal 1 Submission
Link to Course File	Lecture 2-People, Process, and Products
Discussion	Reading Journal 2 Discussion
Assignment	Reading Journal 2 Submission
Checklist	Module 1 Checklist

Module 2—Case Studies in Design Thinking

Content Type	Content Title
Course page	Module 2 Introduction and To-Do List
Discussion	Module 2 Comments, Questions, and Answers
Link to Course File	Lecture 3–4 Case 1
Course page	Case Study Instructions
Link to Course File	Case Report Form
Discussion	Reading Journal 3 Discussion
Assignment	Reading Journal 3 Submission
Quiz	Midterm Exam
Discussion	Case 1 Discussion
Assignment	Case 1 Report

Content Type	Content Title
Link to Course File	Lecture 5–6 Case 2
Discussion	Case 2 Discussion
Assignment	Case 2 Report
Checklist	Module 2 Checklist

Module 3—Design Yourself

Content Type	Content Title
Course page	Module 3 Introduction and To-Do List
Discussion	Module 3 Comments, Questions, and Answers
Link to Course File	Lecture 7A-Design Your Life Pt.1
Link to Course File	Lecture 7B-Design Your Life Pt. 2
Course page	Design Project Instructions
Discussion	Reading Journal 4 Discussion
Assignment	Reading Journal 4 Submission
Discussion	Design Project Pt. 1-Presentation
Assignment	Design Project Pt. 2-Reflective Essay
Quiz	Final Exam Pt. 1
Assignment	Final Exam Pt. 2
Checklist	Module 3 Checklist

When students open any of these modules, the first thing they see is the Introduction and To-Do List, which tells them everything they must do in the order they must complete it. The list also includes tasks not present in the LMS, such as reading assignments and attendance at synchronous meetings. A screenshot of the Module 1 Introduction and To-Do list follows.[42] Underlined text is hyperlinked to items elsewhere in the course. Therefore, students can complete the module by returning to this page and clicking on the hyperlinks to each item, or they can navigate with the arrow tools that appear at the top and bottom of each page.

Every time I build a course, no matter how well prepared I am, I discover additional information I need to include, decide to create supplementary pages of instruction that I think will help students, or choose to modify things that worked well face to face but that won't be as successful online. Uploading a course isn't just a pedagogical task—it's a design challenge. We undertake a process that sometimes feels like we're taking two steps forward and one step back, shaping and molding, adjusting and editing, until all the components are in place.

Step 3: Check and Adjust

Once I think everything is ready, I switch from the instructor view to the student view and click through each module to make sure the flow of information makes sense, everything is visible, there are no mistakes, and there's nothing left that I think I should adjust, clarify, or modify. Perfectionist that I am, I always find things to change. Be careful when you do this, however. We can edit an HTML document (a.k.a. a page in the course) without removing the page from the students' workflow. However, making a change to a file (a document, slideshow, handout, etc.) means removing the file, making the edits, uploading the corrected copy, and then checking the entire module again to locate and repair any hyperlinks to that file. In another course, I discovered that the LMS automatically

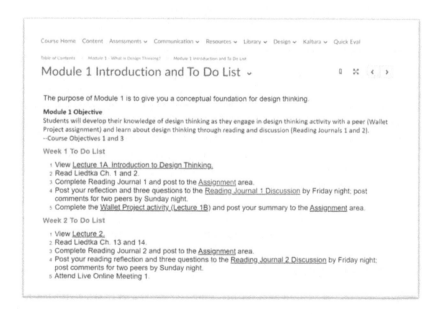

FIGURE 3.1 Design Thinking Module 1 Introduction and To-Do List

converted my PowerPoint lectures into PDFs. However, when I scrolled through the course using "student view," I was dismayed to see that some slides' content had shifted. Textboxes or headings covered images, hyperlinks were illegible, and things just didn't look right. However, when I converted the files to PDF before uploading them to the LMS, everything displayed exactly as I'd created it. You can probably guess what happened next: I converted all my lecture PowerPoints into PDFs, uploaded all the PDF lectures to the LMS, and redid every single link to the lectures in the student workflow.

Authenticity and Intellectual Risk Taking

Will there still be errors even after the course appears to be complete? Of course! Furthermore, students inevitably find them and bring them to our attention. That's why we should remember: each time we teach a course, it's a prototype for the next time we teach it. The course's "maiden voyage" (so to speak) will reveal snags and glitches no matter how diligent, meticulous, and thorough we've been. When students alert me to a problem, I thank them. It takes a courageous student to point out an instructor's mistakes! Then I resolve the problem and email all the students about what happened.

None of us has godlike powers of perfection. Being authentic and allowing students to see that we're human and fallible helps them feel safe taking risks and making mistakes, too. That's the real work of learning: "Intellectual risk-taking is an essential aspect of higher education. Risk-taking is a cornerstone of innovation, lifelong learning critical thinking, and moral and ethical development" (Rowman and Littlefield, 2017).[43] I believe instructors must model intellectual risk taking by trying new instructional activities, whether online or on campus. We should not fear being "wrong" or something not going exactly as planned. Fictional educator Ms. Frizzle, of the 1990s PBS animated television series *The Magic School Bus*, often encouraged her students to "Take chances, make mistakes, and get messy."[44] As instructors, we might resist this advice, especially if we prefer the tried and true. We think mistakes are embarrassing, and we don't find messiness to be at all charming. I feel that way myself, sometimes. It's hard to grow beyond our comfort zones! The opportunity to embrace the risk of trying something new by building all our course content online opens an array of instructional options that might be much more rewarding than we'd have dreamed when staying on the familiar, safe path of face-to-face on-campus instruction alone.

MOVING FORWARD

Without a doubt, creating a high-quality online course is a *lot* of work. It's hard to envision every detail of our instruction, find or develop all the materials we will need, and create varied and engaging learning experiences for our students—and all before the first day of class. We definitely need grit and a growth mindset to make it work.

Circumstances beyond our control forced us to convert our face-to-face courses to an online format in a tremendous hurry, leaving us no time to plan, prepare, or attempt best practices in online course design. We jumped into Zoom, WebEx, and other platforms for synchronous instructional delivery, modified our course content, and adapted our instruction to our new circumstances. We made it work. Nevertheless, these emergency measures were never supposed to be a permanent solution. We might compare it to blowing out a tire while on a cross-country road trip and installing the spare tire by the side of the road. The spare will take us to our destination, but if we don't buy and install a new tire as soon as possible, we risk permanently damaging the vehicle. Likewise, we can't teach online long term using only emergency measures. I've spoken to faculty who rather enjoyed working from home and say they would prefer to continue teaching this way, especially if conditions on campus could put their health at risk. At the same time, they refuse to learn how to use the LMS properly. Unfortunately, we can't have our cake and eat it, too. If we're going to be prepared to teach online, we have to build excellent courses online. Failing to do so shortchanges our students; furthermore, it poses a significant risk for our institutions because dissatisfied students have a distressing tendency to leave college.

I'd like to reiterate that I am adamantly *not* advocating for a shift to all-online learning, nor am I in favor of discontinuing face-to-face instruction. I prefer to teach on campus, and I know it's a superior form of instruction for many reasons. Nevertheless, *building* a course online does not—*at all*—mean we must *teach* it online. The point is to be prepared to pivot between different instructional delivery models by placing all our course content online before the first day of class (or at least as much of our content as possible).

Developing a course is an act of advanced creativity, utilizing equal parts disciplinary expertise and competence in teaching. Moreover, many of us perform this labor in relative isolation while we're also teaching our current course load, meeting our obligations for service to the institution, and maintaining our research or creative practice—a daunting challenge, to be sure. We're having this conversation *because you care* enough to strive for more—to investigate ways to improve your teaching practice so you can provide your students with the best possible educational experience. In doing so, you're demonstrating grit, a growth mindset, and an admirably student-centered teaching philosophy. You're placing your students' success ahead of your own convenience. Comprehensive Instructional Design is neither quick nor easy, but it is the mindful, caring, and student-centered approach our students need from us. I'm very impressed that you've begun this journey.

In the next chapter, we'll examine the range of options available to us once we've established our course in the LMS. I'd also like to refer you to the Appendix

167

Design Connection	
Empathize	•Your students deserve the best educational experience it is within your power to provide. Designing your course for online delivery - even if you will teach it face-to-face on campus - expands your options and allows you to prioritize your students' success. Access to the entire course in the LMS is a matter of empathy and access, supporting all learners' needs.
Define	•Your course may (or may not) not be subject to official quality review, but choosing to employ an evaluative tool such as Quality Matters, OSCQR or the Quality Recommendations presented in this chapter allows you to analyze and define the quality of the course you have designed.
Ideate	•When you build a new course online or adapt an existing course for online delivery, you can expect to invest a considerable amount of creative energy. Use strategies for empathy and ideation as you prepare content that delivers the requisite instruction while also exhibiting best practices in pedagogical and curricular design aligned with quality standards.
Prototype	•The course you design becomes a prototype. The Quality Recommendations checklist allows you to self-evaluate that prototype before you release it to students. Even if you don't teach the course online, building the course online prepares you and your students for success across various instructional models.
Test	•The test of your course design occurs when you teach it. Following the Quality Recommendations in this chapter will help ensure that your course meets your institution's standards and expectations, which we could see as another type of successful test.

FIGURE 3.2 Chapter 3 Design Connection

for a **Quality Recommendations Checklist** you may find helpful as you design your course.

Notes

[1] Associated Press. (2005, September 3). Katrina forces Tulane to cancel fall semester. *NBC News*. Retrieved from www.nbcnews.com/id/9181647/ns/us_news-education/t/katrina-forces-tulane-cancel-fall-semester/#.XvsHNGhKg2w

[2] Meyer, K., & Wilson, J. (2011). The role of online learning in emergency plans of flagship institutions. *Online Journal of Distance Learning Administration, IV*(I). Retrieved from www.westga.edu/~distance/ojdla/spring141/meyer_wilson141.html

[3] D2L (Desire 2 Learn) is an educational software and technology firm that created the learning management system Brightspace. Some colleges and universities began using

D2L prior to the launch of Brightspace, so their LMS may be known by either name. For our purposes, we will refer to Brightspace since this is the name that D2L calls their LMS (www.d2l.com/).

[4] Lovell, J. (2006). *"Houston, we've had a problem." Apollo expeditions to the moon.* National Aeronautics and Space Administration. Retrieved from https://history.nasa.gov/SP-350/ch-13-4.html

[5] As I'm an admitted science fiction fan, I hope the reader will forgive these occasional illustrations.

[6] Lovell, J. (n.d.). Houston, we've had a problem. Apollo expeditions to the moon. Chapter 13.1. History. *National Aeronautics and Space Administration.* Retrieved from https://history.nasa.gov/SP-350/ch-13-1.html#:~:text=With%20the%20wisdom%20of%20hindsight,million%20failure%20of%20Apollo%2013

[7] Counseling Center, University of South Florida. (2020). *Statement on diversity and social justice.* Retrieved from www.usf.edu/student-affairs/counseling-center/what-we-do/statement-on-diversity.aspx

[8] Canvas. (2020). *What are modules?* Retrieved from https://community.canvaslms.com/docs/DOC-10735

[9] Wiley Education Services Center for Teaching and Learning. (2020). *Modular course design.* Retrieved from https://ctl.wiley.com/modular-course-design/

[10] Boise State University. (n.d.). *Modular course design benefits instructors and students. Using a module approach to course design. IDEA shop. Teaching with technology: A primer on course design.* Retrieved from www.boisestate.edu/ctl-idea/teaching-with-tech/primer/using-a-modular-approach-to-course-design/

[11] Boise State University. (n.d.). *IDEA shop. Teaching with technology: A primer on course design.*

[12] McAlvage, K., & Rice, M. (2018). *Access and accessibility in online learning.* Online Learning Consortium. Resource Center for Digital Learning and Leadership. Retrieved from https://files.eric.ed.gov/fulltext/ED593920.pdf; see also Rabidoux, S., & Rottmann, A. (2017). 5 Tips for ADA-compliant inclusive design. *Inside Higher Ed.* Retrieved from www.insidehighered.com/digital-learning/views/2017/05/03/tips-designing-ada-compliant-online-courses#:~:text=The%20Americans%20with%20Disability%20Act,course%2C%20which%20can%20be%20challenging

[13] Centre for Excellence in Universal Design. (2020). *What is universal design?* National Disability Authority of Ireland. Retrieved from http://universaldesign.ie/What-is-Universal-Design/

[14] The Principles of Universal Design. (2008). *North Carolina State University Center for Universal Design.* Retrieved from https://projects.ncsu.edu/ncsu/design/cud/pubs_p/docs/poster.pdf

[15] Peterson, J. (2015). *Smashing barriers to access: Disability activism and curb cuts.* National Museum of American History. Retrieved from https://americanhistory.si.edu/blog/smashing-barriers-access-disability-activism-and-curb-cuts

[16] When used in reference to assessment, *objective* indicates quiz or exam questions with defined right and wrong answers as opposed to subjective questions with open-ended qualitative answers.

[17] Canvas. (2020). *Create quiz. Canvas instructor guide.* Retrieved from https://community.canvaslms.com/docs/DOC-10460-canvas-instructor-guide-table-of-contents#-jive_content_id_Quizzes; Brightspace Help. (2020). *Create a quiz.* Retrieved from https://documentation.brightspace.com/EN/le/quizzes/instructor/create_quiz.htm; Blackboard. (2020). *Test or survey options.* Retrieved from https://help.blackboard.com/Learn/Instructor/Tests_Pools_Surveys/Test_and_Survey_Options

[18] Shuffle order of quiz questions:

In Brightspace: https://documentation.brightspace.com/EN/le/quizzes/instructor/create_quiz.htm

In Canvas: https://community.canvaslms.com/thread/3919

In Blackboard: https://help.blackboard.com/Learn/Instructor/Tests_Pools_Surveys/Reuse_Questions/Random_Block

[19] Illinois State University Department of Education. (2002). *Revised Bloom's Taxonomy—question starters.* Retrieved from https://education.illinoisstate.edu/downloads/casei/5-02-Revised%20Blooms.pdf; Grinnell School District. (n.d.). *Higher order thinking question stems.* Retrieved from www.grinnell-k12.org/vimages/shared/vnews/stories/56117b0592c1e/Blooms%20Question%20Stems.pdf

[20] Blackboard: Release content https://help.blackboard.com/Learn/Instructor/Course_Content/Release_Content

Canvas: Differentiate Assignments https://community.canvaslms.com/docs/DOC-9973

Brightspace: Set Release Conditions https://documentation.brightspace.com/EN/le/assignments/instructor/set_release_conditions.htm?Highlight=extended%20time

[21] Freeman, L. (2015). Instructor time requirements to develop and teach online courses. *Online Journal of Distance Learning Administration*, *XVII*(I). University of West Georgia Distance Education Center. Retrieved from www.westga.edu/~distance/ojdla/spring181/freeman181.html

[22] Baldwin, S., Ching, Y., & Hsu, Y. (2018). Online course design in higher education: A review of national and statewide evaluation instruments. *Tech Trends*, *62*, 46–57. doi:10.1007/s11528-017-0215-z

[23] Baldwin, T., & Ching, Y. (2019). Online course design: A review of the Canvas course evaluation checklist. *International Review of Research in Open and Distributed Learning*, *20*(3). doi:10.19173/irrodl.v20i3.4283

[24] Quality Matters. (2020). *About. Home. Why QM?* Retrieved from www.qualitymatters.org/why-quality-matters/about-qm

[25] Online Learning Consortium. (2020). *History. About.* Retrieved from https://onlinelearningconsortium.org/about/history/

[26] Online Learning Consortium. (2020). *Course design review.* Retrieved from https://onlinelearningconsortium.org/consult/oscqr-course-design-review/

[27] Identifying information has been omitted for the sake of maintaining group members' privacy. Discussion occurred July 2, 2020.

[28] Quirk, J., & Young, M. (2016/2018, January 8). *Lost (and found) in translation: What online students want. Educause review.* From a paper presented at the 27th Annual Ann Ferren Conference on Teaching, Research, and Learning, American University, Washington, DC.

Retrieved from https://govt396.files.wordpress.com/2015/12/what-are-students-saying1.pdf

[29] Hajibayova, L. (2016). Students' viewpoint: What constitutes presence in an online classroom. *Cataloging & Classification Quarterly*. doi:10.1080/01639374.2016.1241972

[30] Kropp, E. (2018, April 20). Using your instructor bio to humanize course, reduce student anxiety. *Online Education: Faculty Focus*. Retrieved from www.facultyfocus.com/articles/online-education/instructor-bio-humanize-course-reduce-student-anxiety/

[31] Cicco, G. (2018). Instructor presence in online course design and delivery: Building rapport and revisiting the "PICCA" model. In *Proceedings of E-learn:World conference on e-learning in corporate, government, healthcare, and higher education* (pp. 1212–1216). Las Vegas, NV: Association for the Advancement of Computing in Education (AACE). Retrieved July 3, 2020 from www.learntechlib.org/primary/p/185334/

[32] Glazier, R. (2016). Building rapport to improve retention and success in online classes. *Journal of Political Science Education*, *12*(4), 437–456. doi:10.1080/15512169.2016.1155994

[33] See Mackh, B. (2018). *Higher education by design: Best practices for curricular planning and instruction*. Abingdon: Routledge, for a detailed, systematic description of how to build a syllabus.

[34] Rumore, M. (2016). The course syllabus: Legal contract or operator's manual. *American Journal of Pharmaceutical Education*, *80*(10), 177. doi:10.5688/ajpe8010177

[35] Senak, E. (2014). *Fixing the broken textbook market: How students respond to high textbook costs and demand alternatives*. US Public Interest Research Group. Retrieved from https://uspirg.org/sites/pirg/files/reports/NATIONAL%20Fixing%20Broken%20Textbooks%20Report1.pdf

[36] I open a Word doc and insert a table with seven columns and as many rows as there are weeks in the course, plus an extra row for the days of the week. I'm sure more sophisticated calendar programs exist, but I prefer the simplicity and flexibility of Word.

[37] Merrill, M. D., & via Pappas, C. (2015, May 16). Instructional design models and theories: The component display theory. *eLearning Industry*. Retrieved from https://elearningindustry.com/component-display-theory

[38] Google Support. (2020). *Use automatic captioning*. Retrieved from https://support.google.com/youtube/answer/6373554?hl=en

[39] Google Docs Editors Help. (2020). *Type with your voice*. Retrieved from https://support.google.com/docs/answer/4492226?hl=en

[40] Feil, H. for Clemson University. (2020). *Leveraging Google voice typing*. Retrieved from https://clemson.instructure.com/courses/49844/pages/leveraging-google-voice-typing

[41] Microsoft.com. (2020). *Live transcription with presentation translator*. Retrieved from www.microsoft.com/en-us/translator/education/lectures-and-presentations/

[42] Taken from the Summer 2, 2020, section of Art 4210-Design Thinking, Valdosta State University, using Brightspace

[43] Kelty, R., & Bunten, B. (Eds.). (2017). *Risk-taking in higher education: The importance of negotiating intellectual challenge in the college classroom* (p. xxvii). Lanham, MD: Rowman & Littlefield.

171

[44] Cole, J., Degan, B., & Martin, K. L. (1994–1997). *The Magic School Bus* (animated television series). Public broadcasting system. *From IMDb*. Retrieved from www.imdb.com/title/tt0108847/ Quotes: www.imdb.com/title/tt0108847/quotes/?tab=qt&ref_=tt_trv_qu

Pivoting Between Instructional Models

CHAPTER 4 SUMMARY

- Criticism of Online Education
- Models of Comprehensive Instructional Design
- How to Pivot
- Reflection

****

Building a course online gives us a firm footing from which we can pivot to various instructional models. Just as basketball players pivot on one foot as they search for an open teammate, building a course online gives it a fixed position in the LMS around which we can pivot easily, with 360 degrees of flexibility from teaching fully online to fully on campus, enhanced by the technologies available to us.

In the keynote address for *REMOTE: the Connected Faculty Summit* hosted by Arizona State University (July 13, 2020), ASU President Michael Crow explained the need for higher education to adapt to the moment we face, when high-speed changes to the social, environmental, and technological landscape demand our response. This is a moment, Crow says, where we must realize:

> The 16th, 17th, 18th century model of universities as only being close-knit faculty clusters with students physically clustered around them—as profound and significant as that model has been—is not adequate for the future sociologically, it's not adequate for the future technologically, and it's not adequate for the future for adaptability . . . [due to] the simplicity

of the design and the inadequate nature of the design for the complexity of the planet we're living on.

If we learned anything from our experiences during the COVID-19 pandemic, it's that our ideal of face-to-face on-campus instruction is ill suited to overcoming unexpected obstacles. We rose to the challenge only by abruptly shifting into unfamiliar instructional models for which the majority of faculty were unprepared. It was not an optimal response, but it was the best we could manage under the circumstances. We are deservedly proud of what we achieved, but we cannot settle for this as a future disaster response model, nor should it suffice as a baseline expectation for course preparation.

Now imagine this: what if *every* course were *routinely* housed on each institution's LMS? Shifting to a different model could then be as quick and easy as sending an email. "Hello, Students: We will be unable to meet on campus for our course on Tuesday due to a broken water pipe under the floor of our classroom. Please use the link below to join me on Zoom at our regularly scheduled class time, where we will discuss the assigned readings. If you have specific questions before class, please email me, and I'll be sure to address them during our discussion."

Without a doubt, this strategy challenges millennia of tradition. Faculty are very comfortable with their routines and understandably resistant to suggestions to alter "the way it's always been," not to mention that it's a great deal of work to build a course online, as we saw in Chapter 3. Now I'd like to address faculty concerns about these issues and explore what's possible if we upgrade our pedagogical practice by building every course online regardless of its intended instructional model. I believe this is more than just a disaster-preparedness measure, as has been suggested in the wake of our experience with Emergency Remote Teaching:[1] it's a path toward a better future for higher education I call Comprehensive Instructional Design—an approach that includes the best of online course design across all instructional models.

CRITICISM OF ONLINE EDUCATION

Given that higher education is populated by the best and brightest minds humankind has to offer, it's curious that so many faculty members still harbor biases against online learning. For instance, critics might say a course is not being taught "solely" on campus if its content is housed on the LMS, adding a technological dimension to the centuries-old model in which all teaching and learning takes place between instructors and students occupying the same temporal and physical space. I'll concede that this is true, but I'll also counter with the fact that **no** classroom is unmediated by technology because we bring it into the learning environment ourselves. Every faculty member, student, staff member, and administrator

I've ever met uses a cell phone and a computer, usually bringing both to campus daily. Those who are of a certain age can remember having land-line telephones in their campus offices, sending and receiving paper memos through intercampus mail, and using the library's card catalog with its many wooden drawers. Technology has fundamentally changed our lives, culture, and society, not to mention our colleges and universities. Furthermore, online courses and programs exist at institutions from the Ivy League to community colleges, giving somewhat of an official seal of approval to this form of teaching and learning. In light of these facts, I am always somewhat incredulous when I encounter faculty members who remain opposed to instructional technologies.

Hands-on Experience: one of the main criticisms of online learning is that it doesn't lend itself well to fields that require direct experience. It's true that certain disciplines might not be able to utilize online instruction as easily as others. Those dependent on installations of highly specialized equipment, such as electron microscopes, or those requiring hands-on practice, such as clinical nursing courses in which students learn how to perform medical procedures, might have few digital correlates. Nevertheless, virtual reality technology is expanding into higher education, offering a viable alternative to the physical classroom in certain situations. Virtual simulation in nursing education, for example, has been shown to improve knowledge retention and clinical reasoning among nursing students as well as increasing their satisfaction with the learning experience.[2]

Nevertheless, virtual simulations cannot substitute for *all* learning done in person. Most of us would prefer that our healthcare provider had practiced starting an IV on someone other than ourselves many times before it was our turn. Few of us would want to board an airplane if we knew the pilot had trained only on a flight simulator but had never actually flown a plane. However, arguments for the irreplaceability of certain types of face-to-face instruction do not delegitimize online learning as a whole.

Questions of Quality and Integrity: Online learning has long been stigmatized as being of lesser quality than face-to-face instruction, but this unfortunately persistent perception is not based on fact. Research shows online instruction to be of equal or greater effectiveness than traditional face-to-face teaching (Means, Toyama, Murphy, et al., 2010; Cook & Steinert, 2013; Sheikh, S. 2016).[3] Likewise, some negativity toward online learning arises from its use by certain predatory for-profit institutions (Shireman, R., 2016).[4] The presence of some bad actors should not be cause to cast aspersions on the entire field any more than the scandals emanating from traditional institutions delegitimize higher education as a whole. Every field of human endeavor contains individuals who prey upon others. The problem lies in human nature, not in the field itself.

Misplaced Exemplars: Perhaps of greatest concern, we should not confuse well-designed and thoughtfully planned online programs with the Emergency Remote Teaching we undertook in the spring of 2020. We achieved remarkable results, to be sure, but due to the speed at which we had to make this transition, our efforts could not possibly have equaled the quality of programs specifically designed for online environments. Saying "Well, it didn't work very well then, so it's not worth doing now" reveals a flawed understanding of what online education can be when approached with quality, rigor, and fidelity.

Therefore, the rationale for universal adoption of online components into all teaching and learning comes to this:

- Our centuries-old model of face-to-face instruction has not kept pace with social and technological developments outside higher education.
- Online teaching and learning are widely accepted across higher education.
- Criticisms of online programs as being of lesser quality or value than traditional on-campus teaching and learning are unfounded. Likewise, predatory or unscrupulous online institutions do not represent the norm of teaching and learning online.
- Emergency Remote Teaching was necessary, but its inability to achieve the quality of well-designed and well-taught online courses does not reflect online education overall, nor should this approach be continued long term.

We have an opportunity to take a bold step into the future of higher education by embracing a fundamental shift in our pedagogical practice, building every course in our institution's LMS regardless of its method of instructional delivery. At first, this proposition was nothing more than an attempt to establish something like a Universal Online Back-up Plan, allowing for nimble transitions between one form of teaching and another in case of emergency. I do not believe that this approach could work in the long run, though, because building a course online is far too much work to be worthwhile if we treat it as nothing but an insurance policy. Fortunately, online design for all courses can be so much more!

As we saw in the previous chapter, building course content online has many benefits.

- It organizes course content for all participants, minimizing wasted time searching for information or materials.
- It eliminates or reduces the need for paper copies of handouts, readings, exams, and other documents.
- It frees instructors to concentrate on teaching instead of the typical faculty practice of building a course while also teaching it.
- It broadens available instructional strategies to include easy access to electronic student resources, supplementary skills practice, expanded collaboration tools, flipped instruction, etc.

- It provides options for individual customization for students who cannot attend class on campus.
- It allows instructors to adapt to changing conditions or student needs flexibly.
- It facilitates annual evaluation and institutional assessment by creating an accessible data archive demonstrating instructional effectiveness.

Despite these clear advantages, some remain unconvinced. Faculty members have expressed two typical concerns after presentations I've conducted about building all courses in the LMS regardless of how they will be taught (Comprehensive Instructional Design). The first involves the amount of work involved in planning and preparing the entire course well ahead of the first day. I cannot deny that this is, indeed, a labor-intensive process. Nevertheless, it's a matter of the old cliché, "Pay me now or pay me later." Whether we design and build the course up front or design and build it as we go, the work must be accomplished somehow.

In the typical process for establishing a new course at many institutions, a faculty member conceives of and plans a course, then completes a form that asks for basic information about the course such as a proposed title, credits, contact hours, course type, prerequisites, technology requirements and so on. The form also asks the faculty member to provide a brief catalog description, a rationale for the course, expected learning objectives and outcomes, a general outline of key topics, and planned assessment methods. The proposal generally goes through a three-part approval process by a departmental curriculum committee, a college curriculum committee, and academic affairs. If approved at all three levels, the course is added to the university catalog, after which the faculty member who created the proposal is assigned to teach the course.

So what concrete resources does the instructor have to work with by this point in the process? A description of the course, objectives and outcomes, an outline of key topics, and a description of planned assessments—basic information included on many syllabi. It's a necessary outline or road map, but this is a far cry from a fully planned course complete with all materials and resources, even if the instructor has begun to develop some of these course components. Complete preparation is simply not the norm. When I was the director of the Mellon Research Project at the University of Michigan, I traveled to 46 different universities and examined courses in every subject, from AAAS to zoology. Far more often than not, I found that instructors had not prepared 100% of their instructional materials in advance.

We seldom question our traditional approaches to course development because they're so familiar. Many of us may have had the graduate school experience of being handed the previous instructor's syllabus and sent off to teach a course. We learned to teach by teaching, just as we learned to develop course content week by week as the semester progressed. This experience became the norm that's been passed down to subsequent generations of faculty. It works because faculty members are disciplinary experts who are so steeped in their fields that they can speak confidently and knowledgeably about topics within their academic domains without a great deal of preparation. Many instructors don't plan ahead, either because they don't feel any compelling need to do so or because they prefer an approach of serendipitous pragmatism, remaining open to emergent developments in their field of knowledge that provide new information they wish to teach.

As a metaphor, the construction of a new house begins by pouring a foundation. Would it make sense to move in when only the concrete was in place? Would anyone choose to live in a home before it had walls or a roof? Before it had plumbing and electrical service? Of course not. Instead, we finish building the house and move in when it's complete, or nearly so. The syllabus is nothing but the foundation and basic structure of the course; it's far from a full-fledged plan.

To consider the matter from a different angle, creating a course while simultaneously teaching it is like building a ship while sailing. Under normal circumstances, ships are built on land in a "dry dock," launched only when they're complete. They're never built in the middle of the ocean and certainly not after the journey has already begun. It would be foolish for a crew to set off on a transoceanic voyage with only a rudimentary raft, attempting to construct the entire ship around themselves as they sailed. Nevertheless, circumstances alter cases. Damaged ships generally head to a port to make repairs, but if the port is too distant, repairs must be completed at sea. Just so, our programs continued even as we made changes in response to the pandemic—we rebuilt our ships while they were still underway. In short, our design-as-you-go approaches to teaching can end up being far more difficult than if we'd taken the time to build the course in the beginning.

Secondly, faculty tend to prefer the traditional design-as-you-go approach because it affords greater freedom to improvise in the classroom, capitalizing on serendipitous moments and taking advantage of unexpected teaching opportunities. The idea of preplanning the entire course feels unacceptably confining or restrictive, like wearing a jacket that's two sizes too small. However, we must also consider that the process under which our course received approval already places constraints on this freedom. Most faculty are not permitted to deviate from the course description or the approved learning outcomes. This prohibition is not just a matter of institutional policy but a best practice. As an example I shared in *Higher Education by Design*, I was enrolled in a doctoral seminar on research methodologies in which the instructor decided to use almost all our class time as a bully pulpit from which she imparted her passionate views on animal rights. When I dared to ask what this had to do with research methodologies, the instructor said (with some annoyance), "That's for *you* to figure out." This instructor assuredly did not model best practice in teaching; moreover, her actions were unethical and contrary to her duty to deliver instruction that helped her students achieve the course objectives and outcomes. I've seen this occur all too often, whether intentionally, as in the case of that graduate seminar; through a lack of attention; or because the instructor is unaware of the constraints placed upon them. Perhaps we lecture too long on a particular topic, or we lose class time discussing issues not directly related to the course, or we run into unforeseen circumstances that result in the cancellation of class sessions. Whatever the reason, we can easily find ourselves at the end of the semester without covering topics crucial to our students' achievement of the course's learning outcomes. Some instructors shrug this off, saying, "Eh, that's just the way it is." But this is not fair to our students and certainly not a best practice in teaching.

Of course, we can and should pursue the intriguing topics that emerge during a discussion, even in a well-designed course taught with fidelity. Some of our best classroom experiences occur this way, and pre-existing plans should not force us to ignore these teachable moments. Indeed, this is where online design can work to our advantage because we can take the time to pursue worthwhile tangents during class, knowing that our students can log onto the LMS later on to view the content we had originally planned for that class session. We continue to meet our obligation to deliver the required instruction while also doing what we do best: leading students on a journey of discovery in our discipline. In other words, a course that has been built online gives us greater freedom, not less.

Furthermore, courses built in the LMS are no more carved in stone than those without technological support. No course designer or instructor can anticipate everything, so we often have to revise directions for assignments or activities, add resources, alter instruction, or re-arrange due dates (provided these choices are consistent with the course description and outcomes, which is the case with any course). For instance, when I was teaching a senior seminar course, several students informed me that the due date for a major project fell on the same day as a capstone exhibition involving more than half the students on the roster, causing them a great deal of stress. It was a simple matter to move the deadline back a week to give them the additional breathing room to finish their projects. Doing so placed me at a bit of a disadvantage since I now had to grade their work later in the semester than I'd have preferred, but as a student-centered educator, I was happy to accommodate their request nonetheless.

To summarize the responses to common criticisms:

- **Time**: All course design takes time, whether we complete it before we begin teaching or as we go. Planning and preparing the course ahead of time allows us to focus on our students rather than splitting our attention between teaching and designing.
- **Flexibility**: A well-designed, well-planned course can still accommodate changes, just like any course we teach.

179

■ *Opportunity*: Instructors can more easily take advantage of unexpected teaching opportunities when their course is backed up in the LMS because students can catch up with regularly scheduled content online if their class time is spent on an unplanned discussion.

■ *Responsiveness*: Online course design also allows us to be flexible and responsive to students' needs and rise with emerging challenges without resorting to emergency measures.

Next, we'll look at seven instructional models empowered by Comprehensive Instructional Design.

MODELS OF COMPREHENSIVE INSTRUCTIONAL DESIGN

Figure 4.1 shows a continuum of instructional models ranging from fully online to the left to fully face to face on the right. Before we begin to examine each of these seven approaches to instruction, please note that this is merely a representative sample of a wide variety of instructional practices. Little consensus exists about specific names for these approaches since each institution, and even each instructor, can define them differently. Terms that frequently occur in discussions about instructional models are defined as follows for our discussion.

Asynchronous Instruction, Interaction, or Activity typically refers to actions occurring at different times in the online learning environment. Asynchronous instruction is often delivered through prerecorded videos or slide presentations. Asynchronous interactions or activities occur through discussion boards, email, text messaging, or voice mail. Students have always completed assignments and readings for their face-to-face courses independently outside class, making this an asynchronous activity. However, when we apply the term *asynchronous* to higher education, it usually implies a context of online teaching and learning.

Blended Learning broadly refers to courses that incorporate both face-to-face and electronic elements.[5] If we fully utilize Comprehensive Instructional

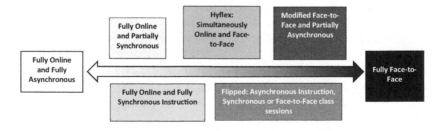

FIGURE 4.1 Models of Instructional Delivery

Design, whereby we build and house all courses in the LMS, including those taught fully face to face, then a course structure that includes *any* face-to-face interaction could be termed "blended." (See also "hybrid.")

Face-to-Face Instruction is the familiar model that occurs when students and instructors meet at the same time and in the same physical space. Descriptors also include on campus, on ground, and bricks and mortar.

Flipped Classroom indicates a departure from the usual pattern in which students complete readings before a lecture, "flipping" the process by requiring students to view asynchronous prerecorded lectures or slide presentations in the LMS before a regularly scheduled class session.[6] Classes may meet face to face on campus, or they may meet synchronously online through the use of a video conferencing service. Because students have already viewed the lecture, class sessions can include supplementary instruction, discussion, or active learning components such as group work, case studies, or other activities. Instructors might check for students' understanding of the pre-class activities through an online quiz or written response, following up by using the next synchronous or face-to-face class session to answer questions or provide supplementary instruction on concepts with which students struggled. The flipped approach can be applied to any course using synchronous or face-to-face class sessions.

Fully Online Learning applies to instructional models that take place only in an electronic environment. Students and instructors never encounter one another in a shared physical location. Fully online instruction can incorporate synchronous or asynchronous components or a blend of both. The difference is that all interaction occurs electronically, never face to face or on campus.

Hybrid Instruction is often used synonymously with "blended instruction," but hybrid learning is distinct in its reference to a course that *replaces* some face-to-face instruction with online components.[7] It may also refer to an online course that incorporates some face-to-face sessions or splits students into sections that rotate between in-person and online instruction.[8]

Hyflex Instruction combines the ideas of "hybrid" and "flexible" into a single term—hyflex. Here, "hybrid" indicates that the course uses both online and face-to-face instruction. "Flexible" refers to student choice. For any given class session, students may choose how to attend among three possible options.

1. Face-to-face on campus
2. Synchronously online through a simulcast of the face-to-face classroom by way of a video conferencing service
3. Asynchronously through a recording of the face-to-face or synchronous class session

Student choice is a hallmark of hyflex learning, affording the flexibility to decide which modality best meets a student's needs on a given day. This model is also more technologically dependent than others since it often utilizes hardware and software beyond what is needed for standard video conferencing. At some institutions, hyflex classes are held in specially equipped classrooms with sophisticated cameras, microphones, and smartboards, with examples found at the University of North Carolina at Chapel Hill, Central Michigan University, and San Francisco State University, among many others.[9]

iCourse refers to a model at Arizona State University in which the faculty member assigned to teach a face-to-face on-campus course may choose to teach the course fully online, substituting synchronous instruction for face-to-face class sessions using any of the digital teaching resources that have been developed for the various fully online degree programs offered through ASU-Online. This model is called an "i" course because ASU's on-campus degree program is known as "campus immersion." Stated differently, iCourses are not part of the ASU Online enrollment and management system. They use tools and resources available to ASU Online but do not contribute to ASU Online degree programs. iCourses are highly flexible with respect to how they are timed and delivered. Faculty members may choose to offer their courses synchronously or asynchronously, although most courses are designed to be experienced asynchronously. ASU Sync is a teaching model applicable to ASU campus immersion classes wherein all lectures are provided digitally so that students may participate synchronously from remote locations.[10]

Split Sections separate students into two or more cohorts that meet in a face-to-face classroom at different times but receive the same instruction. This action may become necessary when student enrollment surpasses limits for safe occupancy in the assigned meeting space. Split sections are integral to the Modified Face-to-Face and Partially Asynchronous model and are an option for the Hyflex Model too.

Synchronous Instruction, Interaction, and Activities are those occurring at the same time. Everyday interactions such as those in traditional face-to-face classrooms are inherently synchronous, but this term generally applies to online interactions conducted through a video conferencing service. Because not all students can attend a synchronous class session, the instructor can record the session through the video conferencing service, posting the video to the LMS (preferably as an mp4) afterward. This strategy helps all students because those who attended can rewatch the session as a study aid, and those who could not attend synchronously can view the recording of the session asynchronously.

However, we should bear in mind that participation in synchronous sessions can become an access issue, penalizing students who cannot participate. Some students do not have a personal computer, their computer may not have a webcam or microphone, or it might be too old to support the requisite software. Some students do not have high-speed internet at home sufficient to livestream the session, or they might not have a quiet, private place from which they can participate. Some students juggle the demands of a full-time job or family, which can prevent attending a scheduled event such as a synchronous class session. Since four of the seven instructional models incorporate synchronous class sessions, this is an issue that instructors should be prepared to address with their students. In certain cases, it may be possible for students to log into the session through a smartphone, although this is not ideal. In others, the student's only option will be to view the recording of the synchronous session. We should respect all students' needs and provide viable solutions without penalizing or discriminating against them either intentionally or unintentionally. The instructor's demonstration of empathy can be the key to ensuring these students' success in the course.

Video Conferencing Services are provided by companies such as Zoom, Google Hangouts, WebEx, Bluejeans, Microsoft Teams, and Blackboard Collaborate, facilitating live video conferencing over the internet. Rather than repeating this list of options or privileging one over the others, we will use the phrase "video conferencing service" to indicate the means by which any synchronous online interaction using such technology occurs.

In the next section, we will examine six aspects of each of these instructional models.

- Description
- Instructor Roles and Responsibilities
- Student Roles and Responsibilities
- Advantages
- Disadvantages
- Recommendations

The discussion will presume four baseline expectations across all seven instructional models to focus more clearly on their similarities and differences while avoiding unnecessary redundancy.

1. Every course has been built in the institution's LMS, following the quality recommendations explained in Chapter 3. Clemson University published an excellent infographic[11] about instructional models. However, one of the "cons" that repeatedly appears on their list is the prohibitive difficulty of preparing and organizing class content on the LMS. Here, we remove that problem by embracing the use of the LMS in every course. When this becomes a standard expectation, it ceases to be an impediment.

2. Instructors' responsibilities always include monitoring students' participation and attendance, informing appropriate university personnel regarding students who are not participating in the course, evaluating students' work, and posting final course grades. These are baseline expectations across all teaching. Therefore, we need not mention them in

every instructional model because they do not change anywhere on the continuum from fully online to fully face to face.

3. Students' responsibilities always include striving to achieve the course objectives and outcomes; adhering to stated schedules, due dates, and deadlines; and upholding standards for academic honesty. Like faculty responsibilities, students must meet these expectations no matter what instructional model the class might utilize.

4. We live and work in a culture of digital connectivity, and digital technologies are integral to the model of Comprehensive Instructional Design. Therefore, every model of instruction we examine presumes that instructors and students will have access to a computer capable of performing tasks in the LMS and the ability to participate in synchronous class sessions, which requires a web camera and microphone, usually integrated into the student's computer, and access to high-speed internet. Even in a fully asynchronous online course, a web camera may be necessary for proctored online exams or creating video discussion posts. Understandably, technology requirements can pose hardships for students who depend on campus computer labs because they do not own a computer and students who do not have adequate internet service when off campus. Moving forward, institutions must address this problem, perhaps providing an up-to-date laptop computer and personal hotspot device to all incoming students, including the cost of these items in standard tuition and fees. Mobile technologies may also expand the availability of online learning to students who lack a computer or internet service, but this has not yet become an ideal (or widely accepted) substitute. Unfortunately, individual instructors do not possess the ability to solve these problems, so for the purpose of this discussion, we will presume students have access to the required technologies appropriate to the course. Instructors should address students' technological needs on a case-by-case basis, working with them and with appropriate campus offices to help them find solutions allowing them to participate in the course fully. We must handle these cases with care, knowing that lack of access to appropriate technologies frequently goes hand-in-hand with matters of diversity, equity, and inclusion. Our traditionally aged, dependent, relatively affluent students are not likely to be those who need our help. Rather, our solutions will have to take our students' unique identities and life circumstances into account. Their barriers may not even be technological. A single mother may not be able to afford childcare during synchronous online classes, limiting her ability to keep her camera or microphone on. A student with social anxiety may find it impossible to tolerate being on camera. A student may have deep concerns about privacy or internet security and refuse to participate in a recorded session. The solution in every case will be found

in the instructor's capacity to demonstrate empathy for the student and work with them to find a mutually acceptable path forward.

Fully Online and Fully Asynchronous Instruction

Description
- All course content and learning activities take place in an online classroom.
- Instruction typically occurs through prerecorded video lectures or slide presentations with or without audio narration.
- Faculty members and students remain more distant from one another in this model than others because they interact through written communication or prerecorded videos alone.

Instructor Roles and Responsibilities
- The instructor monitors the online classroom, communicating with students through email, course announcements, discussion boards, and feedback on assignments.

Student Roles and Responsibilities
- Students watch lecture videos or view slide presentations, read assigned materials, post comments to discussion boards, and take exams at their own rate, subject to predetermined deadlines and due dates.
- Students submit their work through the LMS, interact with each other through the discussion boards, and communicate with the instructor through email or messaging within the LMS.
- Students complete their work independently and stay on pace with the course. They must take the initiative to contact the instructor when experiencing a problem preventing them from meeting the instructor's expectations.

Advantages
- Fully online fully asynchronous instruction is not bound by either time or location, making it ideal for students or instructors who prefer to work at atypical hours, live far from campus, or are unable to be on campus for various reasons.
- This instructional model is well established with ample precedents and examples.

Disadvantages
- The absence of synchronous or face-to-face interaction may cause online students to feel lonely or unmotivated. It is also easy for students to forget about the course because there are no set meeting times.

■ This instructional model is the most labor intensive for instructors because all communication is memorialized, generally in writing, which can be more time consuming and require more thought than spontaneous verbal interactions. Instructors must choose their words more carefully, being more empathetic, instructive, supportive, and thoughtful than we might otherwise be if we spoke to the student face to face.

Recommendation

■ Instruction should include multiple inputs such as readings, podcasts, and videos. Instructors should also provide opportunities for meaningful peer-to-peer and student-to-instructor interaction to increase student engagement.

■ Strategies such as these mitigate the boredom and disengagement that can result when reading and writing are the only forms of communication used in the course. Instructors should frequently communicate with students (usually through course announcements and email) and maintain an active presence in the online classroom.

■ Best practice in teaching includes sending frequent reminders of upcoming due dates, providing supplementary resources as needed, and maintaining a positive and encouraging demeanor in all student interactions.

■ A fully online and fully asynchronous course can also be the most difficult for students since they cannot see or speak to the instructor or one another. Instructors must demonstrate a great deal of empathy and attempt to be intentionally warm and encouraging in their written communications with students. When they cannot see our facial expressions or hear the tone of our voices, it's very easy for students to misconstrue our intended message or meaning.

■ We also need to respond with empathy when students have trouble keeping up with their work, run into personal problems that get in the way of completing assignments, or even when they just forget about the course.

■ Students form lasting memories of the way we treat them. Personally, I'd rather be known as the kind professor who gave a student a second chance than the cold and heartless professor who imposed a grade penalty because an assignment was submitted 45 minutes after the 11:59 p.m. deadline.

Fully Online and Partially Synchronous Instruction

Description

■ This instructional model is nearly identical to Fully Online and Fully Asynchronous Instruction with the addition of synchronous class sessions that supplement instruction and provide real-time interaction between the instructor and students.

186

- These sessions, held through a video conferencing service, may be used for student presentations, open discussion, active learning, and supplementary instruction.
- Students can also use mobile video communication applications such as Skype, Facebook Messenger, Google Duo, WhatsApp, or Discord to work on collaborative assignments, meeting synchronously to complete projects, discuss reading assignments, and so on.

Instructor Roles and Responsibilities

- The instructor schedules synchronous class sessions, informs students of expectations for attendance and appropriate participation, and provides electronic invitations to join the class sessions, depending on the video conferencing service utilized.
- The instructor also hosts the class sessions, facilitates students' participation, answers questions, monitors the chat feature (messages received via text within the application), and establishes structures for the class session appropriate to its purpose, such as placing participants in breakout rooms to foster small-group interaction.
- In many cases, the instructor records the class session and posts the recording to the online classroom for later viewing by students who could not attend with the rest of their classmates or want to review the information presented during class.

Student Roles and Responsibilities

- Students are responsible for attending synchronous class sessions and meeting expectations for participation.
- If they cannot attend the synchronous sessions, the instructor should provide an alternative such as viewing the recorded session and writing a brief response to a discussion board.

Advantages

- Synchronous class sessions increase students' engagement with course content and foster interpersonal connections, mitigating the feelings of loneliness and isolation common to online learning.
- They also provide students with opportunities to receive immediate answers to their questions.

Disadvantages

- Technological requirements (access to high-speed internet, webcam, and microphone) can be prohibitive for some students.
- Synchronous class sessions may be infeasible for students who work full time, have family responsibilities, or face other hardships.

Recommendations

- Using online polling through a provider such as Poll Everywhere[12] or Doodle[13] can allow students to respond to the instructor's questions in real time, increasing classroom interactivity and engagement. Polling can also be an effective tool for taking attendance when students are not physically present, or students can register their attendance by typing their name into the chat window at the beginning and end of the session. If the instructor saves the chat, attendance is recorded along with any messages students sent during class.
- Instructors may choose to provide a grade-based incentive for student attendance at synchronous class sessions, but they should also allow alternatives for those students who cannot attend by recording each synchronous session and allowing students to view the session asynchronously.
  - Instructors must respect the fact that some students will find it impossible to attend the class session as scheduled.
  - Best practice includes recording the class session and sharing it in a file format such as mp4 that is downloadable and accessible across computing platforms and mobile technologies.
  - Students who view the recorded class session could earn participation or attendance points by writing a short summary of the discussion, emailing questions to the instructor, or posting to a discussion board about the recorded class session.
- The same recommendations for demonstrating empathy and kindness also apply to this model because much of the course remains asynchronous and therefore subject to the same conditions as the previous model (Fully Online and Fully Asynchronous Instruction).

Fully Online and Fully Synchronous Instruction

Description

- Fully online courses follow a pre-established schedule of synchronous class sessions that meet via video conferencing, much as a face-to-face course follows a class schedule. ASU's "iCourses" use this model, meeting at the scheduled time, whether online or on campus.
- Fully online and fully synchronous instruction may follow the typical approach that uses class sessions for lectures, demonstrations, or whole-class discussions.
- Conversely, the instructor may implement a flipped classroom method, requiring students to view prerecorded lecture videos or slide presentations before synchronous class sessions, using class time for discussion, group work, and active learning.

188

- Either way, this approach most closely mirrors traditional on-campus teaching and learning while maintaining the physical separation of participants by meeting only online.

Instructor Roles and Responsibilities

- The instructor prepares and delivers instruction, leads discussions, and facilitates active learning in much the same manner as they would in a face-to-face classroom, even though all interactions occur through synchronous video conferencing.
- The instructor is also responsible for scheduling, hosting, and recording synchronous class sessions and monitoring and participating in the LMS, where students post their assignments, take quizzes or exams, and engage in other activities common to online learning, such as discussion boards.
- In effect, the instructor fills a dual role as both a (virtual) face-to-face instructor and an asynchronous online instructor.

Student Roles and Responsibilities

- Students' attendance at synchronous class sessions may be held to the same standards as attendance in a traditional face-to-face classroom setting.
- Asynchronous course components (assignments, discussion boards, quizzes, and exams) occur in the LMS, much like any other online class.
- Students are expected to manage these dual environments independently.

Advantages

- This model most closely replicates the classroom experience in an electronic form since instruction takes place in real time, albeit through video conferencing, allowing the instructor to interact with students much the same as in a traditional face-to-face classroom.
- If necessary, instructors can utilize this model under emergency conditions without having built the course in the LMS, sharing instructional materials and resources with students through email or a mobile application such as Class Updates,[14] especially if the LMS is infeasible or unavailable.

Disadvantages

- Many instructors adopted this model during Emergency Remote Teaching because it meant they could continue their longstanding practice of delivering instruction and course content as it occurs rather than building the entire course in the LMS in advance. However, the absence of prior preparation can result in disorganization, causing difficulties when students cannot find the resources and materials they need.

- As previously mentioned, reliance on synchronous class sessions poses a hardship for some students, especially those attempting to learn from home, when they do not have access to a quiet environment from which to participate in synchronous instruction, lack access to high-speed internet, or do not possess key technologies such as a computer equipped with a web camera or microphone, all of which place such students at a distinct disadvantage.

Recommendations
- As with the previous model, online polling can increase student engagement and interactivity and is also useful for taking attendance.
- Instructors teaching any course involving synchronous class sessions via video conferencing can record each session and post it to the LMS for students to view asynchronously, along with instructions for what students should do if they want to receive credit for class attendance and participation.
- This model can be very successful if the instructor invests the time and energy necessary to build the course in the LMS according to the quality recommendations in Chapter 3 and adheres to best practices in online teaching. However, it is unwise to implement this model in an attempt to avoid building the course online.
- Instructors may think this model allows them to proceed by transposing their usual teaching practice into an online environment, but doing so deprives students of the optimized learning created by a well-planned, high-quality online course. Therefore, it should not be the first choice except when normal face-to-face instruction becomes suddenly impossible, and the instructor has not had time to prepare the course in the LMS as recommended.

Hyflex: Simultaneous Online and Face-to-Face Instruction

Description
- Hyflex instruction allows students to choose whether they will attend class on campus or online, either synchronously or asynchronously. (Some institutions may schedule attendance to provide adequate social distancing.)
- The instructor teaches in the face-to-face classroom while simultaneously broadcasting and recording the class session through a video conferencing service.[15]
- The on-campus classroom may be equipped with cameras and microphones that broadcast a wider view of the physical environment and capture discussions and activities occurring around the room than

is possible with the integrated webcams and microphones on many computers.[16]

■ Whichever of the three attendance options they select (face to face on campus, synchronously online, or asynchronously online), students should receive an equivalent educational experience.

■ Successful implementation of hyflex generally requires institutional support to purchase and install appropriate technologies and provide technical assistance.

Instructor Roles and Responsibilities

■ The instructor plays three simultaneous roles in hyflex instruction:

■ Deliver instruction and interact with students in the face-to-face classroom.

■ Manage the technologies used to broadcast the class session to students attending remotely while recording the session for later viewing by students who choose to participate asynchronously.

■ Monitor and respond to input from students attending synchronously, usually through the "chat" function.[17]

■ Because the instructor is responsible for providing instruction and interacting with students in all three modalities, a higher degree of preparation than usual is required to ensure that all learners' educational needs are met.

■ Instructors must learn how to use the multiple technologies involved, which will vary by institution but may include separate systems. The course profiled in Hinck & Burke's chapter in Beatty's *Hybrid-Flexible Course Design* book (2019) included 13 different technological tools (indicated in bold type):

■ The **Canvas** learning management system, along with **Proctorio** for online test proctoring and **VoiceThread** for online asynchronous discussions

■ A **classroom computer** and **wall-mounted cameras** optimized for live Zoom broadcasting and **Panopto** recording for playback later

■ A KappIQ **Smartboard** to support and capture whiteboard activities

■ SHARP SVSI **video distribution** and the Axis **streaming assistant**

■ An **iPad** to control the **Zoom Room software**

■ A Catch Box **throwable microphone** and instructor **lavalier mic**[18]

■ Furthermore, instructors can expect to spend as much time in the face-to-face classroom as they would in a fully face-to-face instructional model and as much time managing the online classroom and responding to students who participate asynchronously as they would in a fully asynchronous instructional model.

- Therefore, instructors using a hyflex model should be prepared to invest a substantial amount of time preparing to teach and teaching, especially if they are attempting this instructional model for the first time.

Student Roles and Responsibilities

- Because of the high degree of challenge faculty will encounter when implementing this model, students should be patient with instructors who may be distracted by technological difficulties or inattentive to members of either the face-to-face or remote audiences.
- Students should be prepared to self-advocate to ensure their needs are met and questions are answered.

Advantages

- Hyflex increases students' access to courses when they cannot attend class in person or when the classes they want to take are scheduled at the same time. It gives them greater control over their schedules by allowing them to choose whether to attend in person, synchronously online, or asynchronously online.
- Broadcasting systems installed in the classroom can deliver a more authentic audio-visual experience than standard video conferencing, when available.
- Hyflex can also offer increased social distancing by reducing the number of students in the face-to-face classroom while providing simultaneous instruction to students who are not physically present.
- Split sections may be implemented when social distancing requirements are necessary, establishing a set schedule for access to the face-to-face classroom.[19] Nevertheless, students may almost always choose to attend online even when scheduled for the face-to-face classroom, subject to institutional and instructor policies.

Disadvantages

- Hyflex places considerable demands upon the instructor. Because students can choose how they will attend, instructors might not know how many students will be present in the face-to-face classroom on any given day, making it more challenging to plan activities such as collaborative projects.
- Instructors might also face a considerable learning curve if multiple technologies are used to deliver the face-to-face classroom experience to remote learners.
- Early adopters report frustration with attempting to focus on teaching while also ensuring that technologies function properly and providing equal attention to students who are present face-to-face and those attending virtually.

- Students in the face-to-face classroom can become irritated when the instructor is distracted, and students in the virtual classroom can feel overlooked and ignored when the instructor pays more attention to the students in the face-to-face classroom.
- Asynchronous online students may feel left out of interactive experiences such as small-group discussions or online polling.

Recommendations

- Using the LMS strategically helps instructors manage a hyflex classroom.
- For example, regardless of how they choose to attend class, all students should submit assignments to the LMS so that the instructor does not have some paper copies of students' work given to them in person and some submitted online.
- All students could be required to participate in discussion boards on the LMS, even if they mainly attend class in person, simplifying things for the instructor and increasing access for all learners.
- As with other instructional models using synchronous delivery, online polling is a good option for increasing interactivity and taking attendance.
- To include learners who choose asynchronous participation, the instructor could create a discussion board for each class session, asking all students to respond to an open-ended question about the day's instruction. The instructor could create a short quiz to gather information about students' understanding of the content presented in each class session, use a virtual "exit slip" that asks students to answer a question or two before leaving the physical or virtual classroom,[20] or write a "one-minute essay."[21]
- Any of these options place students' responses into the LMS, making them more easily accessible to the instructor and all students.
- The instructor will need a way to capture the discussions and activities occurring around the room so that students attending virtually are not excluded.
  - For instance, those working from home could be assigned a face-to-face partner who uses video conferencing to include the virtual partner in small-group discussions.
  - As another example, the instructor may choose to group virtual students and ask them to conduct discussions and activities through video conferencing while other students work in the physical classroom.
- Ideally, an instructor attempting hyflex (especially for the first time) would have the help of a graduate teaching assistant or staff member who could manage the technologies and monitor the online chat while the instructor focuses on teaching. Hinck & Burke (2019) described how this worked at their institution:

193

One to two students were paid to assist during each class period, helping with set-up, monitoring the Zoom chat and reminding students to use the Catch Box microphone when speaking. They also controlled the wall-mounted classroom camera with a joystick to improve the quality of the video capture when the instructor moved around. One of these student assistants was enrolled in the course and their salaries were paid out of the business school's work-study budget.[22]

- Unfortunately, this will not be possible at many institutions. Instructors may decide to create their own solutions, such as recruiting student volunteers to fill these supporting roles.
- Selection of student assistants and methods for rewarding them for their help would, of course, vary by instructor. Nevertheless, instructors should consider providing some form of recognition or appreciation to their student assistants, such as awarding extra-credit points along with openly expressing gratitude for their help.
- Because of its inherent complexity and high demand load, many instructors will not find hyflex to be a desirable option; however, if the institution chooses to implement hyflex broadly, instructors should take advantage of any and all support available, including training opportunities, informational materials, and technologies.

Flipped Classroom: Asynchronous Instruction, Synchronous or Face-to-Face Class Sessions

Description
- Flipped instruction can apply to any course that uses a combination of synchronous and asynchronous components.
- It is "flipped" because students use the LMS to view prerecorded lectures before class instead of spending class sessions listening to lectures.
- This approach leaves class sessions open for discussion, small-group or partner activities, and to deepen students' learning through supplementary activities.
- The instructor might, for example, ask students to complete a short quiz in the LMS following their pre-class viewing of the lecture and use this formative assessment to provide additional explanation of troublesome concepts during the following class session.
- Flipped instruction can take place whether the class sessions are held synchronously online or in a face-to-face classroom. It can also include hyflex components if face-to-face sessions will be simulcast to students attending remotely.

194

Instructor Roles and Responsibilities

- The instructor creates lectures and other instructional materials, setting up the course in the LMS.
- However, the instructor also plans and delivers instructional activities for the weekly synchronous or face-to-face class sessions that build on, support, enhance, or supplement the asynchronous content that students complete in advance of these sessions.
- If some students attend remotely during the synchronous or face-to-face class sessions, the instructor must remain mindful of their needs and plan to include them in all activities, just as in a hyflex instructional model.

Student Roles and Responsibilities

- Students must complete all pre-class activities and be prepared for the synchronous or face-to-face class sessions.
- They must attend the synchronous or face-to-face classes and participate in the learning activities taking place.

Advantages

- Many educators have experienced the frustration of spending most of a class session in lecture only to run out of time just when a discussion is becoming interesting or when students have more questions than it's possible to answer.
- Flipped instruction removes the lecture component from the minutes spent in the classroom, increasing the time available for activities and discussions.
- This model provides the beneficial structure of an online class with an on-campus class's flexibility, maximizing our ability to pursue emergent or serendipitous topics.
- Students receive instruction without interruption because it occurs asynchronously online, yet the instructor can adapt the face-to-face or synchronous portions of the course to deliver a more personalized educational experience.
- A meta-analysis of research on the effectiveness of the flipped classroom by Shi, Ma, MacLeod, et al. (2020) speaks to its ability to improve students' cognitive learning, especially when accompanied by individualized active or collaborative pedagogies.[23]

Disadvantages

- Because instruction is adaptive to the needs and interests of the students, a higher degree of instructor engagement may be necessary than with fully online and fully face-to-face models, including frequent use of

on-the-spot formative assessments such as instant polls, quick quizzes, short written responses, or reflective posts to a discussion board following the online pre-class instruction.
- If the flipped model includes only asynchronous content paired with face-to-face class sessions, it cannot accommodate the needs of learners who cannot attend the face-to-face class in person.

Recommendations
- Flipped classroom models require the instructor to be responsive and engaged, but they mitigate instructors' discomfort with constraints imposed by a preordained structure in the LMS.
- Flipping the classroom increases instructors' freedom to teach, follow up on emerging topics, and supplement students' learning because they can spend class sessions interacting with students rather than lecturing.
- If synchronous learning occurs through video conferencing, instructors could create breakout rooms to facilitate small-group interaction. They can also record the entire class session for students to view asynchronously later on.
- To prepare for the face-to-face or synchronous sessions, the instructor could embed a short three- to five-question quiz following each lecture in the LMS, with the last question being an open response such as "What questions do you have after viewing this lecture?" or "What would you like the instructor to address during our next class?" A formative assessment like this has two benefits.
  - First, it holds students accountable for watching the lecture.
  - Second, it provides actionable information the instructor can employ when planning discussion topics or other learning activities to address students' areas of difficulty.

Modified Face-to-Face and Partially Asynchronous Instruction

Description
- This model involves a campus-based face-to-face course with modifications for social distancing, such as split sections.
- Generally speaking, students are divided into two or three cohorts that rotate through face-to-face class sessions led by the instructor.
  - For instance, an instructor teaching a course scheduled on Tuesday and Thursday might meet with the first cohort on Tuesday and the second cohort on Thursday.
  - Courses that meet three days a week could divide into three cohorts using the same strategy.

- Participation in face-to-face class sessions may occur less frequently in courses with high enrollment or small classrooms because social distancing rules limit the number of students who can safely occupy the classroom.
  - For example, imagine a course scheduled to meet twice per week with an enrollment of 40 students, assigned to a classroom that can only accommodate 10 students while maintaining safe social distancing.
  - Four cohorts would become necessary, following a rotation schedule in which each cohort meets in the face-to-face classroom in alternating weeks.
- Students complete asynchronous learning activities online when they are not assigned to attend the face-to-face classroom.

Instructor Roles and Responsibilities

- The instructor must plan learning activities for all cohorts—providing instruction for students meeting face to face and those working independently on asynchronous course content.
- The instructor must be present in the face-to-face classroom as per the course schedule while continuing to monitor the online classroom where students complete their asynchronous activities.

Student Roles and Responsibilities

Students must attend and participate in face-to-face class sessions and complete asynchronous learning activities.

Advantages

- This model is well suited to courses that require direct instruction in hands-on processes such as science labs, art studios, music performance, nursing or other health professions, and technical education.
- All students have the opportunity to meet with the instructor while still maintaining recommended social distancing.
- It would also be helpful under circumstances in which a course could not meet in a room sufficient for its enrollment needs.
  - For example, a large lecture course that regularly met in an auditorium would be unable to hold class if that auditorium's ceiling caved in under the weight of heavy snow and ice.
  - Lacking an alternative space large enough to accommodate all students, the institution might decide to move the course to its next-largest space, pivoting to the modified face-to-face and partially asynchronous model.

197

Disadvantages

- This model lacks some of the helpful features present in courses with synchronous online engagement, which means students cannot attend fully online if circumstances prevent them from coming to campus.
- The instructor may need to repeat the same lesson two or three times each week, which might become tedious.
- The instructor would also need to monitor the online classroom to facilitate the asynchronous components of the course.
- In effect, this model may double the instructor's workload in the same manner as hyflex, rendering this an undesirable option from the instructor's point of view.
- Likewise, students may be dissatisfied with meeting face to face less frequently than in a traditional course.

Recommendations

- Care should be taken to ensure that the content of the face-to-face class session and the online learning activities are nonsequential because at least half the students will complete the online activities before the face-to-face class session whereas the other half completes them afterward.
- A flipped model of instruction could mitigate this problem: all students could view a prerecorded lecture online before their face-to-face or synchronous class session, freeing their cohort's valuable time with the instructor for engaged learning, small-group work, discussion, or supplementary learning activities such as demonstrations of hands-on processes.

Fully Face-to-Face Instruction (I and II)

Version I — LMS-Enhanced (Comprehensive Instructional Design)
Description

- Students and instructors meet face to face in an on-campus classroom or other learning space.
- All instruction takes place live in real time.
- Course content exists in the LMS, which houses course materials, quizzes and exams and serves as the repository for students' assignments.
- The LMS also provides the course's organizational and communication system, enhancing the face-to-face learning experience.
- The instructor delivers lectures during regularly scheduled class sessions as usual.
- The instructor may choose to post lecture slides, prerecorded lecture videos, or videos created during face-to-face class sessions to the LMS. These items can serve as valuable study aids before exams and can be a resource for students absent during face-to-face class sessions.

Instructor Roles and Responsibilities

- Instructors teach as usual in their on-campus classrooms, but they utilize the LMS to organize course content and materials that enhance and support students' learning.
- The level to which they utilize the LMS is a matter of personal choice.

Student Roles and Responsibilities

Students must attend face-to-face class sessions and meet the course requirements stated in the syllabus, as usual.

Advantages

- Students can catch up with class sessions they miss by accessing lectures in the LMS.
- Instructors can also direct students to these resources if a face-to-face class session is canceled or if the instructor chooses to utilize class time for a different purpose such as a project, field trip, or other activity.
- Even if the instructor's use of LMS-based content is minimal, the course is still poised to pivot in emergencies. For example, if an instructor were suddenly unable to continue teaching the course, another instructor could easily pick up where the previous instructor had left off since everything is prepared and ready to go in the LMS.

Disadvantages

- Faculty may be reluctant to deviate from the norms of traditional on-campus instruction by preparing the entire course on the LMS.
- Students who cannot attend class do not have access to synchronous simulcasts or recordings of class sessions as they do in some other instructional models (although this has always been the case with face-to-face instruction).

Recommendations

- Because faculty who have always taught face to face on campus (except for Emergency Remote Teaching in 2020) may resist undertaking the work of building their course into the LMS, it might be a good idea to arrange to work with an instructional designer who can assist the faculty member in building a course for the first time. This experience can increase faculty buy-in and raise their confidence, helping them see the benefits of this practice to their teaching and for their students.[24]
- If the institution does not employ instructional designers, working with personnel in the Center for Teaching and Learning (or its equivalent) is helpful, as is working with a colleague who has built online courses before.

199

Version II — Traditional Face-to-Face Instruction

Description

- Students and instructors meet face to face in an on-campus classroom or other learning space.
- All instruction takes place live in real time.
- Course content exists entirely offline, usually dependent on printed materials.
- The instructor teaches only during regularly scheduled class sessions.

Instructor Roles and Responsibilities

Instructors teach as usual in their on-campus classrooms, labs, or studios.

Student Roles and Responsibilities

Students must attend face-to-face class sessions and meet course requirements, as stated in the syllabus.

Advantages

This model is comfortable and familiar.

Disadvantages

- Technological enhancements are not utilized, limiting options for communication, assessment, and interaction.
- Instructors are unprepared to respond if unexpected problems make the on-campus learning environment inaccessible (e.g., severe weather, natural disaster, damage to campus buildings, civil unrest, widespread illness, etc.).
- Instructors have few tools available to meet students' needs.

Recommendations

Although this model is preferred by both faculty and students, having existed for centuries (if not millennia), it may no longer be suitable for 21st-century higher education. Providing faculty development in using the LMS to enhance instruction and meet students' needs could result in a model more appropriate to the present day.

Summary and Comparison

Table 4.1 summarizes these instructional models, comparing their identifying features. The more features that are checked, the more complex the model. Here, hyflex emerges as the most complicated model while fully face to face (version II) is the simplest.

200

TABLE 4.1 Summary and Comparison of Instructional Models

	Housed in the LMS	Asynchronous Components	Face-to-Face Components	Synchronous Interaction Through Video Conferencing	Simulcast of Face to Face Classroom via Video Conferencing	Capacity for Flipped Instruction
Fully Online and Asynchronous	✓	✓				
Fully Online and Partially Synchronous	✓	✓		✓		✓
Fully Online and Fully Synchronous	✓	✓		✓		✓
Hyflex	✓	✓	✓	✓	✓	✓
Online Flipped	✓	✓		✓		✓
Face-to-Face Flipped	✓	✓	✓		✓	✓
Modified Face-to-Face and Partially Asynchronous	✓	✓	✓			✓
Fully Face-to-Face I (enhanced)	✓	✓	✓			✓
Fully Face-to-Face II (traditional)			✓			

Our instructional options have expanded greatly in the past decade, moving well beyond the binary of fully online and fully face-to-face models. Technological advancements have opened new possibilities for teaching and learning that formerly existed only in science fiction. Not only can we design a course using these new options, but we can also move between and among them as needed, enhancing our ability to provide educational continuity even in the face of disasters or emergencies.

HOW TO PIVOT

Distance education and its evolution into online learning have added new options for instruction without significantly affecting the longstanding histories and traditions surrounding campus-based teaching. Our dependence on face-to-face instruction has always left us vulnerable to disruptions, rendering us unable to provide educational continuity when floods, fires, hurricanes, tornados, blizzards, earthquakes, social and political unrest, and—yes—outbreaks of illness make it impossible to continue business-as-usual on campus. By combining the best of what we know about online teaching and learning with new technologies for virtual class sessions, we can create a wider variety of options for meeting the needs of both faculty and students, allowing us to continue to deliver instruction no matter where we might be or what we may be facing.

We might visualize instructional components as a menu from which we choose one or more items in each category, combining them in courses that best suit students' needs and instructors' priorities. If one item on the menu becomes unavailable, we can easily substitute another option.

Clearly, we can't anticipate every scenario, but we can examine a few examples using the formula, "if this . . . then that . . ."

- If face-to-face instruction is not possible because the space where the class usually meets has been damaged, then the class can pivot to meet synchronously online.

TABLE 4.2 Course Component Menu Options

Course Component Menu Options			
Instructional Delivery	Interaction	Learning Activities	Assessment
• Face-to-face • Flipped instruction • Pre-recorded video presentation • Simulcast (hyflex) • Slide presentation (with or without audio narration) • Synchronous instruction via video conferencing	• Asynchronous via discussion boards, email, announcements, and feedback on assignments • Face-to-face • Synchronous via video conferencing	• Case studies • Collaborative projects • Community-based learning • Discussion • Problem-based learning • Project-based learning • Reading • Service learning • Skills practice • Writing	• Objective quizzes or exams • Performance tasks • Practical application • Presentations, exhibitions, or performances • Reflective essays

- If the technologies needed to simulcast a face-to-face class to virtual learners (hyflex) are not functioning properly, the instructor can pivot to a modified face-to-face and partially asynchronous model.
- If the partnering organization cancels a planned service-learning activity, the instructor can pivot to a different activity and ask students to write a short research paper about the population served by that organization.
- If a studio art course was supposed to culminate in an exhibition of students' artworks, but an enormous oak tree crashed through the campus gallery's windows during a recent storm, the instructor can pivot to the LMS, asking students to post photographs of their works to a discussion board so the class can hold its final critique virtually. They could also upload images of their artworks to a portfolio site like Flickr, Behance, or Tumblr. As another alternative, students could create a personal website to display images of their artworks, perhaps using a free web hosting service like Weebly, or all students could upload a file folder of their images to Microsoft Teams. The point is to create an electronic collection of the students' artworks that will be accessible to all class members and the instructor, allowing for synchronous critique through video conferencing in which the instructor displays students' works through screen sharing or asynchronous critique through a discussion board where students post a link to the site where their images are posted, and fellow students can post their comments about their peers' works.
- If instructors worry that students are unlikely to be honest when taking a lengthy multiple-choice exam in the LMS, they can pivot to a different type of assessment by reducing the number of objective questions and adding higher-value subjective options, such as a reflective essay or performance task. As another alternative, they could schedule individual appointments with students to administer a modified oral exam by asking students open-ended questions. Furthermore, many institutions subscribe to an online test proctoring service, although this is not a pivot so much as an added technology.
- If the instructor of a face-to-face course has a family emergency and cannot make it to campus, they can pivot by emailing students with instructions to view the lecture in the LMS and complete the follow-up quiz.

For almost any realistic scenario we could imagine, this menu of options contains a solution. The only potential disaster for which Comprehensive Instructional Design could not prepare us is the abrupt loss of the LMS, electrical service, and the internet, all at once. If a catastrophe of that magnitude were to happen, though, we would be facing a much larger issue than educational continuity. It's not necessary to make contingency plans for the zombie apocalypse, the eruption of the super-volcano under Yellowstone National Park, or a devastating meteor strike, either. All we can do is to be as prepared as possible for the kinds of problems that disrupt higher education most of the time. Comprehensive Instructional Design empowers us to do just that.

REFLECTION

I firmly believe we can find a solution for every problem we might face if we are willing to transform challenges into opportunities by being prepared and maintaining a positive attitude. Comprehensive Instructional Design affords this flexibility.

We might look at the instructional models we've examined in this chapter as successive generations of teaching practice, much as technologies receive periodic upgrades.

- Teaching 1.0: Face-to-Face Instruction
- Teaching 2.0: Asynchronous Online Instruction
- Teaching 3.0: Hybrid Instruction
- Teaching 4.0: Synchronous Online Instruction
- Teaching 5.0: Hyflex Instruction (with appropriate assistance as originally envisioned)
- Teaching 6.0: Flexibly pivoting instruction into and out of any given modality

The abilities, competencies, fluencies, literacies, and skills we've developed as educators allow us to teach effectively in any modality. Reading about Comprehensive Instructional Design is a good beginning. I hope that you will continue to seek input beyond this book, learning more about andragogy (adult education), digigogy (digital education), heutagogy (self-determined learning), pedagogy (teaching practice), and omnigogy (flexible movement between teaching models).

Comprehensive Instructional Design allows us to be better educators because it frees us to focus on teaching rather than trying to design and teach at the same time. It also keeps our courses more organized, which is good for everyone. The biggest hurdles are the problems we create for ourselves by clinging so tightly to the past that we cannot reach toward something new and better. We can remain in Teaching 1.0 if we want, but when there are better options available, why would we choose to do so when more effective models exist?

As another attractive advantage, most courses usually need to be built into the LMS just once. Thereafter, we can simply copy its contents to a new course shell each time we teach it again. Some basic maintenance is required after the course-copy procedure, such as adjusting dates, or we might decide to add or change components based on evidence gathered in the previous iteration of the course, such as deciding to include a study guide before an exam on which a majority of students did not achieve the results we'd expected. However, these changes don't usually require the daunting expenditure of time and energy needed to build the course initially. Subsequent course set-up then becomes a matter of hours, not days or weeks.

A well-designed course built in the LMS has positive benefits extending far beyond the course itself. The design process mirrors the steps of action research, and it's also integral to our efforts toward continuous improvement, as we discussed in Chapter 2. Furthermore, placing the course in the LMS puts valuable data for academic program review at our fingertips, which helps prepare for assessment by regional, national, and disciplinary accrediting bodies, not to mention measures of institutional effectiveness. Finally, it serves as evidence of our effectiveness as instructors, contributing to our annual performance evaluations.

No matter which model of instruction we use—whether by choice or by mandate—we must keep our students' well-being and educational needs in mind. The decision to pivot is not about what's best for us as instructors or even what's best for the institution—it's about **what's best for our students**. Indeed, some of these models, especially hyflex instruction and modified face-to-face and partially asynchronous instruction, are much more challenging and labor intensive for the instructor than we might prefer, whereas they pose little hardship for students if we manage them well.

Assuredly, our institutions should provide upskilling and reskilling through faculty development so that more of our colleagues choose to follow us on this journey. I commend you for stepping into the unknown alone. None of us entered the professorate because it would be easy. We chose this job because we are passionate about sharing our disciplinary expertise with our students, hoping that our efforts will produce graduates prepared to rise to the challenges they will encounter in their communities, workplaces, and personal lives and mobilize their education to solve complex problems. We pour our hearts into our work so our graduates will become adaptable, compassionate, competent, curious, ethical, intelligent, well-informed global citizens who not only aspire to make the world a better place but also possess the knowledge, skills, and competencies to do just that.

Please, never forget that you personify the character traits you hope your students will acquire. Your demonstration of adaptability, firmly founded in your preparation of high-quality courses and embodied by your skill in pivoting when faced with unforeseen challenges, is a powerful tool for achieving this aspiration. You also have the opportunity to exemplify grit and a growth mindset since both are necessary whenever we face the unfamiliar or the unexpected.

Higher education's strong preference for its legacies, histories, and traditions shapes every aspect of our professional lives. I respect the value of these histories.

Design Connection	
Empathize	•Your students rightfully expect the institution and their instructors to fulfill their responsibilties within the social contract of higher education. Students mortgage their lives to pursue a degree, and the weight of this knowledge makes them keenly aware of what they stand to lose if their educational experience is disrupted. Providing continuity by being prepared to pivot helps you uphold your end of the bargain and demonstrate empathy for your students.
Define	•As you read this chapter, you engaged in the "define" stage of the design thinking process, reaching an understanding of terms and models related to Comprehensive Instructional Design. The seven models cannot encompass all possible combinations of instructional delivery, interaction, learning activities, and assessments, but they offer a good place for you to begin ideating strategies to maintain educational continuity in the face of emerging challenges or opportunities.
Ideate	•Instructional models vary depending on institutional mandates, such as a decision to implement hyflex across an entire university. Within these parameters, you must plan and prepare for teaching by using your best judgement. How will you engage in ideation to build your course into the LMS? How can you employ strategies for ideation to the process of ensuring quality and continuity in whatever form your course may take?
Prototype	•In essence, pivoting is an ongoing prototyping process - responding to circumstances by changing your approach, trying something new, and seeing how well it works. You make changes in response to these observations and try again. By approaching challenges in the spirit of design rather than grasping tightly to old models, you move foward while minimizing disruption. It's what's best for your students, but it's also best for you.
Test	•For students, a test marks the end of a course. For instructors, the test never ends. Pivoting to a new model of instruction is merely another iteration, during which you have a chance to gather data that contributes to the quality of your course now and the next time you teach it. A design mindset transforms this process into action research. It also provides you with evidence of your effectiveness as an educator for your annual performance evaluation, and it helps with program review and institutional assessment.

FIGURE 4.2 Chapter 4 Design Connection

I've even written in other contexts about my own discipline's deep roots in the past and the value this lends to present-day scholarship. However, the pull to look back can subsume our need to look forward. We stand at the brink of a priceless opportunity to re-envision higher education. What have we learned from Emergency Remote Teaching that we can apply to our work as educators under normal conditions? What technologies or enhancements can we incorporate into our routine instruction to improve student outcomes?

I've encountered some academic fields' slow acceptance of instructional technologies since I first started consulting. I recall a conversation with faculty members who vehemently rejected any form of digital scholarship even as they consulted their smartphones during our meeting and typed notes into their laptop computers. The cognitive dissonance was astounding.

Perhaps it is time to open our minds to new possibilities as we consider the advantages of building our courses online even when we teach only on campus. Pivoting is but one of the benefits we could realize and perhaps not even the most important. Yes, emergency preparedness is unquestionably good, but unlike an underground bunker full of spider webs, canned goods, and stale jugs of water, a repository of learning resources in the LMS is something we can use to our students' benefit every day.

I propose that our way forward does not lie in returning to the past but in embracing the lessons of the present to prepare for the future. We have amazing tools at our fingertips that our predecessors could only have imagined. We've come a long, long way from early attempts at distance learning like correspondence courses, closed-circuit television broadcasts, and self-paced instruction via video-cassette lectures. Today, we can hold a live class with students anywhere in the world. We are no longer tethered to a single campus or classroom, nor are we restricted to a set schedule. Such freedom is unprecedented, and although its very unfamiliarity is uncomfortable, it's also exciting. Technologies that existed only in science fiction when most faculty were children are now commonplace. Why, then, should we settle for a return to an archaic model of teaching and learning that is so much less flexible and does not meet present or future needs?

In our next chapter, we will consider taking the next steps to becoming more student-centered future-ready instructors and turn our attention to high-impact practices that can offer a better educational experience to our students.

Notes

[1] Hodges, C., Moore, S., Lockee, B., Trust, T., & Bond, A. (2020, Mar 27). The Difference Between Emergency Remote Teaching and Online Learning. *Educause.Edu.* https://er.educause.edu/articles/2020/3/the-difference-between-emergency-remote-teaching-and-online-learning

[2] Hodgson, P., et al. (2019) Immersive virtual reality (IVR) in higher education: Development and implementation. In T. Jung, M. C. tom Dieck, & P. Rauschnabel (Eds.), *Augmented reality and virtual reality: Changing realities in a dynamic world*. New York: Springer.

[3] Means, B., Toyama, Y., Murphy, R., Bakia, M., & Jones, K. (2010). *Evaluation of evidence-based practices in online learning: A meta-analysis and review of online learning studies*. US Department of Education. Retrieved from https://www2.ed.gov/rschstat/eval/tech/evidence-based-practices/finalreport.pdf; Cook, D. A., & Steinert, Y. (2013). Online learning for faculty development: A review of the literature. *Medical Teacher*, 35(11), 930–937. doi:10.3109/0142159X.2013.827328; Sheikh, S. (2016). *Perceptions of faculty member and administrators from on-campus universities regarding online doctorates in education*. Northcentral University, ProQuest

207

Dissertations Publishing. Retrieved from https://search.proquest.com/openview/bcb13358b8e1775ff6880fcd6f8c30b3/1?pq-origsite=gscholar&cbl=18750&diss=y

[4] Shireman, R. (2018). Selling the American dream: What the Trump University scam teaches us about predatory colleges. *Social Research: An International Quarterly*, *85*(4), 767–794. Retrieved from www.muse.jhu.edu/article/716114

[5] Halverson, L. R., & Graham, C. R. (2019). Learner engagement in blended learning environments: A conceptual framework. *Online Learning*, *23*(2), 145–178. doi:10.24059/olj.v23i2.1481; Poon, J. (2013. Blended learning: An institutional approach for enhancing students' learning experiences. *Journal of Online Learning and Teaching*, *9*(2), 271–288.

[6] Seligman, A. (2019). *Blended, hybrid, and flipped courses: What's the difference?* Temple University Center for the Advancement of Teaching. Retrieved from https://teaching.temple.edu/edvice-exchange/2019/11/blended-hybrid-and-flipped-courses-what%E2%80%99s-difference; Roehl, A., Shweta, L., & Shannon, G. (2013). The flipped classroom: An opportunity to engage millennial students through active learning strategies. *Journal of Family and Consumer Science*, *105*(2). Retrieved from https://pdfs.semanticscholar.org/daa3/b94cdc7b52b3381a7c7e21022a7a8c005f84.pdf Shi, Y., Ma, Y., MacLeod, J., et al. (2020). College students' cognitive learning outcomes in flipped classroom instruction: A meta-analysis of the empirical literature. *Journal of Computer Education*, 7, 79–103. https://doi.org/10.1007/s40692-019-00142-8

[7] Seligman, A. (2019). *Blended, hybrid, and flipped courses: What's the difference?* Temple University Center for the Advancement of Teaching. Retrieved from https://teaching.temple.edu/edvice-exchange/2019/11/blended-hybrid-and-flipped-courses-what%E2%80%99s-difference

[8] I taught a dual-enrollment hybrid course that was held online with two scheduled face-to-face sessions held at a regional high school on Saturdays during the eight-week term. Our Saturday classes provided supplementary discussion of concepts in the course but did not replace any of its online components.

[9] Hybrid-Flexible (or Hyflex) Implementation Guide. (2020). *Modes of teaching*. The University of North Carolina at Chapel Hill. Retrieved from https://keepteaching.unc.edu/hybrid-flexible/; Succeeding with HyFlex Instruction at CMU. (2020). *Office of the provost: Curriculum and instruction*. Central Michigan University. Retrieved from www.cmich.edu/office_provost/CIS/Pages/Access%20Course%20Delivery%20Services/Succeeding-with-HyFlex-Instruction.aspx; Beatty, B. J. (2019). *Hybrid-flexible course design: Implementing student-directed hybrid classes*. EdTech Books. Retrieved from https://edtechbooks.org/hyflex/

[10] Personal interview with Derrick Anderson of Arizona State University, conducted via Zoom on May 18, 2020. See also https://asunow.asu.edu/20200710-sun-devil-life-what-difference-between-asu-sync-icourses-and-asu-online

[11] Clemson University. (2020). *Academic program planning*. New Instructional Playbook: See all Models. Retrieved from www.clemson.edu/otei/fall2020-academic-models.html

[12] Poll Everywhere. www.polleverywhere.com/

[13] Doodle. https://doodle.com/free-online-survey

[14] Class Updates. http://classupdatesapp.com/

[15] Beatty, B. J. (2019). *Hybrid-flexible course design: Implementing student-directed hybrid classes*. EdTech Books. Retrieved from https://edtechbooks.org/hyflex/

[16] Hinck, G., & Burke, L. (2019). New technologies deliver on the promise of Hyflex: University of St. Thomas. In B. J. Beatty (Ed.), *Hybrid-flexible course design*. EdTech Books. Retrieved from https://edtechbooks.org/hyflex/hyflex-UST

[17] Beatty, B. J. (2019). Teaching a hybrid-flexible course: The faculty experience in Hyflex. In B. J. Beatty (Ed.), *Hybrid-flexible course design: Implementing student directed hybrid classes*. EdTech Books. Retrieved from https://edtechbooks.org/hyflex/teaching_hyflex

[18] Hinck, G., & Burke, L. (2019). New technologies deliver on the promise of Hyflex: University of St. Thomas. In B. J. Beatty (Ed.), *Hybrid-flexible course design*. EdTech Books. Retrieved from https://edtechbooks.org/hyflex/hyflex-UST

[19] Succeeding with HyFlex Instruction at CMU. (2020). *Office of the Provost: Curriculum and Instruction*. Central Michigan University. Retrieved from www.cmich.edu/office_provost/CIS/Pages/Access%20Course%20Delivery%20Services/Succeeding-with-Hy-Flex-Instruction.aspx

[20] Leigh, R. (2012). The classroom is alive with the sound of thinking: The power of the exit slip. *International Journal of Teaching and Learning in Higher Education*, 24(2), 1890196. https://files.eric.ed.gov/fulltext/EJ996265.pdf

[21] The Minute Paper. (n.d.). *Center for the enhancement of teaching and learning*. Tufts University. Retrieved from https://provost.tufts.edu/celt/files/MinutePaper.pdf

[22] Hinck, G., & Burke, L. (2019). New technologies deliver on the promise of Hyflex: University of St. Thomas. In B. J. Beatty (Ed.), *Hybrid-flexible course design*. EdTech Books. Retrieved from https://edtechbooks.org/hyflex/hyflex-UST

[23] Shi, Y., Ma, Y., MacLeod, J., et al. (2020). College students' cognitive learning outcomes in flipped classroom instruction: A meta-analysis of the empirical literature. *Journal of Computer Education*, 7, 79–103. doi:10.1007/s40692-019-00142-8

[24] Personal interview with Dr. Derrick Anderson, Advisor to the President of Arizona State University, conducted via Zoom on May 18, 2020. Dr. Anderson said that every faculty member at ASU who worked with an instructional designer to create an online course felt it was a very positive experience and shared their enthusiasm with peers, who then followed suit to take advantage of this valuable resource to improve their pedagogical practice.

Chapter 5

Adapting High-Impact Practices Across Instructional Models

****

High-impact practices, or HIPs, are proven strategies for supporting students' success. In my experiences across higher education, I've encountered a lot of talk about HIPs. The topic crops up in situations like committee meetings, when someone (often a dean or provost) says, "We need to start incorporating high-impact practices," and the faculty members nod in agreement. The trouble is, we don't really know how to do this or even what HIPs would look like if we tried to take them from theory to practice. My goal in this chapter is to synthesize this admonition into practical advice that any faculty member could use to make their courses better, stronger, and more effective than ever before.

So far, our journey has taken us from the intersection of tradition-bound face-to-face instruction and Emergency Remote Teaching to the point that we now understand the rationale behind adopting Comprehensive Instructional Design. We're better equipped to build our courses online and to implement flexible approaches to instruction that allow us to maintain educational continuity through nearly all eventualities. Now we'll learn a bit about what HIPs are and think about how incorporating HIPs into our courses can take our practice as educators to the next level.

To accomplish this purpose, the following pages cover a great deal of information, but they may not convey quite the same personal tone as other sections of this book.

A SHORT DEFINITION

For more than a dozen years, colleges and universities nationwide have referenced George Kuh's *High-Impact Educational Practices:What They Are,Who Has Access to Them, andWhy They Matter* (2008, AAC&U). Extensive research supports the efficacy of high-impact practices (HIPs) to increase student engagement and facilitate academic success. It's a simple matter to find literature identifying what these practices are, who benefits most from them, and why they're important. But a crucial element is missing from most of the literature about HIPs: *how?* HIPs tend to be large-scale efforts or university-wide initiatives, so our task is to determine how we can adapt high-impact practices for implementation in our classrooms.

High-impact practices include:

1. First-Year Seminars and Experiences
2. Common Intellectual Experiences
3. Learning Communities
4. Writing-Intensive Courses
5. Collaborative Assignments and Projects
6. Undergraduate Research
7. Diversity/Global Learning
8. ePortfolios
9. Service Learning, Community-Based Learning
10. Internships
11. Capstone Courses and Projects

The Association of American Colleges and Universities (AAC&U) supports a national initiative known by its acronym LEAP—Liberal Education and America's Promise. LEAP encourages dialog about the fundamental nature of higher education, provides guidance for students, and promotes a framework for excellence beneficial to all students in achieving the essential outcomes of a liberal education: "broad knowledge, intellectual and practical skills, personal and social responsibility, and integrative learning," especially for "students who, historically, have been underserved in higher education."[1] HIPs are among LEAP's focus areas, along with essential learning outcomes, principles of excellence, authentic assessments, and an initiative promoting a nationwide requirement that all students complete a "substantial cross-disciplinary project in a topic significant to the student and society."[2]

HIPs share a set of eight key elements.[3] Not every HIP will demonstrate all eight, but they frequently include four or more. These elements also describe high-quality teaching and learning. As you read this list, pause and ask yourself: "Do any of these statements describe my course?" If you can't identify them in your course, do they apply to the program in which your course exists?

- Performance expectations set at appropriately high levels.
- A significant investment of time and effort by students over an extended period.
- Interactions with faculty and peers about significant matters.
- Experiences with diversity, wherein students are exposed to and must contend with people and circumstances that differ from those with which students are familiar.
- Frequent, timely, and constructive feedback.
- Periodic structured opportunities to reflect and integrate learning.
- Opportunities to discover the relevance of learning through real-world applications.
- Public demonstration of competence.

So, why are HIPs important? At their core, HIPs are about building connections. When we strengthen students' relationships with faculty and peers, embed learning in real-world contexts, and increase student engagement with the topics they're studying, we can deliver an educational experience that empowers students' academic achievement and facilitates their ability to form connections between their education and their lives after graduation.

Educational psychologists such as Jean Piaget (1936)[4] and Jerome Bruner (1957)[5] and neuroscientists (Kandel, 2012[6]; Eagleman, 2015)[7] explain that the human brain learns by making connections between new knowledge and prior learning. The more we strengthen those connections, the deeper our learning. We know that practice and repetition help students learn, but the more they conduct this practice within authentic settings, the more effective and satisfying their learning will be. The human brain connects new learning to prior factual knowledge and to emotions, experiences, sensory input, and actions. Conversely, it's far less effective to learn by rote (simple memorization) or in isolation because new knowledge lacks connection to anything other than itself.

Given what we learned about Comprehensive Instructional Design in the preceding chapters, we now have the skills and knowledge to pivot, using what we've learned about design to adapt and scale high-impact practices in our teaching, regardless of the instructional model we may be using at present. George Kuh may have conceived high-impact practices with a model of traditional face-to-face instruction in mind, but they are also adaptable to online learning, as seen in works such as Kathryn Linder and Chrysanthemum Hayes' *High-Impact Practices in Online Education* (2018),[8] aligning with many of the ideas presented in this chapter. Technological tools can add beneficial elements to HIPs, such as facilitating communication across multiple modalities of instruction. They require alignment and planning (which is true of any instructional practice), but adding HIPs to our online instruction extends their impact to students across higher education.[9]

In the next sections, we'll examine each of the HIPs in succession, ending these explanations with **Action Steps** that faculty can take to integrate the principles of the HIP in their classrooms and **Pivot Points** that clarify how we might adapt or adjust each HIP for the range of instructional models we've examined.

First-Year Experiences

The transition from high school to college marks an exciting personal milestone, but it's also a monumental change for which some students are ill prepared. K–12 public education remains a highly structured environment in which students have little choice in what, where, when, how, and with whom they will study. Teachers rarely leave students unsupervised, and rigid systems of rules ensure compliance with performance expectations. College offers a great deal more independence, but this unaccustomed freedom also demands a higher degree of personal motivation and responsibility.

We expect college students to leap from a very structured, highly supervised environment into a setting where they must be self-directed, independent, and responsible, yet we may not provide much by way of personal development or pre-transitional mentoring. Compounding the problem, students may lack essential skills such as time management, appropriate communication, self-care, respect for rules and policies, or character traits such as honesty, integrity, and perseverance.

First-year seminars or experiences arose from institutions' recognition of these problems, beginning at the University of South Carolina in the 1970s.[10] As of 2010, 95% of four-year institutions offered a first-year seminar,[11] and that estimate may well have increased over the intervening decade. Of course, each college or university places its own stamp on the first-year experience, but research by Hickinbottom et al. shows that these programs tend to share the goal of increasing retention by strengthening student engagement and fostering academic success. First-year programs usually seek to help students: (1) develop a connection with the institution, (2) become familiar with the campus's resources and services, and (3) develop academic skills.[12]

An effective first-year seminar helps students understand *why* the topic or skill we want them to acquire is important, *how* to acquire this skill or knowledge, and *what* it looks like outside the course. For instance, we know that teaching students how to write a good topic sentence is worthwhile, but deep learning of this skill is far more likely if the instructor:

- Explains why the skill is important both in students' collegiate experiences and their future professions.
- Provides examples of good topic sentences in disciplinary writing.
- Asks students to practice writing topic sentences for different purposes and share their work with peers.
- Provides feedback on their efforts and opportunities for revision of their writing.

This instructional practice deliberately connects new learning to students' prior knowledge, embeds it within a social and emotional context, and ensures opportunities to receive and develop new skills and knowledge through active learning strategies and practical application. As a result, students are much more likely to perceive the value of instruction, remember what they've learned beyond the final exam, and apply their learning in other contexts.

Generations of students have arrived on college campuses unprepared for what they will face, yet they adapted and moved forward on their educational journeys. Nevertheless, our incoming students, especially (and somewhat surprisingly) those who fit the traditional profile, lack the essential knowledge, skills, and personal characteristics that gave their instructors the ability to navigate the first-year experience. We must also consider that half our students might be adult learners, as we discussed in Chapter 1, whose adjustment to college differs from students who just graduated from high school.[13] Online learning presents yet another hurdle, requiring more advanced competencies in time management and self-discipline to keep up with asynchronous course requirements.

Even if you don't teach introductory courses, the strategies and principles of first-year experiences can improve your students' learning.

Action Steps

- Clearly explain the connection between your course content and students' subsequent coursework or its application to their lives or careers after graduation.

214

- Provide information about campus services or resources that could help students meet course requirements, such as the Writing Center. Even if you included this information in your syllabus already, mentioning it again during a lecture increases the likelihood students will take advantage of available support.
- Incorporate direct instruction of academic skills crucial to your courses, such as critical inquiry, writing, information literacy, collaboration, and teamwork. We'd like to think students possessed these skills before they enrolled in our course, but this is often a false assumption on our part. If there's something students must know or be able to do in your course, you have to teach it to them because complaining that they don't know it just doesn't work. Plan supplementary lessons to provide your students with the competencies they need for success.
- Address personal competencies or abilities such as time management, attendance, study skills, and so on. This information need not always be part of your lectures, but weekly email and course announcements offer good coaching opportunities in an asynchronous environment, as do the moments at the beginning and end of a face-to-face class session. For example, we know that students tend to procrastinate. If a major project's due date is approaching, you could say (or write, depending on the model of your course), "I know that the deadline for our course project seems like it's far in the future, but three weeks will pass very quickly. Here's a sample timeline that will help you get the project done in plenty of time. By the end of next week, you should . . ."
- Make a point of establishing a personal connection with each student by sending an email or asking them to stay for a moment after class to check in with you. A simple inquiry about their well-being or asking an open-ended question like, "What has been the greatest challenge you've faced in this course so far?" can build rapport and let the student know that you care about their success.

Pivot Points

- Communicate important information to your students across multiple platforms, including email, announcements posted to the LMS, and verbally in the face-to-face classroom or synchronous class sessions. It's better to over-communicate even though students might receive a message in more than one modality than to under-communicate and cause some students to miss out on crucial information.
- Treat each student as an individual and invite them to contact you to discuss challenges they may face in assimilating into the classroom environment, even if their concerns are unrelated to your course content.

215

Some online students may need assistance using the video conferencing service, for instance. Face-to-face commuter students may have difficulty finding parking close to the building where your class meets.

■ Consider adding activities that build relationships and increase engagement. You could begin a synchronous or face-to-face class session with a short poll asking an ice-breaker question, for example, or build a discussion board where students can help one another by responding to a quick "question of the week" like, "What advice would you give to someone new to online learning?" awarding extra-credit points to students who respond or comment on peers' posts.

Common Intellectual Experiences

To a certain way of thinking, every learning environment from preschool to graduate school offers a common intellectual experience (CIE) since all students in a class participate in the same educational activities. It's also the purpose of core curricula or general education courses. Nevertheless, traditional instruction represents the barest minimum of what a CIE can offer. Courses or other learning activities classified as CIEs typically include five components.

■ Interdisciplinary theme
■ Shared content between courses
■ Faculty collaboration
■ Co-curricular connections[14]
■ Strategies for active learning

As an example, Michigan State University offers paired courses for first-year students that share a common theme and connect this theme to activities outside the classroom. The 2017 CIE pilot program demonstrated notably positive non-cognitive outcomes among student participants, including enhanced social integration, increased self-efficacy, and establishing a growth mindset. Students participating in these courses also outperformed peers enrolled in non-CIE versions of the same courses.[15]

Although this high-impact practice is geared toward institutions or programs rather than individual instructors, we can draw inspiration from CIEs as we learn more about how they work. CIEs typically incorporate at least four of the eight key elements of HIPs, all of which could be part of our courses.

■ Interaction with faculty and peers about substantive matters.
■ Experiences with diversity, wherein students interact with people and circumstances that differ from those with which students are familiar.

- Periodic, structured opportunities to reflect and integrate learning.
- Opportunities to discover the relevance of learning through real-world applications.[16]

CIEs take many forms. A one-time activity of significant value for a small group of students can be a CIE. A single course or pair of courses can fulfill the requirements of being a CIE. We might link courses horizontally within a major through a shared theme or link them sequentially to provide opportunities for students and faculty to engage in long-term collaborative projects (notably one of the Big Six's goals). CIEs could expand upon general education requirements such as writing across the curriculum or writing in a particular discipline that continues student learning from their introductory English requirements or their first-year experience courses. At their most extensive, CIEs can unify comprehensive integrated programs for large student populations, serving to synthesize learning across general education requirements and co-curricular activities.[17]

The primary benefit of CIEs is their capacity to integrate students' learning across multiple knowledge domains or topics, leading students to think holistically about their educational experiences. Activities facilitating reflection (a hallmark of all HIPs) are particularly important in this regard, helping students identify what they have learned explicitly and implicitly and across both positive and negative experiences. For instance, students who realize they can learn from failure and success develop resilience and persistence—both essential to life in the rapidly changing world of the 21st century.

CIEs present challenges for online learning environments, however. Online or blended models rely on flexibility, student choice, and asynchronous interaction, so students' learning can be more fragmented, limiting common experiences.[18] Nevertheless, we can find common areas to explore even with an increasingly diverse student body and geographical distancing by using the action steps and pivot points that follow.

Action Steps

- Include an activity that builds meaningful interaction between students and the instructor. Reading an impactful book and holding subsequent discussions—a "common read"—is a well-known CIE, but other options are also possible.
- Explore substantive themes and ideas through your course, especially connections to diversity or exposing students to people or ideas with which they are unfamiliar. Make a point of using diverse examples or resources in your instruction, addressing the intersection of diversity and your academic field, or acknowledging how your field needs to

217

improve in this regard. Diversity does not always involve race: the underrepresentation of women in computer science and men in nursing exemplify inequalities in those fields. Every field has room to grow when it comes to diversity, so fostering open conversation about these matters helps all students expand their thinking.

■ Build opportunities for reflection into your course through the discussion board or face-to-face discussion, small-group interactions, or written assignments such as reflective essays. Requiring students to pause and reflect on their learning helps them transfer their knowledge from short-term to long-term memory by linking it to meaning and emotion.

■ Include activities that link your course content to the world outside the university, such as case studies, community-based learning, service learning, job shadowing, or other experiential learning. Students could interview a family member, community member, or professional in your discipline. You could invite a guest speaker who is a professional in your discipline to talk about how they applied their education in the workplace. There are many options for helping students connect what they are learning in your class and its application beyond the real or virtual classroom.

■ The "common read" strategy is as applicable online as it is on campus, and discussions about an impactful text can easily be held through video conferencing or discussion boards.

Pivot Points

■ In a face-to-face course, a common intellectual experience could involve an outing or field trip—something that takes everyone outside their normal instructional context to participate in a shared experience. Online, students might watch an impactful film asynchronously and discuss it afterward (being careful, of course, to obtain necessary permissions or clearances so as not to violate copyright or fair use laws). An online guest speaker could also provide a common intellectual experience.

■ Students may not be able to participate in learning activities at the same time and in the same place, but they can independently conduct variations on the same activity and then discuss the experience through video conferencing or a discussion board. For example, a course on educational history might ask students to interview a person over age 70, asking questions about their elementary school experience. Students could share their findings to form a more comprehensive view of what school was like decades ago. They would have the common experience of conducting an interview while retaining the flexibility and distancing of online learning.

Learning Communities

Alexander Meiklejohn established the first learning communities at the Experimental College of the University of Wisconsin in the late 1920s, followed by Joseph Tussman's Experimental College at the University of California at Berkeley in the mid-1960s, which quickly inspired the founding of Evergreen State College (WA) in 1970.[19] Broadly defined, learning communities enroll a common cohort of students in groups of two or more courses linked by a shared interdisciplinary theme or problem. Learning communities have been common in higher education since the 1990s. Their longevity rests in their effectiveness. Zhao and Kuh (2004) identified a significant impact of student participation in learning communities with their academic success and retention, demonstrating "enhanced academic performance, integration of academic and social experiences, gains in multiple areas of skill, competence, and knowledge, and overall satisfaction with the college experience."[20]

Similarities between learning communities and common intellectual experiences are obvious. However, the primary purpose of a CIE is to deepen students' learning through reflection, application, and integration of knowledge and skills beyond the boundaries of courses or activities in which they exist. The primary purpose of a learning community, on the other hand, is to build a sense of community between and among students, faculty, and staff by placing them in an academic context that exhibits three distinctive characteristics.[21]

- **Shared Knowledge**: students register for a pair or group of courses organized around a central theme, designed to promote higher levels of cognitive complexity than taking unrelated courses.
- **Shared Knowing**: because all students in the learning community enroll in the same courses at the same time, they build relationships as they construct knowledge together. Shared knowing fosters social and intellectual engagement, promotes cognitive development, and nurtures an appreciation for others' perspectives.
- **Shared Responsibility**: coursework offers frequent opportunities to participate in collaborative groups. Students develop essential skills in teamwork, cooperation, problem solving, negotiation, communication, and accountability.

In other words, learning communities provide academic content while also teaching students how to build relationships and how to work with others toward a common goal.

219

Learning communities generally take one of four forms, although many configurations are possible.

- **Linked courses** share a cohort of students and are organized around complementary themes, readings, skills, assignments, projects, or experiences.
- **Freshman interest groups** (also known as FIGs) supplement linked courses by incorporating co-curricular and community-building activities organized around a common interest or shared theme.
- **Meta-majors** cluster courses within a field of interest, introducing students to a broad career field and providing opportunities to explore various possible majors that share a set of prerequisites.
- **Living-learning communities** combine the residential experience with elements of FIGs or meta-majors. Students live in a campus residence with peers who share a common interest and participate in activities, events, excursions, or experiences designed to help them build relationships and acclimate to college life.

The practices listed here are quite common, but we might also consider some innovative alternatives that show how the idea of a learning community can be adapted to suit different student populations. For example, commuter students tend to be left out of learning communities simply because they don't live on campus, which places them at a disadvantage when building peer relationships. Drexel University's LeBow College of Business offers a learning community for commuter students (CLC)[22] that fosters a sense of belonging on campus, helps students develop peer relationships, and enhances the learning experience. The group emphasizes balance, providing high-quality opportunities for meaningful engagement scheduled to align with commuter students' responsibilities and schedules outside the university. Like other learning communities, it includes instruction in time management and other essential skills, but students also participate in off-campus excursions, corporate site visits, career development, and civic engagement. Participants in the CLC are so enthusiastic about this program that they choose to remain part of the group as upperclassmen and alumni.

Like Drexel University, San Diego State University not only has a commuter learning community similar to Drexel, but also established a home base for these students—the Commuter Resource Center: a staffed area with access to amenities commonly found in dormitories, including a kitchen area with refrigerator, sink, and microwaves; comfortable seating; work stations; computers; and free printers. SDSU's commuter students can choose from among several Commuter Success Pathways built around the common goals of building relationships, feeling a sense of belonging on campus, becoming part of a small community of peers who share common interests, and receiving specific academic support.[23] (Having been a commuter student during my undergraduate years, I can attest to the fact that this would be extremely helpful. Many commuters have no space to call their own other than their cars, and for those who commute via public transportation, lack of a "home base" is even more of a problem.)

Instructional models in which students never meet face to face present another level of challenge to building community, but this is not impossible, as we saw in Chapter 3. Online, we need to be more strategic and deliberate, but we can still achieve positive outcomes.[24]

Because we are considering how individual instructors can scale this HIP to their classrooms, our action steps will mirror the three distinctive characteristics of learning communities. After all, each course we teach is a self-contained temporary community, even if we never meet in person (as in the fully online and fully asynchronous models). By taking steps to build a sense of community among the class members, we enhance our students' collegiate experience and deepen their learning.

Action Steps

- **Shared Knowledge**: structure your course around a central theme or topic to create a cohesive, comprehensible, and engaging body of knowledge.
- **Shared Knowing**: build opportunities for peer-to-peer interaction through small-group discussions or collaborative projects that allow students to discover and construct knowledge together. The combination of social and intellectual engagement promotes cognitive development and nurtures an appreciation for others' perspectives.
- **Shared Responsibility**: utilize strategies for active learning such as discussion groups, partner activities, or collaborative projects to help students develop essential skills in teamwork, cooperation, problem solving, negotiation, communication, and accountability as they learn how to distribute responsibilities among participants and fulfill their obligations to the group's successful completion of a project.

Pivot Points

- Incorporate video responses in discussion boards to help students get to know one another.
- Use the chat function in video conferencing, if available. For example, Zoom and Microsoft Teams allow participants to use a text-based chat feature to communicate with one participant or the entire group. During synchronous discussions, allow students to chat a response to a classmate of their choice, or assign students a "chat partner" to whom they respond

to the instructor's questions. In a face-to-face class, this might be called a "turn and talk" response, but we can adapt it to online settings with the chat function.

■ Encourage students to use a few minutes before or after synchronous class sessions for conversations about topics other than the day's lecture. Casual interactions happen quite naturally in face-to-face settings, but an instructor teaching online will need to inform students that the class session will open a few minutes early and encourage students to use that time to talk to one another.

■ Place students into discussion groups that meet in a breakout room during a synchronous class session, meet virtually using video conferencing, or conduct asynchronous conversations through a discussion board. (Blackboard Collaborate and Zoom both offer breakout rooms, as just two examples.)

Writing-Intensive Courses

Adults are aware that we speak differently depending on our audience. The tone, style, and mannerisms we employ when chatting with a colleague tend to be different from the voice we use when lecturing, which differs yet again from the way we speak to our families at home. Students aren't as perceptive of these differences in verbal communication and are even less likely to realize that expectations for writing can be vastly different, depending upon the intended recipient and the context in which the writing occurs. First-year students are baffled when a paper that would have earned an A in high school now receives a C or worse from a college professor. Likewise, students may have completed Composition 101 and 102 successfully but cannot write a coherent paper for a course in their major.

Writing-intensive courses address poor-quality student writing by integrating specific instruction in expectations for written communication across curricular areas, accompanied by frequent opportunities for feedback and revision. Harvard University defines a writing-intensive course as including the following characteristics, similar to those at many colleges and universities.[25]

1. Timely feedback on student writing, both written and spoken, during one or more conferences between the student and instructor.
2. Opportunities for revision of written work, including a sequence of draft, feedback, rethinking, rewriting; peer feedback and evaluation.
3. Multiple or sequential writing assignments throughout the semester or a longer paper completed in installments.
4. Small class sizes or the capacity for small sections within larger classes, ensuring students receive individual attention.

5. A significant portion of the student's grade depends on the quality of thought expressed in good writing.

Writing-intensive courses can exist in any major and pair with virtually any academic content. Of course, written assignments are ubiquitous across most courses, but the decisive factor in being writing intensive is embedding instruction in writing coupled with individual attention to help students become better writers. We don't just assign a paper—we tell them how to write it, give them feedback on their writing at least once during the writing process, and allow them to rewrite and improve the paper before it receives a final grade.

We may be wise to consider that teaching a writing-intensive course is not something best suited to all faculty. Art Young (2006) offers this wise advice:

> If you have little interest in reading student writing, chances are that students will have little interest in writing it. Under such conditions, we teachers create a situation in which writers who don't want to write, write for readers who don't want to read, and we do this in the name of improving communication. . . . Rather, writing across the curriculum suggests that we begin by creating assignments in a classroom environment where students and teachers are eager to read one another's work.[26]

The success of writing-intensive courses has led to "parallel efforts in such areas as quantitative reasoning, oral communication, information literacy, and, on some campuses, ethical inquiry"[27] across the curriculum. Not every course must become a writing-intensive course. However, we can incorporate some of these strategies into every course, especially those in which writing serves as a major component of students' final grades. Writing extends across all instructional models, so we can employ these strategies no matter where our course falls on the spectrum between fully online and fully face to face. By learning how to become proficient writers, students also learn how to identify, process, synthesize, and publish the knowledge they acquire through their studies. In short, making an intentional effort to teach students how to become better writers, even in courses that are not "about" writing per se, has multiple benefits.

Action Steps

- ■ Include specific course objectives for writing in addition to your disciplinary learning goals, and employ formative assessment of students' written work. For instance, instead of assigning one big research paper due on the last day of class, you could scaffold the task incrementally, providing critique and opportunity for revision at each stage.

223

- Identify areas of your course where you could include writing activities. Even courses that generally do not require writing could incorporate a written response. For instance, students in an acting course could attend a play and write a critique of an actor's performance.
- Embed explicit instruction in the modes and expectations for writing in your primary discipline. Instruction could include good examples of disciplinary writing, such as articles from professional journals. We should also teach students how to critique one another's work and effectively use proofreading and editing software.
- Assign only purposeful and meaningful writing tasks. Writing shouldn't only generate a course grade—it should actively engage students' curiosity, creativity, and intellect.
- Provide direct instruction in your discipline's norms for written communication, including key terminology, vocabulary, preferred style guides, and resource materials.
- Choose assignments for which you will provide students with formative and actionable feedback before submitting the final paper or project.[28]
- Embed opportunities for students to read and analyze professional writing in your discipline.
- Create resources, templates, outlines, or other scaffolding for your writing assignments that will allow students to meet your expectations successfully.

Pivot Points

- Fully online and fully asynchronous courses naturally require more writing than instructional models in which some or all interaction occurs synchronously or face to face. Instructors should consider the *entire* writing load—not only written assignments but also requirements such as participation in discussion boards—modifying the writing workload if necessary. Rigor should never mean piling on more work than the student can manage.
- Consider how to use technology to your students' advantage as writers. For example, students could engage in peer editing using Google Docs, allowing multiple users to work on the same document.
- Ask students to read and respond to professional literature in your discipline by posting a PDF or link to an article in a professional journal to a discussion board and asking students to post a reflection about the article and three questions that occurred to them as they were reading.

Creativity-Infused Learning: the Missing HIP

Infusing creativity into students' educational experience is not among the HIPs promoted by the AAC&U, yet research into the advantages of direct engagement in making and doing reveals similar benefits. A few excerpts from *Surveying the Landscape: Arts Integration at Research Universities* (2015)[29] illustrate this point.

> Students in any major field and at every level from undergraduate students to doctoral candidates experience the benefits of hands-on participation in making, doing, creating, and performing, just as faculty members from across the university find that their personal participation in arts practice enhances their work in their major academic discipline.[30]
>
> The arts provide intrinsically engaging content, allowing students to connect with course topics on a more emotional or visceral level than lectures, textbooks, and research papers. Furthermore, making and doing activate different parts of the brain than reading and listening, providing an enhanced learning experience and greater student engagement.[31]
>
> The arts encourage risk-taking, experimentation, and exploration, but university students arrive on campus pre-trained in risk-aversion, having grown up in an academic system rewarding them for achieving 100% on an exam, not for trying an exam multiple times until they "get it right." When students enter the workforce they find no such situation exists in adulthood: life demands a high capacity for iteration, a willingness to try and try again, seeking new means of addressing challenges.[32] Integrating the arts in the university helps to address this need, involving students in participatory investigations simulating likely conditions outside academia.[33]

Of course, making and doing are not the exclusive territory of the arts. Engineering, advertising, web design, writing, product development, publishing, and education are deeply creative fields, among many others. Building our students' capacity for creativity is all the more important as we find ourselves trying to stimulate their suppressed imaginations, held at bay for so long by the pressure to achieve high scores on standardized tests or subsumed by hyper-saturation in media and entertainment that leaves little room for independent thinking.

Businesses constantly cite creativity as a crucial competency, yet our schools produce just the opposite. In an article for *The Guardian*, Tham Khai Meng commented:[34]

> We are not talking about high art, but empowering people to use their imagination. Not everyone can be Mozart, but everyone can sing. I believe everyone is born creative, but it is educated out of us at school, where we

225

are taught literacy and numeracy. Sure, there are classes called writing and art, but what's really being taught is conformity.

Young children fizz with ideas. But the moment they go to school, they begin to lose the freedom to explore, take risks and experiment.

We spend our childhoods being taught the artificial skill of passing exams. We learn to give teachers what they expect. By the time we get into industry, we have been conditioned to conform. We spend our days in meetings and talk about "thinking outside the box," but rarely do we step outside it.

These words, although dire, have the ring of truth. Picasso famously said, "Every child is born an artist. The problem is to remain one as he grows up."[35] We can easily see this in the delightfully unconstrained creative activities of very young children, which become increasingly conventional as they progress through school. There's no hidden agenda among schoolteachers to squash creativity, but public education's norms and practices reward conformity over originality. Once these students arrive in our college classrooms, their creative skills are rusty, at best. In "How Digital Media Has Changed Creativity" (2016), Chandra Johnson reported:

> A 2010 study from the College of William and Mary examining more than 300,000 creativity tests dating back to the 1970s found that creativity has declined generally among American children. Researchers studied results of the Torrance Test of Creative Thinking, an exam often called the "gold standard" for measuring creativity in children. The test is widely trusted because of its high correlation rate between its scores and future accomplishments—high test scores on a Torrance test correlated to three times more lifetime accomplishments than child IQ tests.
>
> The findings stated that children were becoming less humorous, less imaginative and less able to generate unique ideas. While creativity is innate in humans from birth, it's a quality that has to be nurtured to be useful, like any skill.[36]

Reasons for this are many. The high-stakes testing culture of K–12 education has eased somewhat with the expiration of No Child Left Behind in 2015,[37] but today's college students lived with this pressure—and its impact on their schools—through their formative years, long before stepping foot on our campuses. Furthermore, increasing childhood use of technology also hinders creativity. Johnson also reported

> "Focus is the superpower of the 21st century. You need to be able to think deeply to get ideas and put them into action," said creativity researcher and

UC Berkeley sociologist Christine Carter. "But a brain that's used to being highly stimulated can't do deep work. It can write a tweet, it can't write a book."

The consequences of a creativity decline are dire, said Wellesley College psychology professor and creativity researcher Beth Hennessey. "Creativity is what moves civilizations forward. Creativity for its own sake is important, but it's also important for solving the world's intractable problems. . . . Without creativity and imagination, none of those thorny problems will be solved."[38]

Carter said. "Technology really impacts us in that way because it basically steals all our down time. When kids might have been playing, daydreaming or just waiting for your parents to come pick you up—that's high creativity-building time that's now taken up by our devices."[39]

We adults are often guilty of the same thing, of course. It's the nature of today's lifestyle. However, most adults' childhoods were filled with far more unstructured non-electronic play than our current students experienced, which nurtured our creative capabilities when our brains were developing. Now consider this: Kyung-Hee Kim, the principal investigator in the 2010 William & Mary study, found the sharpest declines in creativity among five-to-ten-year-olds.[40] It's not difficult to calculate that these very students are now college age or soon will be. Our students widely believe there is one right answer to a question, and when they find it, they move on. They believe that mistakes are bad and should be avoided at all costs. They study only what will be on the exam. And they are convinced that optimal workflow should proceed in a measured and orderly fashion.[41]

Those of us who teach in creative fields recognize these beliefs as the very antithesis of creativity. We know that there are many potential answers to a given question, mistakes can be cause for celebration, investigations can take us delightfully beyond the beaten path, and workflow is rarely, if ever, predictable. The question is, how do we convince our students of these truths?

Interestingly, public libraries, children's museums, and public schools have begun to combat declining creativity by establishing "makerspaces" where students can experiment with physical materials combined with digital technologies.[42]

Makerspaces are zones of self-directed learning. Their hands-on character, coupled with the tools and raw materials that support invention, provide the ultimate workshop for the tinkerer and the perfect educational space for individuals who learn best by doing. . . . They promote multidisciplinary thinking and learning, enriching the projects that are built there and the value of the makerspace as an educational venue.[43]

227

We can draw inspiration from these efforts and, in the spirit of HIPs, begin to infuse creativity into our students' college experiences. Some institutions require students to complete coursework in fields that provide immersive experiences in making and doing. For example, students at Stanford University can choose from among dozens of courses to meet their Creative Expression requirement, many of which are interdisciplinary. They might create a portfolio of ceramic works as they explore questions of the physics of clay. They could combine computer coding, music composition, and performance as part of the Stanford Laptop Orchestra. Courses like Plein Air Painting, Acting for Non-Majors, or a multifocal music course in which students conduct a "critical and creative exploration of the performing body as captured on film" by viewing musicals, dance, opera, and music videos also meet this requirement, among dozens of other options.[44]

Creativity fits just as easily into online and blended learning. Students in my Design Thinking course engage in a "crash course in design thinking" activity with a partner, conducted through video conferencing. However, the activity itself requires that the students create physical prototypes and sketches to design a solution for their partner. They can show their partner these artifacts through the video conference, but I also require them to photograph their sketches, prototypes, and handwritten notes and submit the images with a short written reflection at the conclusion of the assignment. The assignment doesn't just increase students' knowledge of design thinking. It also builds a peer-to-peer relationship while enhancing their creativity and communication skills and providing an opportunity to reflect on their learning experience—all components of HIPs and all conducted online.

Just as any course can become writing intensive if it incorporates certain practices, we can also develop creativity-infused courses across all instructional modalities, modifying our curriculum by incorporating one or more of the following action steps.[45]

Action Steps

- Write learning outcomes for increasing students' creativity and develop a means of assessment (pre- and post-course survey, reflective essay, creative project, etc.).
- Include opportunities to identify problems or discover multiple solutions to open-ended problems. Problem finding asks students to identify missing information or apply intellectual or imaginative vision, leading students to think deeply and ask critical questions.
- Provide scaffolding for students' learning of design thinking through guided practice, including brainstorming, ideation, and prototyping (a la Stanford University's "Design Thinking Bootcamp")[46] before expecting students to use these skills independently.

- Allow students to fail. Resist the temptation to redirect them or step in to make things right when you can see where they're going wrong.
- Debrief each project with students, encouraging them to reflect on what they learned through both success and failure.
- Ask open-ended questions as students are working. Avoid answering students' questions directly. Saying, "I don't know; what do you think?" sparks further thinking, whereas "Here's a website with a tutorial that shows you how to make a _____" shuts it down.
- Incorporate both individual projects and collaborative work to meet the needs of students with different learning styles.
- Invite guest speakers who are creatives and innovators (in person or via video conferencing), asking them to share their experiences and ideas with students.
- Include required readings about creativity. (Ex: Ed Catmull's *Creativity, Inc.*; Twyla Tharp's *The Creative Habit*; and more.)

Pivot Points

- Allow students to respond to discussions or assignments creatively, using tools such as digital photography, drawing programs, or multimedia to present their work.
- Ask open-ended questions on discussion boards or in synchronous discussions that spark divergent thinking. Questions beginning with, "What if . . . ?" work well for this purpose.
- Rotate the role of instructor among students, asking them to develop a lesson that includes visuals such as infographics, timelines, videos, images, or multimedia. One of the best ways to learn something is to teach it, and the process of planning and preparing the lesson is inherently creative. You could allow the student to teach the lesson through video conferencing by sharing their computer screen, or the student could prerecord a video of their lesson, post it to YouTube, and share the link with their classmates through a discussion board where students could ask or answer questions in the presentation.[47]
- Consider allowing students to respond to an assignment with a creative project or presentation instead of writing a paper. Be sure to state your expectations and grading criteria very clearly before offering this option.
- Case studies or scenarios prompting students to identify an innovative solution to a real-world problem build creativity and foster communication, critical thinking, and collaboration. Students could work in pairs or small groups, in breakout rooms or independently through video conferencing, or they could work together through mobile apps like Skype, Google Hangouts, or Discord.

229

Collaborative Assignments and Projects

The 21st-century workplace is inherently collaborative, despite our society's lingering tendencies to valorize individual achievement.

> Many innovations that seem to have been the work of a lone genius were actually group efforts. Thomas Edison, for instance, built a team of dozens of inventors in his Menlo Park lab, allowing him to work on numerous innovations simultaneously. Indeed, some historians have said Edison's greatest invention was not the light bulb, the phonograph, or motion pictures but the research and development laboratory.
>
> (Belis, 2016)[48]

We place Edison on a pedestal as a penultimate innovator, but we seldom recall the team that made his achievements possible. The same phenomenon occurs with star athletes, actors, and musicians: their achievements are praiseworthy but would not have occurred without the backing of an equally impressive team.

Our cultural preoccupation with individual achievement doesn't fully prepare us to become effective team members once we join the workforce or to work with others in civic organizations or social situations. Collaborative assignments and projects can help bridge the gap. At its most basic, collaborative learning means that students must work together to complete a given task, which can be of any duration. To rise to the quality level of a HIP, however, we must structure collaborative tasks so that they utilize some of the key elements.

- Set group and individual performance expectations at appropriately high levels.
- Expect students to invest a significant amount of time and effort.
- Structure tasks to include interactions with faculty and peers about significant matters.
- Provide opportunities to experience diversity as students are exposed to unfamiliar people and circumstances.
- Build purposeful opportunities to reflect and integrate learning into the project.
- Utilize problems or challenges that lead students to discover the relevance of their learning through real-world applications.
- If possible, end the project with a public presentation demonstrating students learning and competence.

Well-planned collaborative learning has many benefits for students.[49,50]

> Students who work in teams develop better oral communication, self-management, and leadership skills. Team-based or cooperative learning

increases the quality of student-faculty interactions, bolsters students' self-confidence, and allows them to gain a greater understanding of peers from diverse backgrounds or perspectives.[51] Collaborative learning methods are "based on the assumption that learning is an active, integrated, and constructive process influenced by social and contextual factors"[52]—an idea supported by research such as a 2015 study at the University of Haifa revealing that emotions occurring during social behavior directly influence the brain's processes of learning and memory.[53]

Collaborative assignments and projects exist at all scales and all levels, from study groups to team projects lasting an entire semester or more. However, merely instituting a requirement that students work in groups does not automatically result in the benefits of collaboration. Just as we need to adjust our pedagogical practices to teach writing within our disciplines if we expect students to produce good written work, we also need to teach students how to function as a group. They tend to approach a group task from a "divide and conquer" perspective, divvying up the work and simply assembling the pieces just before the due date, with little attempt at synthesis or integration.[54] Although understandable, such an approach subverts the purpose of collaborative learning. Students also remain wary of working with peers who might not shoulder their fair share of responsibilities or those who exert too much pressure on their teammates. These are genuine concerns, but they appear in the workplace, too. Learning how to work with challenging people is an important life skill, so we might want to think carefully before stepping in to smooth interpersonal frictions unless they become intractable.

Several design characteristics and group process strategies can enhance students' experiences with collaborative learning.[55]

1. Groups should be kept small (three to five students) to foster meaningful interactions.
2. Mixed-ability groups tend to support the success of low-performing students.
3. Equal participation increases the likelihood that students will fully utilize one another's knowledge and skills.
4. Heterogeneous groupings support students' acceptance of diversity and increase learning, especially when tasks require creativity.
5. Open or loosely structured tasks promote higher-level interactions, improve reasoning, and develop students' application and evaluative thinking skills. Complex tasks produce deeper-level interactions than simpler tasks.

Scager et al. (2016) found that the kind and quality of students' relationships have a sizeable impact on their learning. Collaborative projects enhance peer-to-peer interaction, interdependence, accountability, ownership, motivation, and engagement.[56]

It's worth repeating that the ability to work on a long-term project is among the Big Six experiences that strongly correlate with students' quality of life and career satisfaction. Likewise, we might recall a well-known IBM CEO study (2012), which revealed that "CEOs regard interpersonal skills of collaboration (75 percent), communication (67 percent), creativity (61 percent) and flexibility (61 percent) as key drivers of employee success to operate in a more complex, interconnected environment"[57]—all skills that can develop through collaborative learning.

Collaborative learning is certainly not limited to face-to-face settings. As I mentioned earlier, students can work together across all learning models, whether they meet in a breakout room during a synchronous class session; communicate with each other through a tool such as Discord, Google Hangouts, or MS Teams; or use text messaging and asynchronous access to a collaborative workspace or project area in the LMS.

Since we can implement collaborative projects and assignments into a wide array of disciplines (all of which have different emphases and purposes), the following action steps ask faculty to consider how they might include a collaborative project in their course.

Action Steps

- Identify an area of your course where you could add a collaborative project.
- Determine the scale that would be most appropriate for this project. (How long should it last? How heavily should it be weighted in the course grade?)
- Choose the components you will include (evidence of group planning, mid-term progress-check, written documentation, peer evaluations, final presentation, other).
- Articulate the extent to which students could utilize interdisciplinary connections and how they might do this (if relevant to their investigation).
- Anticipate the actions you will take as an instructor to help students integrate their learning in and through this project and how you will assess their learning as the result of this experience. (Will you provide additional input, instruction, or resources? Will you include questions about the project on your final exam?)
- Decide what role you will play as students are working with their teammates. (Will you be available as a resource? Will you join their synchronous online meetings?)
- Clarify and articulate your expectations for groups' and individual student's participation or achievement. (What criteria must students meet, and how will you integrate this into the course grade?)

- Ensure equity of access and integrate experiences with diversity to the extent possible in your course. (How will you structure group membership, provide needed resources, ensure clear expectations for participation, and outline procedures to follow if conflict resolution assistance is needed?)
- Plan how you will facilitate students' experiential learning, build connections to the course's topic and discipline, and apply students' learning to real-world issues and needs through the project. (How does the project intersect with professional practice in your discipline or the course's relevance to students' lives or careers?)
- Identify how the project will include, reinforce, or apply co-curricular experiences by articulating what students must do outside class and how you will hold them accountable. (Note: "co-curricular" in this instance means any learning activities occurring outside the class's normal parameters.)

Pivot Points

- Allow students to choose how they will meet to work on their collaborative projects: video conferencing, mobile video app, face to face, or a combination of these, depending on the group members' needs and preferences.
- Post clear instructions for the activity or project to the LMS.
- Create options for how students will submit their group's work: live presentation via video conferencing, recorded video with a link to the presentation on YouTube, a written document submitted to the assignment area on the LMS, and so on.

Undergraduate Research

Not so long ago, hands-on participation in faculty research seemed to be the sole province of graduate students, while undergraduates remained in the classroom to acquire prerequisite skills and knowledge within a research discipline. However, undergraduate participation in faculty-led research and creative activities has become more prevalent over the past three decades, moving outward from the sciences through the full range of research-based and creative fields. The University of Oregon offers this explanation:[58]

Undergraduate research and creative scholarship activities represent one of the stronger examples of a high-impact learning practice that can advance the key characteristics of the university's mission. Mentored research, in which students and faculty work together to discover new knowledge, apply it to their discipline, and share it locally, nationally, and globally, is instrumental in helping individuals think analytically, question critically, and discover the enduring joy of inquiry. Undergraduate research simultaneously strengthens undergraduate education; provides additional outlets for faculty to teach, research, and serve; and fosters the creation of a community of scholars that is essential to the intellectual health of the university.

Students reap several benefits through participation in mentored research.[59,60]

- Increased persistence and gains in skills such as gathering and analyzing data or speaking effectively.
- Understanding that learning can be active and knowledge transferrable to other situations.
- Discovering that they can take responsibility for creating new knowledge and can answer meaningful questions and help solve real-world problems.
- Developing core competencies including responsibility, persistence, synthesis, analysis, attention to detail, teamwork, leadership, commitment, patience, and ethical behaviors.
- Clarifying students' choice of major; developing a stronger sense of connection to an academic discipline.
- Connecting students to a community of practice, including faculty and external practitioners, allowing students to develop a professional identity.
- Encouraging persistence when faced with setbacks.
- Stimulating interest in graduate study and predicting graduate school success.
- Fostering self-confidence, self-efficacy, deep thinking, and intercultural competence.
- Experiencing personal satisfaction with undergraduate education.

According to the Council on Undergraduate Research, two primary types of undergraduate research exist. Course-based research embeds student research participation in a course that includes an emphasis on teaching students the norms and practices of research through a combination of instruction and direct experience.[61] Undergraduate research also occurs in experiential learning settings such as summer seminars, where students and faculty work together on long-term, meaningful projects. Students actively engage in the research process rather than passively observing it, working alongside a mentor who guides the student through the experience, often in an apprenticeship model. The mentor is usually a faculty member but could also be a graduate student, post-doctoral researcher, or upper-class peer.[62]

Undergraduate research aligns with four of the eight key elements of HIPs:

- A significant investment of time and effort by students over an extended period.
- Interactions with faculty and peers about significant matters.
- Opportunities to discover the relevance of learning through real-world applications.
- Public demonstration of competence.

It also reflects elements of the Big Six in the opportunity to work on a long-term project and develop a mentoring relationship with a faculty member who encourages the student to pursue their goals and dreams.

Of course, most institutions maintain expectations that full-time faculty will engage in research or creative practice as part of their contractual duties, based on a presumption that they will bring their scholarship into their classrooms, laboratories, and studios for the benefit of their students' learning. Mentored research expands the efficacy and importance of this expectation. When faculty allow students to work side by side with them on meaningful projects, routine expectations blossom into high-impact practices, benefitting all participants.

Like most HIPs, undergraduate research tends to be an institutional initiative rather than a choice made by individual instructors, but we can scale this to the level of our classrooms when appropriate. For example, the January 2019 First-Year Experience Seminar "Citizen Science" at Bard College focused on water. All 450 participants collected water samples from their hometowns over winter break, and their investigations with these samples became part of the coordinating faculty member's professional research, empowering students to understand their contributions to an ongoing and socially valuable investigation while also building their academic and intellectual competencies in science.[63]

We can also incorporate undergraduate research into online learning environments, although Faulconer and Gruss (2019)[64] point to significant barriers for online students to participate in undergraduate research, including reduced awareness of and access to opportunities, financial limitations, and lack of time. Access to faculty who engage in research is also limited in online programs since part-time, non-tenure-track, and contingent faculty outnumber full-time faculty teaching online courses.[65] Since they may not have the same research obligations as their tenure-track and full-time colleagues, faculty in online programs may not have the ability to involve students in research. Nevertheless, online students can contribute to faculty research through professional and technical writing, data analysis, project management, data visualization, and tasks conducted through specialized software appropriate to a given investigation.[66] It's up to individual instructors to expand their thinking to create opportunities for students to participate across all learning models, whenever possible and appropriate.

Action Steps

- Identify aspects of your research or creative practice that intersect with the content or topic of your course.
- Share your research or creative practice with students, explaining these areas of intersection.
- Include students in your research or creative practice, even if on a small scale.

Pivot Points

- Consider how you could involve your online students in your research or creative practice by delegating tasks such as technical writing, data analysis, or visualization.
- Investigate online research opportunities in your department and share these with your students.
- Encourage colleagues conducting research, especially those working with undergraduate students on campus, to consider how they might also include online students in their activities.

Diversity and Global Learning

The importance of developing students' appreciation for diversity and their ability to work with diverse individuals spans all HIPs. It also undergirds the AAC&U's support of "inclusive excellence," which institutions achieve when they "integrate diversity, equity, and educational quality efforts into their missions and institutional operations."[67] The "Diversity and Global Learning" HIP rests on three practices:

- Increasing the diversity of the student body through equitable admissions policies and practices.
- Providing all students with a clear path toward educational opportunities.
- Embedding diversity in the institution's mission to produce and transmit new knowledge.[68]

"Students often come to college from incredibly segregated residential patterns and K–12 schools, so they don't have a whole lot of preparation for interacting with people different from themselves" (Shaun R. Harper, Executive Director of the USC Race and Equity Center).[69] College might also be the first time students confront various perspectives on a given issue or experience a disruption in the attitudes and beliefs they absorbed from their families.

The more interaction one has with others who hold different views, or the more one learns about various aspects of human diversity, the more likely it is that one will be challenged to think and respond in novel ways. For example, people who interact with more complex social structures exhibit a heightened sense of individuality while simultaneously showing a more complex attentiveness to the social world.[70]

Despite their good intentions or public statements of support for diversity, equity, and inclusion, our institutions may still cause diverse students to feel that they do not belong. Shaun Harper explains:

When in every class you enter, you are the only one or among only a few of your racial group in that class, it might signal to you that you don't belong. Or if in every class, all your professors are white, it might signal to you that smart people of color don't belong here. Or when the only people who look like you are cutting the grass, emptying the trash or frying French fries in the food court that might suggest to you that my people are not thought of as professorial or professional. Not that custodians, groundskeepers and food service employees are not professional; but they are not located at the power epicenter of the campus. That signals to a young Latina that Latinas like her are not highly valued at the institution.

This quote exemplifies **structural diversity** or the institution's demographic profile. Identities of race and gender tend to receive the most attention in this regard, but other dimensions of diversity such as age, disability, socioeconomic status, ethnicity, religion, sexual preference, and gender identity also have a profound impact on students' collegiate experiences.

Classroom diversity involves instruction about cultural practices and issues relating to marginalized, underrepresented, or minority groups.[71] However, merely studying "the other" does little to change students' attitudes toward diverse individuals. Instead, we build classroom diversity when we teach students how to learn *in collaboration with* others rather than learning *about* others.

Classrooms can become incubators for **cognitive diversity**. Individuals bring different tools to solving problems as a group, including ways of representing situations and problems, generating solutions, categorizing perspectives, and inferring cause and effect. These perspectival differences underlie the value of interdisciplinarity: since each of us is steeped in the particular ontologies, epistemologies, and methodologies of our disciplines, we bring different strengths to collaborative work. Cognitively diverse groups can demonstrate super-additivity, meaning that the solutions they generate are greater than the sum of their parts.[72]

237

Just as universities establish writing intensives in disciplinary courses, they also provide intensives in diversity and global learning. Courses might include features such as:

- Diversity content focusing on historically disenfranchised social groups in the US, national identity groups external to the US, or both.
- Assignments and course activities that provoke deep reflection and increased self-awareness of one's own social identity or identities.
- Co-curricular activities involving interactions with peers or groups from different backgrounds, exploring unfamiliar places, or applying new perspectives.
- Infusion of globally or diversity-connected topics across the entire course.
- Facilitated discussions that invite students to share reflections and experiences to improve their communication skills and deepen their knowledge and understanding.[73]

Every course can support diversity by creating a safe space for difficult conversations and ensuring that all voices are heard and all perspectives are valued. Employing critical theory allows students and instructors to examine common disciplinary norms and practices to identify implicit bias and exclusionary practices. We can also analyze the history and practices of our disciplines. How have they affected civilization? Do they empower or oppress various groups? Are they intrinsically or intentionally inclusive or exclusive? Such conversations can open our minds to aspects of our disciplinary identities we have long taken for granted.[74]

We might differentiate between diversity and global learning in their tendency to focus on the composition of our immediate culture and our interactions in a globally connected world. In both cases, critical thinking plays a significant role. Teaching students to think critically is among our goals as educators, but we often stop at criticizing others' ideas. Critical thinking is also a tool for reflecting on one's own assumptions and strengthening one's own understanding. According to the AAC&U:[75]

Engaging with civic knowledge and diversity should mean applying critical thinking to learn about "the other" and to learn about oneself. Students should understand how gender, race, ethnicity, class, and religion affect those who are different from themselves, but they should also understand how these forces affect them. Just as in a democracy, students should analyze and critique the other's and their own positions.

In this context, the parallels between interdisciplinary and intercultural engagement abound, with deep implications for the way we teach and learn. Like diverse groups in society, each academic discipline (and each person within each discipline) provides unique perspectives on significant questions. Likewise, the boundaries of each discipline support faculty identities. Faculty who succeed in interdisciplinary teaching are able to stretch beyond their disciplinary training, taking delight with others in the mutual enrichment of their disciplines and encouraging students to appreciate connections among diverse approaches to knowledge. Interdisciplinary teaching and scholarship provide an opportunity to reflect on, test, and strengthen one's own ideas and assumptions while working with colleagues from diverse disciplines toward mutual understanding and achievement. These benefits are very similar to the benefits of engagement with diversity in a pluralist democracy.

Teaching for global learning should include emphases on shifting one's perspective.[76]

- **Problem framing**: a purposeful examination of how different people define and experience local, intercultural, international, and global challenges to human and environmental well-being and problem solving.
- **Perspective consciousness**: insight into one's own beliefs, values, and assumptions and how these are similar to and distinct from those held by others at home and abroad.
- **Global perspective**: the ability to construct an analysis of a complex trans-border problem that considers multiple interpretations of its causes, consequences, and proposed solutions.

The most powerful tool for opening our students' hearts and minds to diversity lies in building relationships with people who are different from themselves. As I said in *Higher Education by Design*:[77]

When we develop personal relationships with people who are not like ourselves, we grow to care about them, to respect them, reducing our previous fears and insecurities. We begin to experience pity, sympathy, empathy, and even compassion. . . . John Steinbeck wrote, "It means very little to know that a million Chinese are starving unless you know one Chinese who is starving."[78] When we build relationships with individuals from groups different from our own, they cease to be abstract and "other" and become our friends, our co-workers, or our neighbors. I can speak only for myself in this, but I know that my life has been immensely enriched by the relationships I've built and friendships I've made with people from Palestine, Iraq, Iran, Pakistan, India, the Bahamas, and China (among others), as well as friends who are female, Black, Hispanic, LGBTQQIP2SAA, and many combinations of these

239

identities. . . . The more each of us builds relationships that transcend social boundaries, the more we open our hearts and minds to the simple truth that we are all one race—the human race—despite how cliché it admittedly sounds.

Experiential learning strategies, particularly service learning, community-based learning, and study abroad, are powerful. They take students out of their comfortable and familiar surroundings and place them in proximity to individuals within environments they've never confronted before. It's one thing to read about otherness, yet entirely another to experience it for oneself.

Regarding online learning environments, the Reinert Center for Transformative Teaching and Learning at Saint Louis University explains,

> Online courses often attract an intergenerational and geographically diverse student enrollment, which also intersect with differences in gender, race, class, sexuality, ability, and so forth. It is important to be mindful of how these student demographics matter differently in an online learning environment (e.g., Boyd, 2016;[79] Dominique, 2016).[80, 81]

Because of their appeal to students who need the flexibility and affordability that an online learning environment can provide, our online and blended courses can offer valuable opportunities to engage in this HIP as students work and learn together. Nevertheless, we also must keep the needs of these diverse learners in mind, considering that those from lower-income households or those with work or family responsibilities may have difficulty attending synchronous meetings. Diverse students may also face language barriers or have accommodations that must be met if they are to participate optimally. Instructors should keep these factors in mind, especially when forming collaborative groups or establishing expectations for participation during class activities.

Action Steps

- Reflectively and honestly examine your own attitudes toward diversity.
- Teach students to think critically and reflectively, not just examining others' ideas but developing awareness of their own biases and preconceptions.
- Foster cognitive diversity by incorporating opportunities for students to work in diverse groups.
- Create and promote opportunities to participate in experiential learning (service learning, community-based learning, study abroad) that place students in proximity to others who are different from themselves or in unfamiliar cultures and environments.

Pivot Points

- Consider how you identify and meet the needs of diverse learners in your classroom, remembering that diversity is about not only race and gender but also students with special needs, differing ability levels, and extenuating life circumstances such as being employed full time, being a parent, being much older than their peers, and so on.
- Provide readings and multimedia that expose students to the points of view of persons different from themselves, holding a follow-up discussion synchronously through virtual conferencing or asynchronously in a discussion board.
- Create an activity in which student partners interview one another over video conferencing or a mobile video communication app, asking one another to talk about a common experience and structuring interview questions to elicit points of connection and moments of realization. During a subsequent synchronous class session, each partner could share the most significant thing they learned about their partner, or students could post the same idea to an asynchronous discussion board.

ePortfolios

The AAC&U expanded the original list of 10 HIPs to 11 with the addition of ePortfolios in 2016. "The warrant for declaring ePortfolio practice a high-impact activity is that, on average, students who have a well-structured ePortfolio experience exhibit a similar desirable pattern of positive benefits associated with other HIPs."[82]

> As described in the research, HIPs effect enhanced student learning and success by bringing to the teaching and learning process the intentional and integrative characteristics associated with how humans learn; not just in the moment but for sustained use and transferability from one instance to different instances of practice and application. In short, all of the HIPs are HIPs not because they carry the label but because, when done well and with considered thought and implementation, they lead to deeper student learning, especially for traditionally under-served populations of learners.[83]

Despite the perception that ePortfolios are faddish or trendy, their use rests on sound learning theory based on social constructivism, or the knowledge that learning is most effective when students construct systems of knowledge within a social context through dialog and interactions with others.[84] ePortfolios are both a product and a process. As a product, they represent a curated collection of evidence of students' learning as they construct a digital showcase for their achievements and accomplishments. Academic transcripts are limited to bare-bones evidence of courses completed and grades earned. ePortfolios, on the other hand, can include artifacts from coursework and co-curricular activities, work experiences, volunteering, and more. As a process, ePortfolios provide opportunities for students to reflect on their learning but go beyond the simple acquisition of knowledge and skill to incorporate affective, personal, and self-identity dimensions.[85] Such metacognitive engagement enhances student learning, particularly when employed in conjunction with other HIPs, because it amplifies these practices' reflective and integrative activities. Furthermore, ePortfolios foster student agency because they allow the student free rein to select which artifacts to include and how they want to express their thinking about these items, fostering engagement and motivation.[86]

Some institutions adopt ePortfolio platforms, which may be linked to their LMS and allow faculty to access students' sites for grading and feedback. Faculty or departments can also facilitate students' creation of ePortfolios through a free or low-cost web hosting service like Weebly, Squarespace, Wix, Behance, or Google Sites[87]—a strategy long employed by the visual arts, among other disciplines. Professional networking sites like LinkedIn host portfolios, too. Whatever approach we take toward ePortfolios, whether institution wide or limited to a department, faculty can support students' use of this tool.

Students need faculty support when creating their ePortfolios. When students are left to their own devices, their portfolios tend to become "glorified electronic filing cabinets," but when implemented in conjunction with purposeful instruction, portfolios can grow into meaningful and relevant tools for professional success and can support students' learning.[88] An ePortfolio generally includes the following components, but this varies based on individual preferences, disciplinary norms, and the field in which the portfolio owner works or hopes to work.[89]

- **Biography**: a condensed, narrative summary of accomplishments and experiences, usually written in a third-person voice. This section should include contact information and a photograph of the portfolio owner demonstrating a professional appearance. The portfolio owner's resume or CV should be downloadable from this area of the ePortfolio.
- **Educational Background**: a list of degrees earned or other academic achievements in reverse chronological order, detailing institutions attended, honors or awards, certificates, publications, professional licenses, internships, conferences or workshops, study abroad or other experiential learning, scholarships, and so on. This section may include a description of projects, coursework, transcripts, presentations, and student affiliations with professional organizations.

242

- **Professional Experience**: an explanation of how the portfolio owner's skills and experiences are suited to their professional goals and career aspirations. This section can include specific information about jobs held and details about locations, job titles, employment dates, duties, and responsibilities. This section of the portfolio can also include certificates of additional training, workshops, awards and honors, copies of the portfolio owner's resume and transcripts, volunteer work and community service, public speaking, publications, and other accomplishments occurring since graduation. Letters of recommendation and contact information for individuals willing to provide references could be included here as well.
- **Performance, Skills, and Competencies**: evidence of the portfolio owner's skills and competencies, organized by skill area. Activities could include volunteer work, technical skills, proficiency in languages other than English, military service, or participation in clubs or other co-curricular organizations. Evidence might include publications, electronic presentations, projects, assignments, research papers, writing samples, or other artifacts demonstrating knowledge or exhibiting proof of proficiency.

For example, the Professional Practices course I designed and taught online required students to create a professional website meeting a specific set of criteria and to upload a series of items. Students then shared the link to their site through a discussion board, and all students were required to visit at least three peers' sites and provide a critique.

Building a portfolio of any type is an inherently reflective task, involving complex decision making about the items to be included, the order and sequence of these items, explanations that might help contextualize these items, and site formatting, among many other factors. As students make these choices, they gain an appreciation for their accomplishments, seeing how far they've come and what they've achieved. They also make connections between what they've learned and the career they hope to pursue. Furthermore, ePortfolios seamlessly integrate with online learning since both are digitally based activities.

Action Steps

- Incorporate the ePortfolio into the course's outcomes and tie assessments of students' portfolios to their course grade, using a rubric for grading and providing formative verbal or written feedback during the semester.[90]
- Share examples of high-quality ePortfolios created by other students; create and share your own ePortfolio.

243

- Include viewing and commenting on fellow students' ePortfolios in assignment requirements.
- Encourage students to collect artifacts of their learning throughout your course.

Pivot Points

- Post information to the LMS about which assignments will result in items students could use in their ePortfolio.
- In addition to the Action Steps suggestions, provide an area where students can link their ePortfolio to share with their classmates and hold a "virtual open house" event where students can explore one another's work.

Experiential Education

Service learning and community-based learning technically exist as a separate HIP from internships or other workplace experiences. However, all three are forms of experiential education, which is rooted in a set of shared educational theories, including those of John Dewey (1938),[91] David Kolb (1984),[92] and Carl Rogers (1969, 1994).[93] Experiential learning differs from cognitive learning, such as rote memorization of technical terminology or mathematical formulas, by addressing the needs and wants of the learner, resting on the central tenet that "learning is the process whereby knowledge is created through the transformation of experience" (Kolb). Experiential learning places students in contexts where they can take the initiative, make decisions, learn from natural consequences, and be accountable for the results of their choices. A well-designed experiential learning program embeds frequent opportunities for reflection, critical analysis, and synthesis to facilitate the cycle of learning by experience as students encounter genuine social, practical, personal, or research problems.

According to Kolb, experiential learning is a cyclical process in which learners:

1. **Act**: participate in an experience.
2. **Reflect**: think about that experience.
3. **Learn**: form new ideas based on these reflections.
4. **Apply**: test their new ideas in a different situation, beginning the cycle once more.

The instructor acts as a facilitator who establishes a positive climate for learning, clarifies the learner's purpose, organizes learning resources, and makes them available to students. The instructor also balances the learning experience's

244

emotional and intellectual aspects and shares thoughts and feelings with students without dominating their learning experience. Moreover, students participate completely in the learning process, are the primary evaluators of their own learning, and assess their own progress and success.

Classroom learning cannot substitute for the types of experience acquired in a real-world environment. For example, psychology students might listen to a lecture about domestic violence, but it's entirely different from volunteering in a local shelter for abused women and children. Some might argue that academic fields like graphic design are inherently experiential because most learning occurs through doing rather than passive listening. However, the experience of designing something for a class assignment is fundamentally different than working with a nonprofit agency to design a new logo that allows them to raise their visibility among their target audience.

Experiential education provides invaluable opportunities for students to develop, reflect upon, apply, and transfer knowledge in real-world settings, increasing student engagement with the topics they're studying. Service learning, community-based learning, internships, and other methods of experiential education presume a face-to-face campus setting in which the instructor directly facilitates the student experience. Under conditions in which this is not possible, such as a fully online and fully asynchronous instructional model, we must adapt the procedure by placing greater responsibility on the student for identifying opportunities for experiential learning where they live. We will discuss this option after the explanation of the following models.

Service Learning and Community-Based Learning

Most colleges and universities maintain that their mission, at least in part, is to prepare their graduates to become contributing citizens who lead lives of service to their communities. The purpose of service learning and community-based learning is to place students in off-campus situations where they have opportunities to experience the social issues they are studying in the classroom as they interact with community members through activities that allow them to make a difference in the world, albeit on a small scale.

Internships

Many fields require practical experience as a standard part of student learning. For example, education majors conduct student teaching, and nursing students complete clinical hours. Schools of business have practiced this strategy for decades, sometimes with impressive results. For instance, 99% of the graduates of Babson College, a small business school in Massachusetts, acquire full-time jobs within six months of commencement, as do 98.6% of graduates of the University of Pennsylvania's Wharton School of Business and 98% of graduates of Emory University's Goizueta Business School.[94] If these results merely indicated that more jobs are available in the business sector, we could expect to see similarly stellar job placement rates at all business schools, but this is not the case. Students who major in business management experience an unemployment rate of 3.7% overall, on par with the average for all majors of 3.9%.[95] Rather, these institutions attain exemplary alumni outcomes by integrating preparation for the workplace in their curriculum and establishing industry partnerships.

Practical student experiences can exist in many different configurations, including, but not limited to, internships. Although we may use the following terms somewhat interchangeably, differences between them exist in practice. Each may be of benefit when we plan to add practical experience requirements to our degree programs.

- **Internships** involve a short-term, usually part-time position with a company or organization related to a student's field of study. These can last from two or three months to an entire semester or even a full academic year. Interns usually function as employees of the organization, with designated duties and some level of responsibility. They may or may not receive pay or a stipend. Internships may lead to permanent employment since employers can directly observe the student's work ethic and job-related skills.

- **Externships** are shorter than internships, lasting anywhere from a day to a week or occurring during scheduled breaks. Externships are typically unpaid and often consist of workplace observations or job-shadowing rather than authentic work experience. Nevertheless, externships can still help students begin to build a network of professional relationships and may lead to later internships with the same organization. Faculty might choose to incorporate practical work experience into their students' course of study by requiring students to shadow a disciplinary professional over spring break or organizing similar short-term opportunities with a partner organization near campus, rotating students throughout the semester.

- **Co-operative education** (co-op) is a specialized type of internship that provides career training, sometimes with pay, as students work alongside professionals in their major field. Depending on the field, a co-op placement may require the student to take a semester or more away from their studies, especially if it is a full-time paid position. Co-op students have more opportunity to become an integral part of an organization, work on important projects, and receive authentic work experience. Co-op is most common in technology and engineering, but it also exists in other fields such as business and the liberal arts.[96]

■ **Volunteer work** related to a student's field of study can also provide practical experience. Many organizations on and off campus are eager for volunteers. A student majoring in marketing could help design publicity for an upcoming campus event, or a physics major could volunteer to tutor high school students.

Advance planning for experiential learning requires a significant investment of time and effort. The following is a partial list of actions that can help instructors prepare for these activities.[97] As with anything else, though, these steps will vary depending on your institution, your course structure, departmental norms or requirements, and especially your disciplinary field.

Action Steps

1. Identify and establish a relationship with the partner organization (or organizations) with which your students will work.
2. Write student learning objectives and outcomes contingent upon involvement in the planned experience.
3. Address any ethical issues that may pertain to the experience, ensuring the just and benevolent treatment of all persons involved. You may need to work with your institution's IRB to be certain that requirements have been satisfied.
4. Determine how you will handle any logistical issues such as
   a. transportation of students or project materials to and from the worksite.
   b. liability concerns, including drivers' licenses or insurance for those providing transportation.
   c. media coverage, either by informing the local media of the project, creating posts to social media, or publicizing the project through campus communication channels.
   d. clarifying the roles of all participants and providing for student supervision and oversight.
   e. scheduling any training or orientation that might be required by the partner organization before students can participate.
   f. establishing contingency plans for when things don't go as expected, and also ensuring that proper procedures for handling emergencies are in place.
5. Express any expectations and assumptions so that students, community partners, and the instructor hold a shared understanding of what each party hopes to gain from the project. Participants should also verbalize any concerns so that these can be addressed before they become problematic.

6. Compile all necessary information, documentation, and written materials, providing them to all participants:
   a. Information about required training, the work to be performed, what will occur after the completion of the experience.
   b. Broad issues related to the experience, such as the demographics and histories of the target population, including contextualization such as discussions of power and inequality.
   c. All planned activities related to the experience, including calendars, schedules, and logistical information, where applicable.
   d. Incorporate instruction in problem solving, critical thinking, analysis, application, theorization, and reflection as it pertains to the experience.
   e. Plan for how you will assess student learning and how you will assign grades for students' involvement in the experience.
7. Communicate regularly with the partnering organization, visit the site, monitor progress, and ensure that students are functioning appropriately.
8. Incorporate separate opportunities for debriefing and reflection for students and participants in the partnering organization, allowing each person to think critically about their experience, relate it to larger social contexts and issues, recognize their involvement in the project's challenges and successes, and prepare for future engagement if possible.

Pivot Points

When a course is held fully or partially online, it might be impossible for the instructor to be as directly involved in the process as in the previous models, especially if students are geographically distant from campus. However, experiential education is still possible by involving students in identifying their own opportunities. Obviously, these factors will vary depending on the disciplinary orientation and content of your course. Volunteering with a county forest preserve for an environmental ethics course will be a vastly different experience than serving at a food pantry for a sociology course, which will also differ greatly from an unpaid internship in a corporate marketing department for a public relations course. Furthermore, some kinds of formal experiences like student teaching will be subject to additional conditions, possibly requiring more participation by the instructor.

1. Instruct students on how to identify experiential learning opportunities (as appropriate to your course) in the community where they live.
2. Ensure that the experiential learning requirement is reflected in your course objectives.

3. Communicate with students about any ethical issues that may pertain to the experience, ensuring the just and benevolent treatment of all persons involved. You may need to work with your institution's IRB to be certain that requirements have been satisfied. Therefore, the student's selected opportunity must be contingent on your approval to ensure all conditions have been met.

4. Consult with students on how they will handle matters related to scheduling, transportation, liability, required training or orientation, and employer expectations of student participants (dress code, professionalism, restrictions, etc.).

5. Create a document that the student must present to the individual or organization with which they will work, expressing any expectations and assumptions about the experiential learning opportunity so that all parties reach a common understanding. The document should encourage all participants to verbalize any concerns directly to you so that you can address them before they become problematic.

6. Compile all necessary information, documentation, and written materials, providing them to all participants:
    a. Information about required training, the work to be performed, what will occur after the completion of the experience.
    b. Broad issues related to the experience such as a profile of the partnering organization, description of students' activities or work expectations, or limitations of the experience.
    c. How the experience will incorporate problem solving, critical thinking, decision making, analysis, application, theorization, and reflection.
    d. How student learning will be assessed and how grades for students' involvement in the project will be determined.

7. Ask students to provide you with contact information for the person who will directly supervise or facilitate their experience and communicate with this individual to monitor students' progress and ensure that they are functioning appropriately within the project setting. Send this individual a personal note of thanks once the student's experience has been completed.

8. Incorporate an opportunity for debriefing and reflection that asks students to think critically about their experience, relate it to larger contexts and issues, identify challenges and successes, and prepare for future engagement if possible. You might use a discussion board, reflective essay, or short video, deciding whether the reflection should be public, as with a discussion board, or private, as with an assignment.

249

Capstone Courses and Projects

Just as HIPs begin with first-year experiences, they extend through the culmination of students' educational journeys in capstone courses or projects. In general, academic departments incorporate capstone courses or projects into the requirements for a major. This requirement is far from new. For centuries, doctoral students have written dissertations as evidence of their ability to produce new knowledge in a given field of study, and students earning master's degrees have written a thesis or completed a research project. Students of the arts present an exhibition or performance demonstrating their proficiency. For example, a student earning a bachelor of fine arts in visual art will showcase their artworks in a final exhibition just as a student earning a BFA in violin performance will present a senior recital.

Brown University provides this description of capstone requirements.[98]

The overarching goal of the capstone is to provide students with a culminating learning experience through which they demonstrate proficiency and facility with key learning objectives articulated at the level of the concentration as well as the broader general educational goals of their institution. As culminating learning experiences, capstones are integrative, reflective, and transitional.[99] They are integrative in that they require students to synthesize across discipline-specific content and research methods, apply knowledge to novel problems and contexts, and often experiment with different forms of scholarly and public presentation. They are reflective in that they prompt students to think about and account for the developmental trajectory of their learning within the concentration and discipline. They are transitional in that they frame, with varying degrees of explicitness, opportunities and pathways in post-college life: graduate school, professional career, public service, etc.

The National Survey of Senior Capstone Experiences[100] identifies several options.

- ■ Capstone course
  - ■ Department- or discipline-based course
  - ■ General education–focused course/campus-wide capstone requirement
- ■ Exam
  - ■ Comprehensive exam
  - ■ Exam leading to certification or professional licensure
- ■ Arts performance or exhibition in performing, musical, or visual arts
- ■ Project
  - ■ Senior integrative portfolio
  - ■ Senior integrative or applied learning project
  - ■ Senior thesis or research paper

- Experiential learning
  - Service learning or community-based learning project
  - Internship
  - Student teaching
  - Other supervised practice

These examples are not mutually exclusive. Combination or hybrid options also exist. However, their common thread lies in their inclusion of high-impact practices such as reflection and integration of learning through research, community-based learning, collaborative assignments, internships, and so on. Capstones involving more intensive faculty supervision and feedback correlate with the greatest gains for students.[101] Furthermore, the learning outcomes supported by capstone experiences demonstrate a high degree of correlation with skills and competencies valued by prospective employers. A survey by AAC&U found that employers place the greatest priority on five knowledge areas and skill sets (out of 17 types):

- Oral and written communications (85% and 82%)
- Teamwork skills (83%)
- Ethical decision making (82%)
- Critical thinking and analytical reasoning (81%)
- Applying knowledge and skills in real-world settings (80%)[102]

Capstones provide an opportunity to demonstrate that individual students have achieved program learning outcomes and developed proficiency in their majors. They have an additional benefit in generating useful data for assessing program quality, based on the logical assumption that an outstanding program produces students who demonstrate excellence.

We can scale capstone experience to our courses by incorporating a culminating activity that allows students to understand what they have learned, how it can apply beyond the classroom, and how it relates to their lives after graduation. We might use something as simple as a final discussion board, a question on the final exam, or a reflective essay. Or you could incorporate reflective questions into an existing culminating activity. The point is to prompt students to think about what they have learned and what it means for their futures.

Action Steps

- Select or create an activity or assignment to serve as the course capstone.
- Embed a requirement that students reflect on what they learned as the direct result of their participation in the course.

251

TABLE 5.1 Comparison of HIPS and Eight Key Elements

	Performance expectations	Student time investment	Interaction with faculty and peers	Experiences with diversity	Constructive feedback	Opportunities for reflection and integration of learning	Real-world application	Public demonstration of competence
First-Year Experiences	X	X	X	X	X	X	X	
Common Intellectual Experiences	X	X	X	X	X	X	X	
Learning Communities	X	X	X	X	X	X	X	
Writing-Intensive courses	X	X	X		X	X	X	
Creativity-Infused Learning	X	X	X	X	X	X		X
Collaborative Projects	X	X	X	X	X	X	X	

Undergraduate Research	X	X	X	X		X	X
Diversity and Global Learning		X	X		X	X	X
ePortfolios	X	X	X	X		X	X
Service and Community-Based Learning		X	X		X	X	X
Internships		X	X			X	X
Capstone Courses and Projects		X	X	X		X	X

■ Include an additional requirement that students articulate or explain how they can apply their learning in the course to personal or professional contexts after the course has ended.

Pivot Points

■ Hold a virtual exhibition of students' final projects, requiring that they post the project to a discussion board and comment on one another's work.
■ Set aside time during the last synchronous class period for students to make a reflective statement about what they learned in the course. Students who attend asynchronously could post their responses to a discussion board.

Design Connection	
Empathize	•High-Impact Practices are proven to support students' success, reflecting the student-centered philosophy of teaching and prioritization of empathy at the heart of design thinking. Adding HIPs to your course won't make your job as an educator easier, but it shows that you care about delivering the best possible educational experience to your students.
Define	•It's up to you to determine which High-Impact Practices will be the best fit for your course and decide how you will incorporate them into your instruction. Consider how you could scale and adapt one or more of these strategies. Even adding one HIP will improve your students' learning and demonstrate your empathy, creativity, and willingness to innovate.
Ideate	•When you implement an HIP at a scale appropriate to your course, you'll ideate solutions that suit your course content and your students'needs while also supporting students' achievement of your course's objectives and outcomes. The set of design constraints you'll encounter may be challenging, but you'll end up with an exemplary course.
Prototype	•As with any new effort, adapting HIPs into your course will have a learning curve, necessitating adjustments throughout your initial efforts. The point is to *begin*, drawing upon the design thinking principle of "bias towards action." There will never be a time when trying something new will be easy. Even in times of uncertaintly, it's never wrong to take action that makes your course better.
Test	•The true measure of your efforts to implement HIPs will be realized in your students' future success. Additionally, building your course in the LMS allows you to gather evidence of students' achievement through the reflection and application activities integral to all High-Impact Practices. If you've improved your course with your students' success in mind, their statements will testify to the value and efficacy of your efforts.

FIGURE 5.1 Chapter 5 Design Connection

SUMMARY

Table 5.1 compares the 12 HIPs with the eight key elements based on the information and ideas presented in this text. An X indicates that the element is usually associated with the HIP at left.

Notably, interaction with faculty and peers, opportunities for reflection and integration of learning, and real-world application span all 12 HIPs. True impact arises when we embed learning in high-quality human interactions, we deliberately engage in metacognitive processing of what we've learned, and we apply our learning beyond the walls of the classroom in authentic contexts. At all levels, from individual classrooms to entire universities and from campus-based face-to-face settings to fully online and asynchronous courses and programs, HIPs produce an outsize impact on our students.

REFLECTION

High-impact practices don't immediately appear to have anything to do with Comprehensive Instructional Design. HIPs don't help us build our courses into the LMS so that we can pivot easily from one model of instruction to another. However, they enhance our courses' content and effectiveness in whichever model we may teach. Placing our courses in the LMS is the baseline expectation, and under conditions that force us to pivot, it's perfectly fine if that's all we can manage as we're dealing with the unexpected. However, when our professional situations stabilize a bit more, we're better prepared to build on the firm foundation we've created to reach higher and achieve even more.

High-impact practices support students' achievement and improve their collegiate experience, career outcomes, and personal well-being after graduation. They strongly correlate with a student-centered philosophy of teaching and align with our institutions' mission and vision statements. Their benefits are widely understood, yet we seldom think of them as strategies we can employ for ourselves. It's time we changed our opinion! HIPs are within every instructor's reach if only we approach them in the spirit of design.

Are HIPs a mandate of Comprehensive Instructional Design? No. They're not even required by most colleges or universities. Can you create a well-designed course and teach it skillfully without them? Of course, you can. Nevertheless, building HIPs into your course at whatever scale is appropriate takes your teaching practice above and beyond the levels of "good enough" and "very good" to *outstanding*. We've acknowledged the intense effort involved in using Comprehensive Instructional Design. Incorporating HIPs adds an extra level of challenge to an already-strenuous process. It's an extraordinary achievement that exemplifies a student-centered perspective and showcases your grit and growth mindset as an educator. I sincerely commend you for contemplating how you can add HIPs to your course. You will truly become someone who demonstrates the excellence we hope everyone will achieve across higher education.

Notes

[1] Kuh, G. (2008). *High-impact practices: What they are, who has access to them, and why they matter.* Washington, DC: Association of American Colleges and Universities.

[2] Kuh, G. (2008). *High-impact practices: What they are, who has access to them, and why they matter.* Washington, DC: Association of American Colleges and Universities.

[3] Kuh, G., O'Donnel, K., & Reed, S. (2013). Ensuring quality & taking high-impact practices to scale. Washington, DC: Association of American Colleges and Universities.

[4] Piaget, J. (1936). *Origins of intelligence in the child.* London: Routledge and Kegan Paul; Piaget, J. (1957). *Construction of reality in the child.* London: Routledge and Kegan Paul; Piaget, J. (1958). The growth of logical thinking from childhood to adolescence. *AMC, 10,* 12.

[5] Bruner, J. (1957). On perceptual readiness. *Psychological Review, 64*(2). doi:10.1037/h0043805

[6] Kandel, R., et al. (2012). *Principles of neural science.* New York: McGraw-Hill Education.

[7] Eagleman, D. (2015). *The Brain,* Television Documentary Series. Public Broadcasting Corporation. Retrieved from www.eagleman.com/thebrain

[8] Linder, K., & Hayes, C. (Eds.). (2018). *High-impact practices in online education.* Sterling, VA: Stylus Publishing.

[9] Linder, K. (2019). *Implementing high-impact practices across modalities.* Oregon State University Ecampus (faculty presentation). Retrieved from https://und.edu/academics/ttada/_files/_docs/session-documents/implementing-hips-across-modalities.pdf

[10] Hunter, M. S., & Murray, K. A. (2007). New frontiers for student affairs professionals: Teaching and the first-year experience. *New Directions for Student Services, 117,* 25–34.

[11] Brownell, J. E., & Swaner, L. E. (2010). *Five high-impact practices—research on learning outcomes, completion, and quality.* Washington, DC: Association of American Colleges and Universities.

[12] Hickinbottom-Brawn, S., & Burns, D. (2015). The problem of first-year seminars: Risking disengagement through marketplace ideals. *The Canadian Journal of Higher Education, 45*(2), 154–167.

[13] Morris, P. L., Cobb, C., & Higgs, M. (2019). High-impact practices and adult online learners. *World Journal of Educational Research, 6*(4). Retrieved from https://core.ac.uk/reader/268085366

[14] Co-curricular refers to any activity occurring beyond the classroom. These include participating in or attending special events on or off campus, providing shared experiences, taking excursions off campus, and engaging with the community through special projects, volunteering, or service learning, among others.

[15] Bruner, J. (2017). *Cognitive and non-cognitive findings from the fall 2017 first-year common intellectual experience.* Retrieved from http://www.scholink.org/ojs/index.php/wjer/article/view/2299

[16] Kuh, G. (2008). *High impact practices: What are they, who has access to them, and why they matter (eBook Version-PDF)*. Washington, DC: Association of American Colleges and Universities.

[17] Kuh, G. (2008). *High impact practices: What are they, who has access to them, and why they matter (eBook Version-PDF)*. Washington, DC: Association of American Colleges and Universities. High impact practices in online education. Sterling VA: Stylus Publishing.

[18] Baker, J., & Pregitzer, M. (2018). Ch. 3 common intellectual experience. In K. Linder & C. Hayes (Eds.), *High impact practices in online education*. Sterling, VA: Stylus Publishing.

[19] Otto, S., Evins, M., Boyer-Pennington, M., & Brinthaupt, T. (2015, October). Learning communities in higher education: Best practice. *Journal of Student Success and Retention*, *2*(1).

[20] Zhao, C., & Kuh, G. (2004). Adding value: Learning communities and student engagement. *Research in Higher Education*, *45*, 115–138.

[21] Tinto, V. (2003). *Learning better together: The impact of learning communities on student success*, Higher Education Monograph Series, 2003–1. Syracuse, NY: Higher Education Program, School of Education, Syracuse University.

[22] Drexel University, LeBow College of Business. (n.d.). *Undergraduate programs*. Retrieved from www.lebow.drexel.edu/academics/undergraduate/student-life/learning-communities/commuter-learning-community

[23] San Diego State University. (n.d.). *Commuter life. Student life & leadership*. Retrieved from https://newscenter.sdsu.edu/student_affairs/sll/commuter-learning-communities.aspx

[24] Berry, S. (2019). Teaching to connect: Community-building strategies for the virtual classroom. *Online Learning*, *23*(1), 164–183. doi:10.24059/olj.v23i1.1425

[25] Harvard Writing Project: Guidelines for Writing-Intensive Courses. (n.d.). Retrieved from https://writingproject.fas.harvard.edu/pages/guidelines-writing-intensive-courses

[26] Young, A. (2006). *Teaching writing across the curriculum* (4th ed., p. 32). Upper Saddle River, NJ: Prentice Hall Resources for Writing.

[27] Kuh, G., O'Donnel, K., & Reed, S. (2013). *Ensuring quality & taking high-impact practices to scale*. Washington, DC: Association of American Colleges and Universities.

[28] Please see Ch. 6 of *Higher Education by Design* for an explanation of strategies for providing feedback on students' writing.

[29] Mackh, B. (2015). *Surveying the landscape: Arts integration at research universities*. Ann Arbor: University of Michigan.

[30] Mackh, B. (2015). *Surveying the landscape: Arts integration at research universities*. Ann Arbor: University of Michigan.

[31] Mackh, B. (2015). *Surveying the landscape: Arts integration at research universities*. Ann Arbor: University of Michigan.

[32] Robinson, IBM CEO survey, Preminger, Hardiman, Burnaford, and others.

[33] Mackh, B. (2015). *Surveying the landscape: Arts integration at research universities*. Ann Arbor: University of Michigan.

[34] Meng, T. (2016, May 18). Everyone is born creative but it is educated out of us at school. *The Guardian*. Retrieved from www.theguardian.com/media-network/2016/may/18/born-creative-educated-out-of-us-school-business

[35] Widely attributed to Picasso but subject to question: https://quoteinvestigator.com/2015/03/07/child-art/

[36] Johnson, C. (2016, November 23). How digital media has changed creativity. *Deseret Media*. Retrieved from www.deseret.com/2016/11/23/20600988/how-digital-media-has-changed-creativity#corrina-harrington-3-of-eau-claire-wis-plays-with-air-blowers-in-the-forces-at-play-exhibit-at-the-minnesota-childrens-museum-in-st-paul-minn-on-tuesday-nov-22-2016

[37] Turner, C. (2015, December 8). No child left behind: An obituary. *National Public Radio, Education*. Retrieved from www.npr.org/sections/ed/2015/12/08/458844737/no-child-left-behind-an-obituary

[38] Johnson, C. (2016, November 23). How digital media has changed creativity. *Deseret Media*. Retrieved from www.deseret.com/2016/11/23/20600988/how-digital-media-has-changed-creativity#corrina-harrington-3-of-eau-claire-wis-plays-with-air-blowers-in-the-forces-at-play-exhibit-at-the-minnesota-childrens-museum-in-st-paul-minn-on-tuesday-nov-22-2016

[39] Johnson, C. (2016, November 23). How digital media has changed creativity. *Deseret Media*. Retrieved from www.deseret.com/2016/11/23/20600988/how-digital-media-has-changed-creativity#corrina-harrington-3-of-eau-claire-wis-plays-with-air-blowers-in-the-forces-at-play-exhibit-at-the-minnesota-childrens-museum-in-st-paul-minn-on-tuesday-nov-22-2016

[40] Zagursky, E. *Smart:Yes. Creative: Not so much*. Research & Scholarship: College of William & Mary. Retrieved from www.wm.edu/research/news/social-sciences/smart-yes-creative-not-so-much.php

[41] Markman, A. (2016, January 4). Four things you learned at school that make you less creative. *Inc.com*. Retrieved from www.inc.com/art-markman/4-things-you-learned-in-school-that-make-you-less-creative.html

[42] Makerspace for Education. (n.d.). Retrieved from www.makerspaceforeducation.com/makerspace.html

[43] Makerspace for Education. (n.d.). Retrieved from www.makerspaceforeducation.com/makerspace.html

[44] Stanford University. (2020). *Explore creative expression (CE)WAYS courses:Ways of thinking/ways of doing*. Retrieved from https://undergrad.stanford.edu/programs/ways/choose/explore-creative-expression-ce-ways-courses

[45] Schulman, R. (2018, November 19). Ten ways educators can make classrooms more innovative. *Forbes Magazine*. Retrieved from www.forbes.com/sites/robynshulman/2018/11/19/10-ways-educators-can-make-classrooms-more-innovative/#10f611327f87

[46] Design Thinking Bootcamp. Stanford University d.school. Retrieved from https://dschool.stanford.edu/resources/the-bootcamp-bootleg

[47] Ellis, J. (2016, February 8). 7 Ways to tap into learner creativity via E-learning. *iSpring Solutions*. Retrieved from www.ispringsolutions.com/blog/7-ways-to-tap-into-learner-creativity-through-e-learning

[48] Bellis, M. (2016, August 16). Thomas Edison's 'Muckers.' *ThoughtCo.* Retrieved from http://inventors.about.com/library/inventors/bledisonmuckers.htm; Padgett, K. (n.d.). *Thomas Edison's research laboratory.* Retrieved from http://agilewriter.com/Biography/EdisonLab.htm

[49] Mackh, B. (2018). *Higher education by design: Best practices for curricular planning and instruction.* Abingdon: Routledge, offers an in-depth discussion of strategies for collaborative learning. The material included in this section is only a short excerpt from the book.

[50] Mackh, B. (2018). *Higher education by design: Best practices for curricular planning and instruction.* Abingdon: Routledge.

[51] Cornell University Center for Teaching Excellence. (2017). *Collaborative learning: Group work.* Retrieved from www.cte.cornell.edu/teaching-ideas/engaging-students/collaborative-learning.html

[52] Stanford University "Speaking of Teaching" Winter 2001 Center for Teaching and Learning. PDF.

[53] Science Daily. (2015, August 6). *How emotions influence learning and memory processes in the brain.* Retrieved from www.sciencedaily.com/releases/2015/08/150806091434.htm

[54] Scager, K., et al. (2016, Winter). Collaborative learning in higher education: Evoking positive interdependence. *CBE Live Sciences Education*, 15(4), ar69. doi:10.1187/cbe.16-07-0219. Retrieved from www.ncbi.nlm.nih.gov/pmc/articles/PMC5132366/

[55] Scager, K., et al. (2016, Winter). Collaborative learning in higher education: Evoking positive interdependence. *CBE Live Sciences Education*, 15(4).

[56] Scager, K., et al. (2016, Winter). Collaborative learning in higher education: Evoking positive interdependence. *CBE Live Sciences Education*, 15(4).

[57] IBM. (2012, May 22). IBM CEO study: Command and control meets collaboration. *IBM Press Release.* Retrieved from https://www-03.ibm.com/press/us/en/pressrelease/37793.wss

[58] University of Oregon. (n.d.). *Benefits of undergraduate research.* Undergraduate Research Program. Retrieved from https://urop.uoregon.edu/for-faculty/considering-undergraduate-research-and-creative-scholarship/benefits-of-ugr/

[59] University of Oregon. (n.d.). *Benefits of undergraduate research.* Undergraduate Research Program. Retrieved from https://urop.uoregon.edu/for-faculty/considering-undergraduate-research-and-creative-scholarship/benefits-of-ugr/

[60] Hensel, N. (Ed.). (2012). *Characteristics of excellence in undergraduate research.* Ann Arbor, MI: The Council on Undergraduate Research.

[61] Hensel, N. (Ed.). (2012). *Characteristics of excellence in undergraduate research.* Ann Arbor, MI: The Council on Undergraduate Research.

[62] Elon University. (n.d.). *Center for Engaged Learning: Undergraduate research.* Retrieved from www.centerforengagedlearning.org/doing-engaged-learning/undergraduate-research/

[63] www.bard.edu/news/releases/pr/fstory.php?id=3134

[64] Faulconer, E., & Gauss, A. (2019). Undergraduate research for online students. *Quarterly Review of Distance Education*, 20(3), 45–47. Information Age Publishing.

[65] Ortagus, J., & Stedrak, L. (2013). Online education and contingent faculty: An exploratory analysis of issues and challenges for higher education administrators. *Educational Considerations*, 40(3), 30–33.

66 Faulconer, E., & Gauss, A. (2019). Undergraduate research for online students. *Quarterly Review of Distance Education, 20*(3), 45–47.

67 AAC&U Making Excellence Inclusive. www.aacu.org/making-excellence-inclusive

68 Doscher, S., & Landorf, H. (2018). Universal global learning, inclusive excellence, and higher education's greater purpose. *Peer Review, 20*(1). Association of American Colleges and Universities. Retrieved from www.aacu.org/peerreview/2018/Winter/FIU

69 Gordon, L. (2018, January 3). Racial minorities feel like outsiders at some colleges, USC diversity expert says. *College & Careers: EdSource.* Retrieved from https://edsource.org/2018/racial-minorities-feel-like-outsiders-at-some-colleges-usc-diversity-expert-says/591725

70 Umbach, P. D., & Kuh, G. D. (2006). Student experiences with diversity at liberal arts colleges: Another claim for distinctiveness. *The Journal of Higher Education, 77*(1), 169–192. doi:10.1080/00221546.2006.11778923

71 Umbach, P. D., & Kuh, G. D. (2006). Student experiences with diversity at liberal arts colleges: Another claim for distinctiveness. *The Journal of Higher Education, 77*(1), 169–192. doi:10.1080/00221546.2006.11778923

72 Umbach, P. D., & Kuh, G. D. (2006). Student experiences with diversity at liberal arts colleges: Another claim for distinctiveness. *The Journal of Higher Education, 77*(1), 169–192. doi:10.1080/00221546.2006.11778923

73 University of Colorado at Denver. (2016). *Diversity and global learning: HIP best practices guidelines.* Retrieved from www.ucdenver.edu/student-services/resources/ue/HIP/Documents/D%20GL%20Best-Practices%20Guidelines%2012-2016.pdf

74 Mackh, B. (2018). *Higher education by design: Best practices for curricular planning and instruction.* Abingdon: Routledge.

75 Meacham, J. (2009). *Teaching diversity and democracy across the disciplines: Who, what, and how.* Association of American Colleges and Universities. Retrieved from www.aacu.org/publications-research/periodicals/teaching-diversity-and-democracy-across-disciplines-who-what-and-0

76 Doscher, S., & Landorf, H. (2018). Universal global learning, inclusive excellence, and higher education's greater purpose. *Peer Review, 20*(1). Association of American Colleges and Universities. Retrieved from www.aacu.org/peerreview/2018/Winter/FIU

77 Mackh, B. (2018). *Higher education by design: Best practices for curricular planning and instruction.* Abingdon: Routledge.

78 Preface to the script of *The Forgotten Village* (1941) and the inspiration behind *The Grapes of Wrath* (1939).

79 Boyd, D. (2016). What would Paulo Freire think of BlackboardTM: Critical pedagogy in an age of online learning. *International Journal of Critical Pedagogy, 7,* 165–186.

80 Dominigue, A. D. (2016). Online and blended pedagogy in social justice education. In M. Adams & L. A. Bell (Eds.), *Teaching for diversity and social justice* (3rd ed., pp. 369–396). New York: Routledge.

81 Reinert Center for Transformative Teaching and Learning. (n.d.). *Inclusive online teaching. Saint Louis University.* Retrieved from www.slu.edu/cttl/resources/resource-guides/inclusive-online-teaching.pdf

260

[82] Watson, C., Kuh, G., Rhodes, T, Light, T., & Chen, H. (2016). ePortfolios—the eleventh high impact practice. *International Journal of ePortfolio*, 6(2), 65–69. Retrieved from https://eportfolios.capilanou.ca/devcomm/wp-content/uploads/sites/425/2017/02/ePortfolios_Eleventh-High-Impact-Practice-IJEP_6.2.2016.pdf

[83] Finley, A., & McNair, T. (2013). *Assessing underserved students' engagement in high-impact practices*. Washington, DC: Association of American Colleges and Universities.

[84] Finley, A., & McNair, T. (2013). *Assessing underserved students' engagement in high-impact practices*. Washington, DC: Association of American Colleges and Universities.

[85] University of Waterloo Centre for Teaching Excellence. (n.d.). *ePortfolios explained: Theory and practice*. Retrieved from https://uwaterloo.ca/centre-for-teaching-excellence/teaching-resources/teaching-tips/educational-technologies/all/eportfolios

[86] Tosh, D., Penny Light, T., Fleming, K., & Haywood, J. (2005). Engagement with electronic portfolios: Challenges from the student perspective. *Canadian Journal of Learning and Technology, 31*(3).

[87] Davis, V. (2017, November 17). Eleven essentials for excellent digital portfolios. *Edutopia: Classroom Technology*. Retrieved from www.edutopia.org/blog/11-essentials-for-excellent-eportfolios-vicki-davis

[88] Reynolds, C., & Patton, J. (2014). *Leveraging the ePortfolio for integrative learning: A faculty guide to classroom practices for transforming student learning*. Sterling, VA: Stylus.

[89] Hovis, S. (2017, July 12). Six essential components every ePortfolio needs. *Instructure*. Retrieved from www.instructure.com/portfolium/blog/6-essential-components-every-eportfolio-needs; Montana State University. (n.d.). *Tips for creating a compelling ePortfolio*. Retrieved from www.montana.edu/engcommtoolkit/e-portfolio/

[90] Elon University. (2016, July 27). ePortfolio as high-impact practice. *Center for Engaged Learning*. Retrieved from www.centerforengagedlearning.org/eportfolio as high-impact-practice/

[91] Dewey, J. (1938). *Experience and education*. New York: Kappa Delta Pi.

[92] Kolb, D. (1984). *Experiential learning: Experience as the source of learning and development*. Upper Saddle River, NJ: Prentice-Hall.

[93] Rogers, C. R. (1969). *Freedom to learn*. Columbus, OH: Merrill; Rogers, C. R., & Freiberg, H. J. (1994). *Freedom to learn* (3rd ed.). Columbus, OH: Merrill and Palgrave Macmillan.

[94] Jones, R. (2017). 30 Colleges with the most impressive job placement rates and career services. *Online School Center*. Retrieved from www.onlineschoolcenter.com/30-colleges-impressive-job-placement-rates-career-services/

[95] Federal Reserve Bank of New York. (2019, February 6). *The labor market for recent college graduates*. Retrieved from www.newyorkfed.org/research/college-labor-market/college-labor-market_compare-majors.html

[96] Boyington, B. (2015, March 21). Understand the differences between a co-op, internship. *U.S. News: Higher Education*. Retrieved from www.usnews.com/education/best-colleges/articles/2015/03/31/understand-the-differences-between-a-co-op-internship

[97] Band, J. (2017). *Community engaged teaching step by step*. Vanderbilt University Center for Teaching. Retrieved from https://cft.vanderbilt.edu/guides-sub-pages/community-engaged-teaching-step-by-step/

[98] Brown University. (2018). *Crafting meaningful culminating experiences: Best practices for capstones in the concentration*. Report for the College Curriculum Council. Retrieved from www.brown.edu/academics/college/support/faculty/sites/brown.edu.academics.college.support.faculty/files/uploads/Capstone%20Report_Revised%20with%20Ex%20Sum.pdf

[99] Cuseo's widely-used definition describes three overarching goals for capstones: "(1) offer an opportunity for integrative reflection, (2) make meaning of the college experience, (3) assist with transition to postcollege life" (p. 22). Cuseo, J. B. (1998). Objectives and benefits of senior year programs. In J. N. Gardner & G. Van der Veer (Eds.), *The senior year experience. Facilitating integration, reflection, closure, and transition*. San Francisco, CA: Jossey-Bass.

[100] Young, H. S., et al. (2016). *National survey of senior capstone experiences* (p. 14). Columbia, SC: University of South Carolina National Research Center for the First-Year Experience.

[101] National Survey of Student Engagement. (2007). *Experiences that matter: Enhancing student learning and success, annual report 2007* (p. 20). Bloomington: Indiana University Center for Postsecondary Research.

[102] Hart Research Associates. (2015). *Falling short? College learning and career success* (p. 4). Washington, DC: Association of American Colleges and Universities.

Chapter 6

A Culture of Care

CHAPTER 6 SUMMARY

- A Culture of Care
- Elements of Care
- "Just Send Me an Email"
- Challenges to Care
- Strategies for Care
- Crisis and Change
- The Trim Tab

****

Our journey has taken us a long way. We now understand more about who our students are and what they need from us. We know why we should adopt a student-centered philosophy of teaching and reject the notion that our students ought to be college ready. We have learned why we should build our courses into the LMS, how we should do this in a way that meets high standards of quality, and how to take that course in the LMS to pivot between different models of instruction as needed. We even know how to take our instruction to the next level by incorporating high-impact practices in our classrooms.

I commend you for taking all this advice to heart and designing an exemplary course that you're prepared to teach on campus, online, or any combination in between. The work involved in this task is immense, and those who have accomplished it have good reason to be proud of what they have achieved.

In this final chapter, we will consider what might just be the most important aspect of excellence in teaching. The work we've done with our heads and our hands is important, and it's a good beginning. Nevertheless, the best-designed course taught by the most conscientious instructor will fail to deliver on its promise if the instructor does not treat students with care, respect, empathy, and compassion.

A CULTURE OF CARE

Demonstrating care for others has seldom been a top priority in higher education, but its absence is increasingly evident in traditional approaches to teaching and learning. In decades past, university professors often delivered an introductory speech containing variations on the same theme: "Look to your right. Look to your left. One of you will not be here by the end of the course." This disheartening message was meant to warn students that a course would be difficult, and only the brightest and most motivated students would be found worthy of a passing grade, inspiring a spirit of competition intended to prompt students to be one of the select few who would make it through the course. Although not many of us make the same claims on the first day of class any longer, an excerpt from a discussion on the College Confidential website shows us this attitude has not entirely disappeared:[1]

> Some colleagues were reminiscing last night and noted that the old "look to your right, look to your left, one of you won't be here by the end of the year" speeches that used to be commonly given at some colleges are long dead. Those warnings were a point of pride by universities. Which is kind of appalling. Today of course universities brag about retention rates. How times have changed.
>
> (~Maya54)

> The "point of pride" in that saying in past decades was the implication that the school did not water down its courses and curricula to accommodate weak students who may have gotten in due to much lower admission standards back then. Yes, students whose high school records only barely indicated college-readiness found it easy to get into many colleges back then, but they really needed to turn around their motivation and study habits to succeed in college . . .
>
> (~ucbalumnus)

> I don't understand why some people have a problem with sink-or-swim environments. . . . There is only so much these colleges can do, in their control, to provide high quality academics, and that means students either sink or swim. "We'll let you in, but you are expected to keep up." Furthermore, these less selective schools generally provide a range of tutoring/support services to help struggling (but motivated) students stay on top. And the ones that get weeded out? Too bad so sad. . . . [T]hey had their

chance. . . . Diluting the academics to accommodate less-prepared students is far more concerning than giving them a second chance to prove
themselves. . . . Above all else, I think colleges need to maintain quality . . .
whether that means a) making it harder for students to get in, or b) making
it harder for students to get out.

(~fracatlmstr)

The member who posted the initial discussion thread, Maya54, indicates that
the "look to your right, look to your left" attitudes prevalent in higher education
in the past "are long dead." After having interviewed and worked with over a
thousand faculty members, I'd have to disagree. Instructors may not deliver this
disheartening speech any longer, but for too many, the underlying callousness
remains.

The discussion thread also illuminates some common attitudes about the institution's role in student success, shown in Table 6.1.

Based on the attitudes expressed in that online discussion forum, we might
infer that most students who leave college have failed academically through
sheer laziness or incompetence. However, a study by Oakton Community College[2] revealed that only 20% to 30% of students discontinue their studies due
to academic difficulties. The other 70% to 80% leave for a variety of other
reasons:

TABLE 6.1 Faculty Attitudes and Implications

Overt Attitude	Implication
Providing academic support weakens academic quality and rigor.	Student support means "watering down" courses and curricula to accommodate "weak" students.
Students must turn themselves around, increase their own motivation, and figure out how to study.	The instructor is responsible only for presenting course content to students, not for helping students learn.
There's nothing wrong with a "sink or swim" attitude regarding student success. It should be difficult to get into college and difficult to graduate.	A college degree is a badge of honor reserved for a select group of individuals who possess the personal fortitude, intelligence, and motivation to make it through an intentionally challenging process.
"The ones who get weeded out? Too bad so sad. They had their chance."	Nobody in the institution needs to care if students succeed or fail. Success is entirely up to the student.

265

- Financial: they cannot afford tuition, fees, books, and other expenses. Financial aid does not cover all costs. Students must often work while taking classes, which becomes overwhelming. Unexpected setbacks in parental finances can create insurmountable financial barriers for students.
- Instructional: they don't understand what to do in their courses and do not ask for help because they perceive their instructors as being inaccessible.
- Social: they are unable to make friends or find a social group on campus. Loneliness and isolation undermine their motivation to continue with their studies.
- Institutional: they do not understand how to navigate academic systems such as course registration or financial aid. They do not know where to go for help or how to receive the available support.
- Personal: they lack skills such as time management or study strategies. They may face unforeseen problems such as an extended illness, a death in the family, a challenging personal circumstance such as a breakup with a significant other, lack of reliable childcare, or conflict within their families, all of which create barriers to devoting the necessary attention to their studies.

So, what do all these problems have in common? The attitudes expressed in (but by no means limited to) the discussion thread quoted at the start of this chapter are glaringly devoid of care, equity, and equality. Elitist attitudes embedded in our higher education system began generations ago when many adults didn't even earn a high school diploma, let alone a college degree. Such pejorative attitudes still exist across our society: we have not yet achieved genuine equality in terms of gender, sexuality, race, religion, ethnicity, or other aspects of identity despite the 19th Amendment, the Civil Rights Act, Title IX, the Marriage Equality Act, and other legislative landmarks. Higher education, like all other sectors of society, must continue to work toward becoming more compassionate, accepting, and inclusive, beginning by exposing the implicit prejudice that we need not demonstrate care for our students because only the strongest, smartest, most self-motivated, or most hardworking individuals are *worthy* of a college degree.

The very structures of higher education reflect this bias. As we discussed in Chapter 1, the more restrictive the admissions policy, the more likely the institution will enroll students who are young, white, and from relatively affluent families headed by parents who are college graduates themselves. These students generally received an exemplary K–12 education filled with opportunities for extracurricular achievement. In contrast, incoming students at institutions with more open admissions policies are likely to be older, to exhibit divergent identities and cultures, to come from lower-income households, or to be the first in their families to enroll in higher education. Our institutions have become more aware of the need to accommodate these differences, but many are still unsuccessful in providing the necessary level of care to support all students' success.

As an example, a friend of mine attended an elite private college that, like its peer institutions, had no systems in place to demonstrate care for struggling students. My friend contracted mononucleosis during the second semester of her sophomore year, and at the same time, her parents were embroiled in a divorce. Due to these difficulties, she failed her required physics course. Per institutional policy, the failing grade remained on her transcript even after she successfully retook the course, which prevented her from gaining admission to a graduate program in physical therapy, shattering her dreams and altering the entire trajectory of her adult life. Many institutions of higher learning maintain similarly rigid policies—the grade is the grade, no matter what. We think this is "fair." But is it? The college could have mitigated my friend's negative outcome by demonstrating care through a more humane policy that would expunge a failing grade from a student's academic record upon successfully completing the course in the next semester. Do we really have our students' best interests in mind when we value inflexibility over student success? Couldn't we strive for something higher?

I am not suggesting we give every student a free pass whenever they fail to meet expectations or requirements. Our programs should remain rigorous, maintaining high expectations that students earn their degrees through persistence, hard work, and intellectual engagement. By no means does caring for our students imply sacrificing academic quality. However, we must also look at every student as an individual human being who deserves kindness and respect.

Oxford's Lexico online dictionary defines *care* as:[3]

(noun)

1. The provision of what is necessary for the health, welfare, maintenance, and protection of someone or something.
2. Serious attention or consideration applied to doing something correctly or to avoid damage or risk.

(verb)

1. Feel concern or interest; attach importance to something.
2. Look after and provide for the needs of.

Those who work in higher education do not always provide what is necessary for the health, welfare, maintenance, and protection of their students. They might not apply serious attention or consideration to avoiding damage or risk in the task of educating their students. They sometimes exhibit a lack of concern or interest in their students. They may not choose to look after or provide for their students' needs. These actions (or inactions) result in a failure to care in every sense of the word.

ELEMENTS OF CARE

In *Designing and Creating a Culture of Care* (2018), editor Susan L. Groenwald shares an anecdote from Susan King, the president of Chamberlain College of Nursing's Chicago campus.

> As I exited Stroger Hospital after visiting [a student hospitalized for chemotherapy], one of the resident physicians asked if I was from Chamberlain. He said that the Stroger staff and physicians have discussed how "Chamberlain treats the students like family." The young resident said, "As a student, I have needed someone to care for me and wish I had that type of experience in my learning environment." . . . I realized that our roles are so important to the lives of so many—we have many opportunities to make a difference every moment of every day. I am humbled to work for an organization that truly walks the walk.[4]

King tells of how she and her faculty supported the student throughout the illness, from arranging to take course exams from the student's hospital bed to teleconferencing lectures to sending assignments to the student's home. In doing so, they not only supported the student's academic success—they sent a clear and powerful message to everyone who witnessed their actions that they care unequivocally for their students and will do everything they can to empower their students' success.

If we are to transcend the norms and structures that have caused higher education to retain its exclusionary and uncaring practices—the sink-or-swim, survival-of-the-fittest mentality of past centuries—we must deliberately set out to create a new and more inclusive cultural model built upon a multifaceted view of care.

Care for Self: Most of us tend to immerse ourselves in work, but professions as intellectually and emotionally demanding as teaching carry a grave risk of burnout, unmanageable stress, and exhaustion if we fail to make a conscious effort to care for ourselves. Studies have shown the professorate to be a very lonely career, with a significant amount of our time spent in tasks other than teaching, such as sending and responding to email and attending meetings. We must also find time to engage in research or creative practice, professional development, and service activities.[5] No one can effectively engage in caring for others when their physical, intellectual, and emotional reserves are depleted, at least not for long. Many workplaces offer employee assistance programs, gym memberships, and paid time off, such as sabbaticals, for these reasons. It's why higher education still

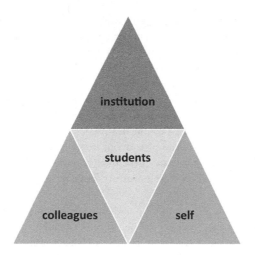

FIGURE 6.1 The Culture of Care

operates on an agrarian calendar in which we teach for just 30 or 32 weeks per year, not counting summer terms. Academic breaks provide time to meet expectations for research or creative practice, but they also serve as a primary mechanism for self-care—to rest and replenish our energies for the coming term.

Care for Students: On the surface, our duty of care for students seems clear. We teach our courses and fulfill our other obligations as educators, but this is only the beginning. We also have valuable opportunities to demonstrate care for our students by exercising empathy, sometimes based on the experiences we had when we were students ourselves. I spent eight years as a student in higher education. Among all the faculty members with whom I studied, I can immediately identify those who demonstrated care for me and those who did not. I imagine names come readily to mind for you, too.

We cannot overestimate the impact of caring for our students, as we noted in the discussion of "The Big Six" in Chapter 2. I've often heard instructors oppose suggestions that they should be more compassionate, usually justifying their choice to maintain a brusque and imposing demeanor with statements like "In the real world, nobody is going to coddle these students. We have to prepare them for life!" I see two problems with this line of thinking. First, the instructor's primary responsibility is not to teach life skills unless these directly relate to the course content. If so, they must be included in the course's objectives and outcomes, linked to an assessment mechanism of some sort, explicitly stated on the course syllabus, discussed on the first day of class, and reinforced throughout the course. Second, thinking we must "prepare students for life" conveys the condescending attitude of "in loco parentis," a legal term meaning "in place of a parent." Extremely few of our students are minors. Although they may be very young adults who lack relevant life experience, it is not within our rights or responsibilities to take on the role of parent.

Another justification I've often heard is "It's not my job to be their friend." That's true. In fact, it would be inappropriate if instructors treated students as though they were close friends because friendship is a relationship based on equal status, which is definitely not present between students and instructors. Nevertheless, nothing ought to prevent us from being friendly, kind, approachable, and compassionate. We appreciate these qualities when others extend them to us. Why wouldn't we choose to demonstrate them to our students, who depend upon us for so much?

Caring is not the same as coddling, babying, or acquiescing to our students. Indeed, sometimes the most caring decision is to uphold our stated policies because it can provide a teachable moment. For example, I taught a studio photography course in which class attendance was linked to the course grade, a common and unremarkable policy in many programs. A student skipped a class where I demonstrated an important process. When I asked why he hadn't joined us, he said, "Well, I was tired, so I took a nap instead." Since it wasn't the first time this student had missed a required class period, I quickly calculated the university's tuition rate per credit hour, divided by the number of class periods, and asked him, "How would your parents react if you called them to say you'd just taken a $300 nap?" He was quite taken aback at this and agreed to complete an extra assignment to make up for the grade points he'd missed by skipping class.

As a counterexample with which I'm familiar, a graduate student knew that she would be late for class one evening due to a parent-teacher conference. She sent the instructor an email explaining that her son's conference time had not been under her control, apologized in advance for being tardy, and attached the assignment that was due that evening. The instructor penalized the student's grade because her policy stated that both early and late submission of assignments were unacceptable, and she applied an additional penalty for being late to class. When the student questioned this decision, the instructor became irate, and the situation spiraled downward. Had the instructor chosen to demonstrate care for the student rather than insisting upon enforcing the letter of her policies, especially since the student showed good faith by making every effort to be proactive and responsible, the outcome could have been much better for all concerned.

Jeffrey Selingo, in an editorial for the *Washington Post*, relates the story of chemistry professor David Laude of the University of Texas at Austin. Laude noticed a strong correlation between students' demographic characteristics and their performance in his chemistry courses (emphasis added).

In fall 1999, [Laude] pulled 50 students from his 500-seat chemistry class who came from low-income families, from families whose parents did not go to college, or had low SAT scores. He enrolled them in a smaller 50-seat class he taught right after the larger class. **"It was the same material, it was just as hard, but I changed my attitude about these students,"** he said. **"We beat into their heads that they were scholars, that they were great."** In addition, he assigned these students advisers and peer mentors. When the semester was over, the students in the smaller class had achieved the same grades as those in the larger section. "These were students I would have failed a year earlier," Laude recalled.

Over time, Laude made other changes to his instruction as well.

He puts most of his lecture material online for students to watch in advance and spends class time in discussions. . . . **"It's about creating a culture that I'm on your side,"** Laude said. To some that might sound like he simply made his course easier so more students could pass. **"The class is just as hard,"** Laude [said], **"but instead of having this adversarial relationship with students, now we're nice to them."**

Laude demonstrates a fundamental truth: we can maintain academic rigor without being harsh or uncaring. We can help our students believe in their own ability to master difficult course material and uphold their success. We can empower our students by focusing on accountability and self-determination. We can embolden our students as we instill self-confidence and assist them in developing a professional identity.

Mentorship is another area with powerful opportunities to demonstrate care for students. Those who major in our particular discipline should know there is a faculty member who is a kindred soul—someone who understands their hopes and dreams and will work actively to help achieve them. Mentorship goes well beyond standard duties for student advising. Mentors take a personal interest in the student's success. They initiate conversations about what the student plans to do after graduation. They work with the student to explore graduate programs, complete grant applications, or prepare a resume. They write letters of recommendation, celebrate their students' successes, and help them through their disappointments. They express belief in their students' potential to succeed. The more skillful we are in building appropriate mentoring relationships with our students, the better the chance that students will develop a positive view of their educational experience.

Caring for students is not solely the responsibility of faculty. Everyone in the university has the opportunity to contribute to the culture of care. I'm reminded of a campus dining service worker who greeted me every day with a warm smile, saying, "Hey, baby, how you doin' today?" I'm a rather physically imposing person with an unconscious scowl—not someone whom others associate with a nickname like "baby," yet when I interacted with this worker, I genuinely felt that she cared about me. She made the two years of my master's program much more pleasant than they might otherwise have been. Another example, albeit fictional, is Boothby—a groundskeeper at Starfleet Academy in the *Star Trek: The Next Generation* and *Star Trek: Voyager* television series, who profoundly impacted the lives of several characters during their years as cadets. Each of us has opportunities to care for students without regard to our rank or responsibilities, from the campus president to the custodial staff.

Care for Colleagues: One might think that a group of like-minded scholars would create an ideal sense of community in the workplace. After all, we share a passion for our discipline, similar educational backgrounds, and the decision to become educators. It seems only logical that this unity of purpose would generate a bond between group members. Sadly, this is often untrue. Human nature being what it is, we tend to become competitive rather than cooperative. We establish hierarchies, vie for dominance, and belittle one another's accomplishments. At institutions where faculty members' career advancement depends on their peers' favorable evaluation, outright bullying may even ensue. A culture of care establishes the opposite. We come to see one another as colleagues rather than competitors. We celebrate one another's achievements. We build each other up instead of tearing each other down. We rally together when one of our colleagues faces personal difficulty, and we celebrate life's milestones together. Most of us establish friendships with a few individuals wherever we work, but within a culture of care for colleagues, we can count on every member of our department for support even if they're not close friends.

Care for Institution: Each of us is part of a larger institution, and its success determines our continuing employment. If we take a myopic view, focusing solely on our immediate concerns, we fail to care for our institution. Care exists through our participation in professional organizations, where we serve as ambassadors for our institution. Likewise, engaging with the community as representatives of our institution demonstrates care. Assisting with marketing and recruiting new students exemplifies care for the institution since student enrollment is crucial to its sustainability. Care includes expressing positivity about the institution when conversing with individuals in the community or our broader professional circles. It also means refraining from complaining about the institution even to our work friends and colleagues since negativity spreads like a virus and undermines everyone's morale. Certainly, we all become frustrated in our workplace at times, but conversations that focus on finding solutions are productive, whereas those intended just to express negativity are contrary to the culture of care we hope to build.

Compare this to an interaction that might occur in a family. Let's say a teenage child has once again returned the family car with the fuel indicator on "empty," compounding the problem by forgetting to inform the parent that the car would need gas in the morning. The parent, running late the next day, becomes angry that they will now be even later for work because they must take time to put gas in the car. The parent then has two choices: to vent their understandable anger at the guilty party or to demonstrate care by calmly discussing the problem and potential solutions. Being human, perhaps we do a bit of both. Nevertheless, we should prioritize the relationship with our child above our negative emotional response. The same is true at work. Conflict arises in every human relationship and at every institution, but choosing to manage workplace conflict with care speaks volumes about our integrity.

"JUST SEND ME AN EMAIL"

As reported in the *Chronicle of Higher Education* (2018),[6] Reesa-Marie Dawkins, an adjunct professor in the University of Alaska system, regularly included a message in the course syllabus that encouraged her students to seek her help when they confronted personal challenges during the term. "Just send me an email. I will help you get through it, no matter what it is."

> As much as I hate to admit this, we have very little (if any) control over most of the things that happen in our lives. Most mornings we arise and think we have a good idea of how we have planned for our day to unfold. Enter Life! There is always something that will not go how we wanted and that, if we allow it, will throw us into survival mode instead of our normal thrive mode.
>
> I have been at this long enough to have seen many difficult things happen to my students. Instead of reaching out, they sit silent! When life happens, just send me an email. I am here to help you in any way possible, so let me know if you need me. My students have lost family members, gone through breakups and divorces, and one even called to tell me she was homeless. (We got her in a dorm the same day.) You may welcome a new baby into the world, get married, or graduate, and you need a few days to regroup. (These are all stressful events, too.) Your kids will get sick, and a spouse may be in the hospital. Just send me an email.
>
> I will help you get through it (no matter what it is). I can give extended grace periods, tutor you one on one by phone, be a good listener, offer a list of campus resources, and help you catch back up, if you have fallen behind. Your success in our classroom is very important to me. If you drop off the radar, I worry, and I will be calling you. So, if during this semester you experience any "Life Happens Events," do not suffer through them alone. Please, just send me an email.

I've adopted this technique in my courses, and it has markedly decreased students' tendency to disappear and encouraged them to communicate with me

273

more openly about the challenges they face. Students who might have avoided contacting me now choose to reach out when they're experiencing difficulties, and we're able to work together to find solutions that allow them to complete the course successfully.

Reciprocity applies to our professional relationships, too. When we extend care to those around us, we not only make the campus a better place, but we also build social capital that comes back to us through reciprocal care from those to whom we demonstrated kindness and empathy.

CHALLENGES TO CARE

Most of us know the Golden Rule—to treat other people the way we want to be treated—but applying this with our students and colleagues is much more difficult when it contradicts longstanding professional practices or institutional policies.

For example, when I was new to online teaching, one of my digital photography students informed me that he was about to be deployed as part of his military service and could not complete the course. He had already contacted his academic advisor to withdraw from the course, but this status change did not appear in my roster. Weekly grades were due a few days later, but I left his grades blank because I felt it would be disrespectful and unfair to give him a failing grade for work he should not have been expected to complete. My administrator noted this omission and informed me that I was required to enter a grade for all students on the roster, even if I was aware of extenuating circumstances. I protested, saying I strongly felt the student should not receive a failing grade when he had followed the correct institutional procedure. My administrator sympathized with my point of view but insisted I adhere to policy nonetheless.

All instructors encounter inflexible institutional requirements. We have little choice about when and how to post grades, grant students an Incomplete, or waive certain course requirements for students in distress. Individual instructors might discover ways to work around these obstacles, but most policies are beyond our control. An institution-wide culture of care would allow us to reconsider punitive policies through conscientious and open discussion toward finding solutions.

Loyalty to habits, histories, and traditions can also become a significant barrier to establishing a culture of care. Statements such as, "But we've always done it that way," or "That was good enough when I was a student, and it's good enough today!" are common, demonstrating how difficult it is to alter habituated behaviors. Even when we begin to make progress toward something new, it's all too easy to slide back into familiar patterns.

Ultimately, the only person we can change is ourselves. Our colleagues' pessimism, fear, arrogance, or false assumptions can undermine our best efforts to establish a culture of care that supports all members and upholds the institution itself. Nevertheless, each of us faces a choice in every interaction. We can be kind and caring, or difficult and demanding. We can demonstrate empathy or choose rigid adherence to punitive practices. We can work toward policies that support a culture of care or fight to keep the status quo.

STRATEGIES FOR CARE

Each of us can take steps to make our institution a more caring place, beginning in our classrooms, whether we teach on campus or online.

1. **Choose kindness.** The hardest battle may lie in overcoming our ingrained reactions to difficult situations. We can choose to modify our responses in favor of kindness rather than thoughtlessly acting on our feelings of anger, disappointment, and frustration. We can prioritize others' needs above our own desires. For example, when a student sends a last-minute email to ask for an extension on an assignment, your first response might be an emphatic "No." Caring asks that we initiate a discussion with the student to determine the best possible course of action. Yes, it takes more effort. Yes, it's inconvenient. However, the student will benefit from this interaction even when your answer remains no *if* you explain your rationale kindly and provide the support the student needs to overcome the problem that prevented them from meeting the stated deadline.

2. **Increase the frequency, quality, and warmth of your contact with students.** Don't limit your outreach to brief reminders of upcoming due dates or obligatory messages when students fail to turn in an assignment. Answer questions thoroughly. Send out interesting articles you've found related to your course content. Wish students a happy birthday. Communicate your belief in their ability to succeed before an important exam or assignment. Remind them that you're available to help when they need it. The more and varied the messages you send, the stronger the rapport you build, and the more successful students will be in your course.

3. **Educate students about your expectations, and clarify the difference between caring and enabling.** Faculty may resist suggestions to be more kind because they suspect students will take advantage of their largess. However, when we carefully explain our policies and expectations from the beginning of the course, we mitigate this possibility. I tell students that I am happy to help them in whatever ways might be necessary, but I also might require documentation of the mitigating circumstances they're experiencing. I emphasize that my number one priority is their successful learning of the course content and that when

275

they are unable to meet a requirement, we will work together to find an acceptable alternative that supports their learning.

For instance, in the online photojournalism course I taught, students were required to create visual documentation of a community event spanning three weeks, with specific photographs to be completed in each of the three stages of the project. A student informed me that she was housebound due to a chronic illness and lived in a rural area far from the nearest small town, so she had no access to anything that could meet the course requirements. We brainstormed together and identified a topic she could pursue in her own backyard. The other project specifications remained the same for her as for every other student in the class, but she was then able to complete the course successfully despite being unable to leave her home.

4. **Find a balance between providing instruction and personalizing that experience for students.** Because most instructors tend to set up our courses independently from our fellow faculty members, we occasionally create difficulties for students when our expectations conflict with those in their other courses. Many of us schedule the due date for major projects or papers in the last week of the course, but this practice can create a disheartening overload for our students. We can demonstrate care by setting the deadline for a high-point-value assignment earlier in the term or breaking it up into smaller increments to redistribute its impact on students' workload.

None of us, alone, can establish a culture of care in the department or college for which we work, but each of us has the power to create a caring environment in our classrooms and offices. By caring for ourselves, our students, our colleagues, and our institution, we make our world a better place, one interaction at a time.

CRISIS, CHANGE, AND CARE

Crises are never welcome. No one wants to experience life-threatening or catastrophic events. Nevertheless, moments of crisis open us to the opportunity for change. We'd much rather keep things the same, which is proven time and again across higher education.

The word *crisis* comes from the Greek term indicating "a point at which change must come, for better or worse"[7]—an apt description of what we faced when Pre-K to post-doctoral programs had to reinvent instructional delivery practically overnight. The sudden migration to online interaction presented us with an opportunity disguised as a formidable challenge. What can we learn from this experience to enact a culture of care during trying times?

Care for Self

Isolation and uncertainty take a heavy toll on our bodies and minds. Therefore, it's essential that we take time to care for ourselves. Educators who are attempting a new model of instruction might feel especially overwhelmed and anxious. So do instructors who have begun a position at a new institution or those who are frantically preparing a dossier for promotion or tenure, to say nothing of times when we struggle with personal hardships. Reaching out to friends and colleagues for emotional support is beneficial, as are the usual self-care strategies such as adequate sleep, a healthy diet, and outdoor exercise.

Care for Students

Demonstrating care for our students is perhaps our most important duty. The more we can communicate care and support for our students, the more likely they will persist in their studies. We possess the ability to make their educational experience just as meaningful and valuable no matter which model (or models!) of instruction we employ while they are enrolled in our courses. To do this, we must first ensure that our instruction remains engaging, and we maintain rigorous expectations while also accommodating students' circumstances, delivering value equivalent to that which students expected when they enrolled at our institutions. When students experience hardships, we should increase the frequency and quality of our communications—sending email, text messages, or phone calls to conduct well-being checks, asking if the student has questions or needs help.

We can also find tangible ways to improve the lives of others. *Inside Higher Ed* held a webcast on April 24, 2020, titled "The Great (Forced) Shift to Remote Learning." One of the speakers was Will Austin, president of Warren County Community College in New Jersey. Besides moving all courses entirely online, as most institutions had done, Austin took steps to support students' physical needs. Realizing that "there's no toilet paper in New Jersey," he ordered from industrial sites and distributed thousands of rolls to students, faculty, and staff. He contacted donors, using the funds to purchase gift cards for local restaurants, disbursing them to students who had lost their jobs. Not only were the students able to eat, but this effort also helped keep the restaurants in business. He made sure every student received at least three phone calls checking on their well-being.

> Our students at Warren are learning the most important thing is not what my professor knows, it's how much my professor cares. . . . Warren will be stronger, better, and more together when this is over. And we will excel because we have no other choice.

Our positivity and warmth make a difference! We might not be able to express care for students in the same way as if we were still on campus, but alternative models of instruction need not prevent us from being empathetic and compassionate. In doing so, we help all students live their potential and continue to pursue their dreams, even during an unprecedented moment of history.

Care for Colleagues

Under normal circumstances, many of our peer interactions occur informally. We drop by one another's offices, pause to chat in the hallway, and meet for lunch or coffee. When we teach only online, we can find ourselves missing these casual conversations and feeling the absence of normal interpersonal interactions with our friends at work. True, we still talk to one another in meetings through video conferencing, but even so, there are differences. Virtual meetings aren't conducive to small talk before the meeting begins, nor to continuing a discussion once the host or facilitator closes the online platform. Caring for one another has to become a more deliberate act, reaching out through phone, text, or email to engage in friendly conversations, offer words of encouragement, and maintain our collegial relationships. Even when there's no crisis, and we're going about our business on campus as usual, our colleagues may be struggling personally or professionally. A friendly word, a cup of coffee, or a quick email expressing support can truly make someone's day a little brighter.

Care for the Institution

Make no mistake: our institutions remain under extreme duress. Administrators worry about declining enrollment, students' expressions of dissatisfaction, concerns for the campus's physical structures, the impact of recent events on their budgets, and more. They know they will be forced to call upon everyone to make sacrifices if conditions do not improve. We can demonstrate care for our institution by pitching in to help when needed, maintaining a positive attitude, and refraining from voicing complaints. The last thing anyone wants to say or hear when the institution is struggling is that pay will be cut, positions lost, services reduced, or budgets slashed, yet those are the complications with which many of our institutions must contend. We went through this in the aftermath of the 2008 recession and again following the pandemic of 2020. Institutions around the country have closed their doors due to insufficient enrollment and outdated business models that cannot keep pace with the demands of the 21st century. The way we choose to respond to such unwelcome news testifies to our willingness to care for our institution as well as to our integrity—to put the greater good ahead of personal concerns so that we can all come through the crisis united by the institution's values, vision, and mission.

CARE IS A CHOICE

Care is *not* some thinly veiled deep-on-the-surface, popular philosophical or administrative construct. It's not a buzzword or bumper-sticker slogan. Care cannot occur by institutional mandate, nor is it fostered through flowery rhetoric. As a prime example, a college in one of the universities with which I'm quite familiar publicly espoused a philosophy of care, but it proved to be nothing more than a pretty platitude. The department in which I worked was torn apart by bickering and interpersonal conflict, the college was dysfunctional as a whole, and scandals abounded across the university to the point where it made international headlines. All the while, the college advertised the message that this was a place with a culture of care.

Care is not an emotion, nor is it an idea. It is an action and a state of being. It is a choice each of us makes in every human interaction, reflecting the quality of our character. We enact a culture of care by accepting personal responsibility to demonstrate all four aspects of care. In so doing, we set an example for others and initiate conversations about spreading the culture of care through our program, department, college, and university. It is a mindset each of us must choose to adopt. We must deliberately turn our backs on the stereotype of the aloof, pretentious professor who uses clever rhetoric to put students down in an attempt to maintain our intellectual superiority. We must reject our old habit of upholding rules and policies instead of prioritizing our students' success.

You might be asking yourself, but what if no one else cares? Then your students and colleagues will still benefit from *your* decision to care. You will take better care of yourself, and you'll do a better job of caring for the university. Your little corner of the world will be a better place than it was before you shifted your mindset and your actions.

THE TRIM TAB

In a 1972 interview, philosopher, inventor, and architect Buckminster Fuller was asked how people could live with "a sense of the individual's impotence to affect events, to improve or even influence our own welfare, let alone that of society"—quite a dark and depressing thought, really, given the circumstances of the world at that time. I remember 1972. It was the year of the Watergate scandal, of the murder and kidnapping of Israeli athletes at the Munich Olympics, and of mass protests against the Vietnam War, all occurring beneath the omnipresent shadow of the Cold War, which threw fears of imminent nuclear holocaust over all our lives. (Today, school-age children participate in active shooter drills. In the 1970s, we had bomb drills, as though sheltering under our desks could save us from a nuclear attack!) It was every bit as frightening a time to live, in its way, as we've experienced in recent years. The interviewer's question reflected the spirit of the times: things are so bad, how do we live with knowing that one person can't even help themselves, let alone make the world a better place? Buckminster Fuller's response was nothing less than brilliant.[8]

279

Something hit me very hard once, thinking about what one little man could do. Think of the Queen Elizabeth—the whole ship goes by and then comes the rudder. And there's a tiny thing at the edge of the rudder called a trim tab. It's a miniature rudder. Just moving the little trim tab builds a low pressure that pulls the rudder around. Takes almost no effort at all. So I said that the little individual can be a trim tab. Society thinks it's going right by you, that it's left you altogether. But if you're doing dynamic things mentally, the fact is that you can just put your foot out like that and the whole big ship of state is going to go. So I said, "Call me Trim Tab."

The truth is that you get the low pressure to do things, rather than getting on the other side and trying to push the bow of the ship around. And you build that low pressure by getting rid of a little nonsense, getting rid of things that don't work and aren't true until you start to get that trim-tab motion. It works every time. That's the grand strategy you're going for. So I'm positive that what you do with yourself, just the little things you do yourself, these are the things that count. To be a real trim tab, you've got to start with yourself, and soon you'll feel that low pressure, and suddenly things begin to work in a beautiful way. Of course, they happen only when you're dealing with really great integrity.[9]

I first heard the phrase "trim tab" in a weekly newsletter for online faculty called "Trim Tab Tuesday" from Karen Rintamaki, coordinator of faculty and course support at Central Michigan University's Global Campus. To be honest, I first thought it had something to do with an internet browser or word-processing program, but at the bottom of the page, Ms. Rintamaki included a quote by Fuller and a hyperlink. My curiosity was piqued, so I followed the link and found the marvelous quote by Fuller cited here.

"[J]ust the little things you do yourself, these are the things that count. To be a real trim tab, you've got to start with yourself." In other words, change starts with me. It starts with you. It starts with the decisions we make in our homes and our departments and our classrooms, day by day, course by course. We need to "get rid of the things that don't work and aren't true," even if they're the very things that our colleagues hold on to so tightly. If they want to keep teaching their courses the same old way, keep believing they should be gruff and uncaring toward students, keep competing with their colleagues, and publicly complain about their institutions, they can do that. Being a trim tab doesn't mean pressuring our colleagues or shouting inspirational messages from the campus bell tower. Nevertheless, we are equally free to change our own behavior. We can choose to do better by being the trim tabs that begin to turn the enormous ocean liner of higher education in a new and better direction.

I'm always a little taken aback when students express surprised disbelief that I'm willing to waive late penalties or accept missing work. Their responses seem out of proportion to a very simple response on my part, making me suspect they've encountered many other instructors who were not at all willing to be flexible or forgiving. I'm saddened to know that their experience with other professors has been so negative. My bottom line as an instructor is always about students' learning. If the student does not do an assignment, they cannot receive the learning experience the assignment was supposed to provide. Penalizing the assignment so heavily that there's no reason to complete it causes the student to miss out on that learning. But if I tell the student, "Yes, you can still turn in your work and receive credit," they participate in the learning experience, and their subsequent grade reflects the quality of their work, not the number of days that elapsed since the due date. I still put due dates on my syllabi, and I list the late penalties that could accrue. I impose those penalties sometimes, too. But when a student contacts me to ask for help, I always give it because their success is the motivation behind everything I do.

Buckminster Fuller wasn't just waxing philosophical about being a trim tab. He lived that credo and did, indeed, make the world a better place. Fuller coined the phrase "Spaceship Earth" and led the world to understand the idea of a global community. He invented the geodesic dome, worked to end poverty and world hunger, and championed renewable energy. He popularized the idea of synergy and promoted holistic healthcare that encompasses "psychology, problem solving, planning, thinking, and systems design." The words "Call me Trim Tab" are carved into a granite marker at his gravesite, reflecting his lifelong quest to make a difference.[10]

I hope that this book will be a trim tab that inspires readers to take steps to improve their practice as educators: to adopt a student-centered philosophy of teaching, to embrace the idea of building every course in their institution's LMS according to the quality recommendations, to be prepared to pivot between different instructional models so that we can maintain educational continuity no matter the circumstances, to incorporate high-impact practices into their teaching, and to contribute to a culture of care.

Dr. Martin Luther King said, "Darkness cannot drive out darkness; only light can do that. Hate cannot drive out hate; only love can do that."[11] Just so, negativity cannot overcome negativity; only positivity can do that. Apathy cannot overcome apathy; only caring can do that. Holding fast to tradition and legacy cannot meet the challenges we face today. Only reaching out for something better can do that.

No matter how uncertain or difficult it may be, this very moment is a priceless opportunity to embrace change—to begin building the foundations of a culture of care and growing as educators, becoming the people our students need us to be. It begins with you and with me, and it continues in every interaction we have with our students, colleagues, and the others we encounter every day.

My fondest hope is that this book has caused you to reconsider your teaching philosophy, instructional practices, and approach to relationships with your

Design Connection	
Empathize	• A culture of care and the design principle of empathy go hand in glove with being an outstanding educator and faculty member. We've all had times when we needed someone to demonstrate care for us. After reading this chapter, you may have begun to see how you could demonstrate care for others, too.
Define	• How might you define "care" in the context of your department, college, or university? How does care apply to your interactions with your students? How would you characterize your efforts to care for your colleagues? For your institution? For yourself?
Ideate	• Each of us exists within a web of relationships, and even small efforts to care can have a positive ripple effect. Think of something you could do tomorrow to show your students you care about them as people. Think of a colleague who needs a boost of care and decide how you could act on this idea. Consider what you could do to show care for your institution, like refraining from joining your colleagues in complaining about an administrator.
Prototype	• The "Trim Tab" is a metaphor for the idea that just one person can have a positive impact on the world. Make a list of ways you could be a trim tab. Choose one. Create a plan for implementing one of those ideas, and enact that prototype over the next few days or weeks, noting the result.
Test	• You've been exposed to many ideas in this book that run contrary to traditional faculty-centered norms and practices in higher education. The test of those ideas is up to you, as you choose to enact them in your workplace. You may not see immediate results, but even the smallest step in the right direction is still worthwhile. You can be a force for change. You can make a tremendous difference in your students' and colleagues' lives. Along the way, you'll find it makes a difference in your own life, too.

FIGURE 6.2 Chapter 6 Design Connection

students, colleagues, and the institution for which you work. It's people like you and like me who will make a difference in higher education! I hereby invite you to join me on this grand adventure.

Notes

[1] From June 2015, https://talk.collegeconfidential.com/parent-cafe/1782136-look-to-your-right-look-to-your-left.html

[2] Cited by McAughtrie, D. (2016, June 8). Ten strategies to increase student retention. *Unit4.com*. Retrieved from www.unit4.com/blog/2016/06/10-ways-to-increase-student-retention

[3] Lexico. (2020). *Care*. Retrieved from www.lexico.com/en/definition/care

[4] Groenwald, S. (2018). *Designing and creating a culture of care*. League of Nursing. Philadelphia, PA: Wolters Kluwer.

[5] Flaherty, C. (2014, April 9). So much to do, so little time. *Inside Higher Ed*. Retrieved from www.insidehighered.com/news/2014/04/09/research-shows-professors-work-long-hours-and-spend-much-day-meetings

[6] Supiano, B. (2018, August 20). One way to show students you care—and why you might want to try it. *The Chronicle of Higher Education*. Retrieved from www.chronicle.com/article/one-way-to-show-students-you-care-and-why-you-might-want-to-try-it/

[7] Online Etymology Dictionary. (2020). *Crisis*. Retrieved from www.etymonline.com/word/crisis

[8] Popova, M. (2015, August 21). Buckminster Fuller's brilliant metaphor for the greatest key to transformation and growth. *Brain Pickings*. Retrieved from www.brainpickings.org/2015/08/21/buckminster-fuller-trim-tab/

[9] R. Buckminster Fuller: A Candid Conversation. (1972, February). *Playboy Magazine*, *19*(2), 59–70. Retrieved from www.bfi.org/sites/default/files/attachments/pages/CandidConversation-Playboy.pdf

[10] Buckminster Fuller Institute. (n.d.). *About Fuller*. Retrieved from www.bfi.org/about-fuller/biography/fullers-influence#:~:text=Buckminster%20Fuller%20was%20one%20of%20our%20world's%20first%20futurists%20and%20global%20thinkers.&text=Fuller's%20global%20thinking%20led%20him,as%20the%20Whole%20Earth%20Catalog

[11] Martin, J., & Sainz, A. (2018, January 14). King's words still inspire nearly 50 years after his death. *Associated Press: AP News*. Retrieved from https://apnews.com/be-7faf7879724e8da237cb6c7f72d58c/King%27s-words-still-inspire-nearly-50-years-after-his-death#:~:text=Darkness%20cannot%20drive%20out%20darkness,only%20love%20can%20do%20that

Epilogue Part 1

A Letter to Administrators and Academic Leaders

To say that we live in uncertain times is such an understatement it borders on the ridiculous. Higher education—a system so averse to change as to have maintained its histories and traditions for more than a millennium—stands at the brink of complete and utter transformation. This shift has been a long time coming, shaped by forces in existence well before any given crisis. The economic recession of 2008 and subsequent decimation of state funding led to rising tuition costs and massive student debt loads even as earning a college degree is increasingly a baseline expectation for the 21st-century workplace. Our students have changed and will continue to change, with the so-called "traditional" undergraduates quickly becoming a minority group on our campuses.

The fact is, we were already in peril before COVID-19. Small private liberal arts colleges and stand-alone art schools had closed or were on the brink of closure. Major universities closed or were considering closing programs in the arts and humanities while increasing STEM programs. Our operational model has not kept pace with the changing world in which it exists, leading to vociferous criticism by politicians, complaints from students and families, and expressions of dissatisfaction by employers who do not feel that our graduates are nearly as ready for the workforce as we believe them to be.

Some of us take pride in our imperviousness to change, believing that if we just hold on to our histories, legacies, and traditions, the storms will abate, and we can quietly return to doing what we've always done in the way we've always done it. This attitude worries me greatly because I believe we are on the verge of as monumental a shift as has ever occurred—a fundamental transformation of what higher education means, how it works, and what our institutions' roles in society will be.

What if you were standing on the edge of the field near Dayton, Ohio, watching the Wright brothers make their first flight? What if you were walking down the street in Detroit and saw Henry Ford rolling toward you on his first Quadricycle? Would you have recognized these moments as the start of a revolution?

I believe we're in exactly this kind of moment now. History assures us that the pandemic we experienced will surely follow the same course as other devastating diseases like polio or smallpox or the bubonic plague. I am more concerned that the ground beneath our feet has been rumbling for quite some time, a portent of the cataclysm to come. It's high time we wake up and recognize it for what it is.

Academic administrators must be prepared to lead their institutions to pivot between operational models just as much as our faculty must be ready to pivot between instructional models. Two types of institutions are likely to survive what awaits us. First, elite colleges and universities will continue with business as usual because they have substantial endowments and loyal (wealthy) alumni who will continue sending their children to receive the same traditional education that they received themselves. Next, institutions like Arizona State University and Southern New Hampshire University will also survive because their leaders have the will to adapt to changing conditions and break free from the paralyzing bonds of history and tradition. Neither of these institutions has completely abandoned the residential college model, but both have expanded well beyond this norm to meet the needs of diverse learners within a rapidly changing society.

For so long, we've clung to the romantic ideal of the residential liberal arts college experience. It's deeply embedded in our culture, and we remain passionately committed to it. Nevertheless, it is far less prevalent than it once was. At California State University-Fullerton, only 6% of its nearly 35,000 undergraduates live in campus housing.[1] At the City Colleges of New York, just 2% of students live on campus.[2] What we envision as the "typical" college experience just doesn't exist for most of our students—at least, not anymore.

Many such norms have faded into the past. In a 1994 article for *The Atlantic Monthly*, noted business theorist Peter Drucker addressed the issue of social transformation, noting that farmers were the largest single group of workers in every country before World War I, followed by domestic servants. Indeed, the census category of "lower middle class" was defined as households with fewer than three live-in servants.[3] Today, farming makes up only 1.3% of US employment.[4] Domestic workers account for about 1% of the workforce, mainly as childcare providers, house cleaners, or health aides working in private homes.[5] Just 18% of parents do not hold a job outside the home.[6] As portrayed in media from *Leave it to Beaver* to *The Simpsons*, the romanticized ideal of the nuclear family has become increasingly rare, declining from 42% of all households in the 1970s to 22% today.[7] Our lives and our society are fundamentally different in more ways than we can count.

Drucker explained how the class of industrial workers rose in the 19th century and fell in the 20th century, giving way to today's knowledge economy. His analysis of more than 25 years ago seems especially prophetic today. Drucker said we would "redefine what it means to be an educated person." Instead of being defined by having earned a traditional liberal arts education, an educated person will be somebody who has learned how to learn, and who continues learning, especially by formal education, throughout his or her lifetime. . . . Learning will become the tool of the individual—available to him or her at any age—if only because so much skill and knowledge can be acquired by means of the new learning technologies.

Drucker believed the knowledge of the knowledge society would be "fundamentally different from what was considered knowledge in earlier societies—and, in fact, from what is still widely considered knowledge." Knowledge of the liberal arts, according to Drucker, "had little to do with one's life's work. It focused on the person and the person's development, rather than on any application—if, indeed, it did not, like the nineteenth-century liberal arts, pride itself on having no utility whatever." Instead of the general education that used to be the norm, Drucker predicted a shift to preparing students for specialized careers, saying that "generalists, in the sense in which we used to talk of them [would come to] be seen as dilettantes rather than educated people."

Drucker's predictions are more accurate than many of us may be aware. For example, our mission statements often refer to "lifelong learning," and our academic programs are increasingly specialized, not to mention technologically dependent. Nevertheless, our organizational systems and our deeply held beliefs about higher education remain firmly rooted in the Industrial Age rather than the knowledge economy, even though our very stock in trade is knowledge itself. As academic administrators, therefore, it is time we come to grips with a deeply ontological question: what role will higher education play in a "world economy in which knowledge has become the key economic resource and the dominant, if not the only, source of comparative advantage?"[8]

Some of our most venerable institutions are also engaged in fundamental transformation. What will a library become in a world where most information exists electronically rather than in printed texts? For that matter, what happens to the paper industry when books, magazines, and newspapers give way to electronic media? As the demand for paper decreases, what of the logging industry or managed forestry operations?[9] Bookstores such as Barnes & Noble, Book World, Borders, and Crown Books have closed their doors forever. Amazon, however, began as an online bookseller and is now one of the largest companies in the US, second only to Walmart in terms of annual revenue.[10] What's the difference? Amazon knows how to innovate and adapt to the changing economy.

Like the print industry, higher education stands on the brink of change. Transformation is upon us whether or not we welcome it. Institutions such as Arizona State University have decided to be part of that change, to grow and adapt to the new demands of the knowledge economy and provide more than the traditional residential liberal arts experience. Those who want that experience will still be able to find it if they can afford it or are willing to go deeply into debt to obtain it. But the vast majority of our future students need something different out of higher education. Affordable tuition, flexible degree paths, the ability to jump into and out of study over many years, the opportunity to re-enroll and re-skill after changing careers—all these and more must become part of our future if our institutions are to survive. The catchphrase "innovate or die" has never been more apropos.

Our hands are more than full just with the problems we face today. Nevertheless, I wrote this book because we are in a moment when our choices will shape our institutions' long-term stability.

In my youth, one of my favorite television programs was *The Six Million Dollar Man*. In the opening credits, astronaut Steve Austin is introduced as "a man barely alive" following a horrific plane crash. A voice-over intones, "We can rebuild him. We have the technology. We can make him better than he was. Better . . . stronger . . . faster."[11] Many of our institutions are in crisis, whether because of the shifting sociopolitical and economic landscape or the lasting effects of the global pandemic, but we *do* have the technology and the human capital to become better than we were before. We can be stronger. We can be smarter. We can follow the lead of Amazon and Arizona State University rather than allowing ourselves to go the way of Blockbuster Video or Borders Books.

Please don't misunderstand: I am not at all advocating for the closure of residential colleges, nor do I believe we should move to an entirely online model of education. The classic "college experience" is intrinsically valuable and should continue to remain available to those who want it and can afford it, just as Amazon still sells paper books. But we must also face the fact that most of our students have different needs and expectations than our present programs or systems can accommodate.

Much has been made of dismal success rates among our students and poor career prospects for our graduates. We in higher education respond by blaming students' poor college preparedness, their economic disadvantages, or the low quality of the high schools from which they graduated. We bemoan rising costs and shrinking state contributions and rail against growing demands that college should prepare students for careers instead of our beloved focus on becoming better people through the liberal arts. Perhaps we should look at this differently. Maybe we need to consider that the educational experience we offer and the operational model that sustains it no longer meet the challenges of the world in which we now live.

The road ahead will be difficult. Farsighted administrators will shepherd their institutions through these transformations one way or another. But as I said in the last chapter, the most crucial factor will be to establish a culture of care that supports everyone from the university's president to the groundskeeping and custodial staff, from post-doctoral students to dual-credit high school students and senior citizens taking non-credit courses for personal enrichment. Leaders can be fairly confident that every person in the institution will resist transformation and innovation. "We like things the way they are, thank you very much. Let us do our jobs. Leave us alone." Many (even most) leaders would like nothing better than to comply, but knowing what we know—that failing to act is tantamount to refusing to run for shelter when the tornado siren sounds—we cannot give in to these pleas. However, we can pitch in and work alongside our faculty, staff, and fellow administrators to do whatever is necessary to make it through this time of change. We can be unfailingly kind. We can respond with understanding, respect, and support when people voice their frustrations. In higher education, even hinting at change can cause an uproar. When change is upon us, we can be assured of backlash, at the very least, yet the alternative leads inexorably to layoffs, program closures, or the shuttering of entire institutions. There will soon be no choice but to change or close our doors forever.

A culture of care eases this transition. We know this will be an unprecedented imposition on our faculty, but we can ease their burden by implementing policies that reward faculty for re-developing their courses to put all their content into the LMS. For example, we could recognize this activity as research by embracing the Boyer's S·M·A·R·T model for faculty evaluation that blends the scholarship of teaching and learning with goal setting toward professional development. We can provide faculty development opportunities for using this model as well as in Comprehensive Instructional Design. We can offer stipends for summertime course development or course release time during the semester. We can take on some of the course redevelopment activity ourselves, too. Most of all, effective leadership through times of change relies on three actions: listen-listen-listen, connect-connect-connect, and communicate-communicate-communicate.

I never sought to become a harbinger of change, yet every year I spend in higher education makes it clearer that change is upon us, and our opportunity to act grows shorter every day. We should have begun to take a new direction decades ago. Nevertheless, we now have the skills, technologies, and hopefully, the motivation to undertake this task. In a knowledge economy, higher education should be the primary engine of social, cultural, and economic development—a powerful, dynamic, inexhaustible spring from which new knowledge flows, perpetually nourishing everyone who works in knowledge-based fields while improving the lives of every person on Earth.

Our role can be exponentially greater than ever before, but only if we are willing to move beyond our historical models to meet these new challenges head-on with vision, passion, and courage. We need academic leaders who are willing to become the next Chuck Yeager (the pilot who broke the sound barrier) or William Beebe (the first person to reach the Deep Sea in a steel bathysphere); to be the Copernicus or Galileo of higher education. We need people who can fundamentally change our understanding of what higher education is and how it works. I believe that Dr. Michael Crow of Arizona State University and

Dr. Paul LeBlanc of Southern New Hampshire University meet this description. They have led their institutions well beyond their original boundaries and are tackling the kinds of education Peter Drucker described in 1994. Nevertheless, ASU and SNHU are but two of the 4,298 degree-granting postsecondary institutions in the US[12] and more than 18,000 in 180 countries worldwide.[13] I hope that more of our institutions raise up leaders who can also demonstrate vision, passion, purpose, and empathy as they take their colleges and universities from what they have been to what they must become.

Notes

[1] US News Best Colleges: www.usnews.com/best-colleges/california-state-university-fullerton-1137/student-life

[2] Kerr, E. (2020, July 28). Eleven universities where most freshmen commute. *US News.* Retrieved from www.usnews.com/education/best-colleges/the-short-list-college/articles/universities-where-most-freshmen-commute

[3] Drucker, P. (1994). The age of social transformation. *The Atlantic Monthly, 274*(5), 53–80.

[4] www.ers.usda.gov/data-products/ag-and-food-statistics-charting-the-essentials/ag-and-food-sectors-and-the-economy/#:~:text=Agriculture%20and%20its%20related%20industries,1.3%20percent%20of%20U.S.%20employment

[5] www.nytimes.com/interactive/2019/02/21/magazine/national-domestic-workers-alliance.html

[6] www.pewresearch.org/fact-tank/2018/09/24/stay-at-home-moms-and-dads-account-for-about-one-in-five-u-s-parents/#:~:text=The%20stay%2Dat%2Dhome%20share,about%20a%20quarter%2Dcentury%20earlier

[7] www.ozy.com/news-and-politics/the-nuclear-family-is-in-decline-but-did-it-ever-represent-america/258493/

[8] Drucker, P. (1994). The age of social transformation. *The Atlantic Monthly, 274*(5), 53–80.

[9] www.washingtonpost.com/business/2020/07/30/wisconsin-paper-mill-shutdown-coronavirus/?arc404=true

[10] https://fortune.com/fortune500/

[11] www.imdb.com/title/tt0071054/characters/nm0027323

[12] www.usnews.com/education/best-colleges/articles/2019-02-15/how-many-universities-are-in-the-us-and-why-that-number-is-changing#:~:text=The%20short%20answer%3A%20There%20were,institutions%20have%20opened%20satellite%20locations

[13] https://monitor.icef.com/2019/07/oecd-number-of-degree-holders-worldwide-will-reach-300-million-by-2030/#:~:text=The%20International%20Association%20of%20Universities,institutions%20in%20180%20countries%20worldwide

Epilogue Part 2

A Letter to Faculty

Before I begin, I want to thank you for everything you've done as a faculty member. Faculty seldom receive thanks for the difference they make in their students' lives or the essential tasks they perform through their committee service. So, **thank you**. You have already gone above and beyond all that could have been expected. You've overcome monumental challenges and done more than your fair share of the work to keep your institution going through crisis and provide your students with an education despite obstacles that no previous generation of faculty could have imagined. You've spent countless hours modifying your curriculum, often without compensation. You've found ingenious workarounds for technological challenges, and you've supported your students through all manner of heart-wrenching personal crises. I salute your efforts, honor your commitment, and commend your achievements.

I wish I could assure you that an end is in sight. Instead, I must tell you that all of us will likely have to dig even deeper because the task ahead is far from easy. If given a choice, I would opt for a return to normalcy, too. I love teaching face to face. Video conferencing allows us to maintain some semblance of immediacy in our teaching, but I agree that it's just not the same as the experience we achieve on campus.

Nevertheless, the world does not stand still. Sometimes, all we can do is choose how we'll respond to the forces confronting us. On the one hand, we can wait until someone or something compels us to alter our longstanding habits, just as we had to comply with Emergency Remote Teaching, like it or not. We can grudgingly obey or just refuse to participate, but neither of these options works to anyone's advantage when the change we're compelled to make is a matter of necessity rather than choice. Returning to the analogy I used in the previous letter to administrators and academic leaders, if an administrator shouts, "The river is

291

rising! Come out and help us with the sandbags!" it's not productive to reply, "No. That's not part of my job description. Call maintenance."

On the other hand, we can try to find the good in what we're asked to do and try our best to adapt. I hope you might freely choose to adopt Comprehensive Instructional Design because you can see that it's best for students if we're able to maintain educational continuity. I hope you will choose to start building all your courses online because you now understand that being as fully prepared as possible will be advantageous to your teaching and your students' learning. To extend our analogy, if you're like me, you'd see the truck full of sand drive up and run outside to start filling the sandbags. When your administrator thanked you for being the first faculty member on the scene, you'd reply, "No problem. Lots of my friends have offices on the first floor. Protecting the building from a flood is important to me, too."

I would like to encourage every faculty member to look beyond the confines of our offices, classrooms, laboratories, and studios and begin to contemplate the nature of higher education in the 21st century. It is incumbent upon all of us to think deeply about how our activities as educators, scholars, researchers, artists, performers, practitioners, and professionals intersect with the world outside our doors—not the way we remember it or wish it could be, but the way it really is, right now, today. We should all understand that the norms that have given shape to higher education for centuries may no longer serve it as well as they once did. In Chapter 1, we talked about how our students have changed, and as a result, we must change from a "college-ready" to a "student-ready" mindset. We also discussed the need to move from a faculty-centered perspective that asks, "What's best for me?" to a student-centered mindset that asks, "What's best for my students?" I remain hopeful that some of you have made this shift and have begun to approach your work as educators with a new, more empathetic perspective.

Now I invite you to take a step further. As much as we love our disciplines and departments, as devoted as we are to the histories, legacies, and traditions of higher education, I ask you to consider: are our present system and model of higher education sufficient to meet the changing needs of the world around us? Is clinging to tradition the *best* we can do? Can we truly make a difference in the quality of human life on Earth through the advancement of knowledge—the central mission of most of our institutions—if we don't ask whether our beloved model still works?

The idea of the trim tab is as appropriate here as when thinking about making a difference in our students' lives. Neither you nor I may be the president or provost of our respective institutions, but we can still have an impact, as small as it may be. We can move beyond what's familiar, even if it's daunting or strange. Each of us, in our own small way, can be change makers.

I believe that the shifts we've experienced in higher education since at least 2008 (if not earlier) have led us to this moment. Certainly, the pandemic accelerated and complicated the situation, but if our highest aspiration is only to go back to normal, I think we've missed a valuable opportunity to make some long overdue course corrections. Each of us may face a day when we must decide whether to embrace transformation and innovation or choose to oppose it. Assuredly, not all changes are good, and not all innovations are worthwhile, but in my letter to administrators and academic leaders, I mentioned Amazon as an example of a company that could navigate change and thrives as a result. With you, my faculty colleagues, I'd like to use the example of Kodak. I originally went to college because I wanted to become a photography professor, and in both my BFA and MFA programs, I worked in black-and-white traditional darkroom-based photographic processes. Kodak film was crucial to my creative practice. I graduated with my MFA in 2008, just when all the economic changes were about to unfold, but Kodak was still the unquestioned industry leader in film photography. How, then, could Kodak plunge into bankruptcy just four years later, narrowly avoiding a complete shut-down? Because Kodak chose not to let go of their production of photographic films even though they had invented the first digital camera, and they did not anticipate how quickly cell phone photography would displace digital cameras.[1] Kodak still exists today and is slowly rebuilding its brand. But the company's history serves as a cautionary tale for organizations that cannot let go of the past enough to embrace the future.

Most of our institutions will survive the changes coming toward us, but like Kodak, we may find ourselves in smaller departments with fewer students and even fewer colleagues, a shadow of our former selves. The very last thing I want to do as an administrator is to tell people they no longer have a job. It's certainly the very last thing we want someone to say to us! What if Kodak had the foresight to recognize that they stood at the edge of a precipice and needed to make a change of unprecedented proportions?

I think we're in just such a moment, unwelcome as this may be. Adopting Comprehensive Instructional Design will help us through what is yet to come, not just because of the pandemic, but as we come to grips with the changing nature of higher education itself. Yes, we'll still teach on campus, but we will also serve more students who need the flexibility and affordability of online or blended instructional models, while fewer students choose the traditional model of a residential college experience.

Our willingness to hold lightly to the past while working wholeheartedly toward the future will be crucial to sustaining our programs and departments. If our disciplines are to remain vital and viable, we must make sure that they actively contribute to the good of our institutions. Moving into an uncertain future is hard, but I'd say it's less disconcerting than what may befall us if we cannot (or will not) adapt to the changes that lie ahead.

I remain confident that each of us has the intelligence, capability, and courage to embark on this new adventure. Working together as a unified whole, side by side with our colleagues, administrators, and staff, we can transform higher education into what it needs to be—finally—to meet the demands of the 21st century. I'm glad we're in this together, and I hope that reading this book has helped you prepare for the task.

Note

[1] A Brief History of Kodak. (2020). Retrieved from www.1ink.com/blog/history-of-kodak-a-brief-look-with-1inkcom/#:~:text=The%20Eastman%20Kodak%20Company%2C%20known,its%20headquarters%20are%20located%20today

Appendix

Quality Recommendations Checklist

Welcome
- ■ Created a message warmly welcoming students to the course (video preferred) and posted it as an announcement to the online classroom.
- ■ Included instructions to read the entire Start Here module, post to the Meet & Greet discussion, and take the short quiz at the end of the Start Here module.

Meet & Greet Discussion
- ■ Created a "Meet & Greet" discussion area.
- ■ Provided instructions for students to introduce themselves (video preferred; insert photo if a video is unavailable).
- ■ Instructed students to post comments on one or more peers' posts (video or audio responses preferred).
- ■ Posted own response to the discussion.

About the Instructor
- ■ Created the "About the Instructor" page in the Start Here module. Page includes:
- ■ Instructor's preferred name and pronouns
- ■ Contact information
  - ■ Email address
  - ■ Phone number
  - ■ Alternative contact information (text messaging, Skype, etc.)
  - ■ Contact preferences and hours of availability
- ■ Short academic biography
- ■ Short philosophy of teaching

Course Orientation
- Created "Course Orientation" page in the Start Here module.
- Posted a video (preferred) or written instructions that include the following information:
  - Explanation of how to navigate the online classroom.
  - Statement about course prerequisites (if any).
  - List of all textbooks and required materials, including links for purchase or download.
  - A printable copy of the syllabus (link or attachment).
  - Course calendar (link or attachment).

Objectives and Outcomes
- Created "Objectives and Outcomes" page in the Start Here module.
- Wrote objectives and outcomes for the course that are:
  - Suited to the level of the course.
  - Stated clearly.
  - Measurable.
  - Written from the student's point of view.
- Wrote objectives for each module that align with those for the course as a whole.

Overview of Activities, Assignments, and Assessments
- Created "Course Overview" page in the Start Here module that explains:
  - How each assignment, assessment, or learning activity aligns with course and module objectives and outcomes.
  - How the course provides multiple opportunities for students to demonstrate learning through varied assessments.
  - How the course includes opportunities for students to review their own performance and assess their own learning (self-graded tests, practice quizzes, reflective assignments, etc.).
  - The weight or value of each graded item in the course.
- Ensured gradebook is well-organized and up to date.

Policies and Expectations
- Created "Policies and Expectations" page in the Start Here module that explains the instructor's policies and expectations for
  - Late work, make-up work, and resubmission of work
  - Grading policies
  - Attendance and participation

- Communication
- Netiquette and classroom civility
- What the instructor expects from students
- Clarified what students can expect from the instructor
    - Where and when feedback will be provided
    - When grades will be posted
    - What students can expect from the instructor
    - How students can provide feedback about the course
- Provided links to relevant or required university policies.

Student Support

- Created the "Student Support" page in the Start Here module that provides a brief explanation, contact information, and links to each of the following campus units:
    - Technology help
    - LMS support
    - Tutoring services or online tutorials
    - Writing center or academic support services
    - Library
    - Health, wellness, and mental health services
    - Office of Disabilities Services
    - Link to the university's accessibility policy

Technology

- Created the "Technology" page in the Start Here module that includes:
    - Explanation of course format (online, hybrid, blended, hyflex, face to face, etc.)
    - List of minimum hardware, software, and equipment requirements, including information on how to obtain required hardware and software
    - How the varied technologies used in the course support students' achievement of course objectives and outcomes, deliver content, and facilitate active learning, communication, engagement, and collaboration
    - List of technological skills and knowledge required in the course along with resources such as video tutorials for required skills
- Page includes links to privacy policies and vendor accessibility statements for all technology tools used in the course.

Instructional Materials
- Verified that all the instructional materials in the course:
    Support students' achievement of course objectives and outcomes
    - Demonstrate up-to-date theory and practice in the discipline
    - Model expectations for academic integrity by clearly stating copyright or licensing status, permission to share (where applicable), and include correct citations or references
- Where possible, free or low-cost student materials are used.

Course Content, Activities, and Interaction
- Ensured the following statements about the course are true:
    - All learning activities promote students' achievement of the course objectives and outcomes.
    - Course activities develop students' higher-order thinking and core competencies such as critical thinking, problem solving, reflection, and analysis.
    - Course includes activities that link to the real-world application of the discipline, such as experiential learning, case studies, or problem-based activities.
    - Activities provide opportunities for interaction:
        - Peer to peer
        - Student to instructor
        - Student to content
    - Course incorporates active learning, collaboration, and peer-to-peer sharing of knowledge and resources.
    - Content is organized logically and follows a clear progression from the beginning to the end of the course.
    - Instructions clarify where to find necessary resources and how to use them to complete assignments, activities, or assessments.
    - Every graded item is associated with clear written directions and includes a rubric, checklist, or other transparent grading criteria.
    - Due dates and submission requirements for all graded items are clear and evident.

Online Environment Design
- Ensured the following descriptions of the course's online environment are true:
    - Frequently used tools are apparent and convenient.
    - Navigation and learning paths are evident and intuitive.

- Page layouts are consistent and uncluttered.
- Color schemes and icons are consistent on all pages.
- Related content is organized together.
- Large blocks of information are divided into manageable sections.
- All instructions are clear, well written, and free from grammatical and spelling errors.

Readability
- Ensured the following descriptions of the course's readability are true:
  - There is sufficient contrast between text and background.
  - Formatting uses titles, headings, and other visual organization.
  - Sans-serif font of no less than 12 points is used for all text.
  - No flashing or blinking text is present.
  - Slideshows:
    - Use a pre-determined slide layout.
    - Slides have unique titles.
    - Simple, non-automatic transitions between slides.
    - Adhere to the same readability requirements as the rest of the course.

Access for Diverse Learners
- Ensured the following descriptions of the course's accessibility for all learners are true:
  - Text is the primary means of conveying information.
  - All text is:
    - Available in easily accessed format (HTML preferred).
    - Readable by assistive technology, including PDF files and any text contained in images.
    - Displayed as in-line text rather than tables whenever possible.
    - Tables are accompanied by a title and summary description.
  - All visual elements in the course are understandable when viewed without color.
  - A text equivalent is provided for every non-text element (alt-text tags, captions, transcripts, etc.) in all documents, files, LMS pages, multimedia, and web pages.
  - Visual presentations include audio narration.
  - Hyperlinks are descriptive and make sense if seen out of context.
  - Students are informed of assessments with time limits and have been provided sufficient lead time to arrange accommodations.

Index

Note: *Italicized* page numbers indicate a figure on the corresponding page. Page numbers in **bold** indicate a table on the corresponding page.